A Tumultuous

LIFE

A Story of a Little Girl Who Rose Above Adversity

Andrea Sherman

ISBN 978-1-0980-9159-0 (paperback)
ISBN 978-1-0980-9160-6 (digital)

Christian Faith Publishing, Inc.
832 Park Avenue
Meadville, PA 16335
www.christianfaithpublishing.com

Printed in the United States of America

Introduction

H i, my name is Andrea, and this is my story. Come and take this journey with me called "Life."

> To everything there is a season, and a time to every purpose under the heaven. (Ecclesiastes 3:1 KJV)

> For I reckon that the sufferings of this present time are not worthy to be compared with the glory which shall be revealed in us. (Romans 8:18–19 KJV)

My life began much like any normal child. I had a mother and a father. My mother, Joyce, had two children from a previous relationship. My sister, Jennifer, was five years old at the time of my birth, and my brother, Jordan, was four. I was named after my mom's dad who was a WWII vet in the Navy. His name was Francis Samuel Bush. My mom wanted one of her kids named after her dad, so I became the lucky one to carry his name for the rest of my life: Andrea Francis Wilber.

Growing up, I always hated my name. Francis was a boy's name, and even the male spelling is masculine. And Wilber? Well, that is a whole other story. I mean, who wants a name after a pig on *Charlotte's Web*? It was a recipe for mean jokes by mean kids. And the name Andrea? There were a lot of girls named Andrea, and I was not like most girls. I wanted a name more original than the girl next door.

As a child growing up, I always fantasized about what life would be like as someone else and what my name would be. Why couldn't I be named Ondrayonnah or just Drea or something more original? I wanted to be really rich, and I was going to have a mansion with a lot of bedrooms so that I could have a bunch of kids, not only from my own womb but kids who were in foster care that needed a loving home and a family of their own. I wanted to provide a safe refuge for kids who grew up much like I did. Adopting from the foster care system has always been a dream of mine. I wanted to be that person who made a difference in someone's life just like others have made a difference in mine.

I wanted the perfect husband who was also wealthy. He was going to be a lawyer or a doctor, have dark hair and a goatee, and were going to live happily ever after.

All I knew as a child growing up was that my life was going to be different once I reached adulthood and had control over the way my life was going to be. I was going to be like Cinderella who met Prince Charming and got whisked into a better life.

What I went through in my childhood was far from normal, but looking back, I realize that God had a purpose for my life, and He was there with me every step of the way. I made it through every valley and overcame every mountain, and the times I felt like life was victorious over me, I had a heavenly Father who picked me up and carried me through the fire and trials of this life.

I wish I had a time machine—not to change anything from the past as hard as my life was but to go back and encourage little Andrea and let her know that *she made it! It was going to get better!* And her life turned out just as God planned it, and the trials and tribulations she had to go through made her who she was supposed to be: a strong and courageous woman, a warrior of life, full of love and compassion for people, a person who understood the plight of others.

Most of the time in this life, it is the future and the unknown that is most unsettling. We have a lot of questions that we don't know the answers to, and we are blinded by the storm clouds that seek to consume us that we can't see the sunny forecast ahead, and we lose sight of the one who created us in the first place.

Sometimes, life and the fiery darts that are thrown at us have us questioning God's purpose and have us asking why we are here in the first place. "Why, God? Why *me?*" And these questions will have us questioning God's love for us. "If God really loved me, then why is this happening to me?"

We live in a fallen world, and because God didn't make us robots, he gave us all free will. Because sin entered the world and God gave us free will, sometimes *we fall victim to someone else's sin. Yes, we fall victim to someone else's sin.* That is the fallen world that we live in.

> And not only so, but we glory in tribulations also; knowing that tribulation worketh patience, and patience, experience, and experience, hope. (Romans 5:3–4 KJV)

God is our *hope!* He is our anchor in the storm, and no matter what this life throws at us, He will be there right beside us every step of the way and He will never forsake us. What I have learned in this life is this: sometimes it will take a whole lifetime to figure out God's purpose for your life, and sometimes you won't see the bigger picture until the end; but one day, you will look back, and it will be a lot clearer to you. We just have to take this life one day at a time and one stride at a time and trust that God will see you through to each tomorrow. Today only lasts for today, but there is always a tomorrow, and tomorrow is a fresh new day and a fresh start.

> Now the God of hope fill you with all joy and peace in believing, that ye may abound in hope, through the power of the Holy Ghost. (Romans 15:13 KJV)

1

All Innocence Is Lost

I was born on February 4, 1988, on a cold winter Thursday in Erie, Pennsylvania, to Joyce Anne Bush and Clayton Harvey Wilber. I had a five-year-old sister, Jennifer, and a four-year-old brother, Jordan, from a previous relationship that my mother had. Clayton also had many older children who were already grown from previous relationships. My father was twenty-five years older than my mother.

After me came two little brothers. Joshua came eight months after me and was born premature, and then Theodore came a year after that. The three of us had bright orange hair and freckles. We lived in the projects in Erie, Pennsylvania. A Puerto Rican family lived on our left, and the rest were all black besides this grumpy old white man at the end that was always chasing us kids out of his yard.

My mom's best friend lived next door. She was a Black lady that always had on bright red lipstick. She loved to kiss Theo on the cheek, and every time he had a pair of red lips on his cheek, we knew that ol' Lucy got a hold of him.

Lucy had a little girl named Danielle. We always rode our bikes up and down the sidewalk with our parents watching us from the porch. Danielle and I were best friends. We always played together. We were big into Barbies. She had Black Barbies, and I had white Barbies. I remember playing with our Barbies together on a blanket on the grass in front of our houses.

I also loved to play with baby dolls. I took my dolls everywhere and had to have a diaper bag for them too. Being a mother has always been the one thing I knew I wanted more than anything in this world. I've wanted to be a veterinarian, a lawyer, a doctor, and an author. At one point, I also considered a mortician, but one thing that has always remained the same was wanting to be a mother. Being a mother has always been something I wanted more than anything in this world ever since I was a small child, and I even picked out all of my children's names. They were going to have original uncommon names. Names have always been something I have been obsessed with.

I was a happy little girl and a big daddy's girl. I remember bouncing on his knee. I remember him chasing me around the house playfully. I remember the tickle fights. I remember him teaching me how to draw bunny rabbits and how to make paper airplanes. He was an artist, and I inherited his talent. I remember his hat collection. He must have had two hundred or more ball caps sitting on shelves that bordered my parent's bedroom walls. I remember him playing the guitar and me singing "Take Me Out to the Ball Game." My mom captured it on video. I was such a chatterbox and was very outgoing and could talk an ear off a fly.

When I was seven, my parents decided that the city and the projects were no place to raise children. My mother's side was from Erie, but my father's side was actually from the thumb of Michigan. When the U-Haul truck arrived, and we packed up everything we owned and loaded up our station wagon, I was devastated. I didn't want to move. Change was a pretty scary thing for a seven-year-old. I had to say goodbye to my friend, Danielle. She gave me this Troll doll to remember her by.

Little did I know that my life would be forever changed that day. Would things still end up the way they did had we stayed in Erie?

We ended up living with my Aunt Goldie in Vasser, Michigan, for the summer until we found our own place. Aunt Goldie was my father's sister. She was a very short woman with straight short red hair and was big busted. That woman had a temper to match her hair and told us stories about taking her bra off to beat her kids with it when they got out of line.

Aunt Goldie lived in a single wide trailer on a farm. She had pigs, chickens, goats, cows, cats, and dogs. I'd never seen a farm before, much less lived on one. I remember not being able to sleep at first because of the lack of city noise. There was no train going by at night and no traffic noise. The ever chatter of crickets and the rooster crowing in the morning was something I was going to have to get used to. This was my life now as a country girl—a Michigander.

Before school started, we did find a place of our own. It was a four-bedroom, two-bathroom, single wide trailer. It was in Deckerville on a busy road, the M53. My sister and I shared a room, the two boys shared a room, Jordan had his own room, and my parents had a room. Jenny and I got the master bedroom. She was such a sloppy roommate. I hated sharing a room with her. My side of the room was always neat and clean. She had clothes shoved between her bed and wall, under her pillow, and in between clothes hung up in the closet.

We got enrolled in Marlette schools. I was going into the second grade. Marlette was a far cry from the big city school in Erie. In Erie, my father walked us to school every day. In Deckerville, we had to ride the school bus. I had never ridden on a school bus before.

On the first day of school in Mrs. Anthony's class, we were all sitting in Indian style on the floor. There was this little brown-haired girl sitting in front of me. I tapped on her shoulder and asked her, "Will you be my friend?"

Her name was Amy Berlin. Her big brown eyes looked back at me, and she smiled and said, "Sure." And we became inseparable. We played together on the monkey bars and sat next to each other in class.

Our trailer was on a busy road on M53, so our bus dropped us off on a side street, and we walked across the neighbor's yard to go home. One day, Jordan, Joshua, Theo, and I were dropped off. Jenny was not on the bus that day, which was strange because she rode the bus to school with us. Did she go home sick? Theo was not in school yet, and he was home by himself and was only six years old. Why weren't Mom or Dad home? They were usually both home when we got home from school. Jenny wasn't home either, and why didn't she ride the bus? My six-year-old little brother was very eager to tell us what was going on.

"The cops came and took Daddy away," Theo said.

Since Jordan was the oldest, twelve at the time, he was left in charge. Me being a daddy's girl, I was very upset and confused. Why would the cops take my daddy away? He wasn't a bad guy. He loved us. He loved me. I was his girl. My daddy wasn't a bad man. They must have been mistaken. They had the wrong guy. Maybe they would sort it out and he would be home soon. When I got the news, I went to my room and cried myself to sleep in my pillow. Life was a blur after that. I do, however, remember going to school the next day, crying, and Mrs. Anthony asked me what was wrong after sitting me on her lap, holding me, and trying to console me.

"My daddy went to jail!" I sobbed. I was very heartbroken,

That same year, tragedy struck again as if my daddy going to jail wasn't enough. What did he do anyway to be taken away from us? I just didn't understand, but soon I would find out. Soon I would know why he was taken away from us. The star quality I saw in him as an eight-year-old girl, the role model that I once looked up to, the endless love that a little girl had for her daddy would soon be crushed and replaced with confusion, anger, hatred, betrayal, and utter disgust in a man I soon became ashamed to call my father.

I soon became a very depressed little girl and spent a lot of time in my bedroom. Little did I know at the time just how bad things were about to get.

One day, when Jordan was left in charge of us, my world has become a much darker place. My mom and Jenny were gone a lot more since my dad went away, so it became normal that my twelve-year-old older brother was left in charge of us. Jordan and I were never really close. My two younger brothers and I were more close since we were all closer in age, and we played together a lot.

Joshua and Theo were outside playing in the dirt. I was in my bedroom when Jordan came and asked me if I wanted to go to his room and listen to the radio with him. Jordan being nice to me and including his little sister in something was very odd to me, but I agreed and followed him to his room and sat at the end of his bed to listen to the radio. Jordan sat next to me on the bed before he began touching me. He began by touching my leg and touching me all over on top of my clothes. Then he pushed me back onto his bed on my back and got on top of me. He tried kissing me, but I kept sinking my head as far back into the pillow as I could to get away from him. I didn't understand what he was doing to me, but I knew that it wasn't appropriate, and it made me feel uncomfortable and scared. I kept shaking my head back and forth to avoid him.

"No!" I cried. "Stop!" I pleaded as I shook my head back and forth to avoid his lips on mine. He was my big brother. Why was he doing this to me? The more I fought him and tried to avoid his advances towards me, the more aggressive he got with me, and he pinned me down and started dry humping me with our clothes on and was grinding himself on me.

Jordan dragged me down the hallway to the bathroom. He shut the door and pushed me against it and forced his tongue into my mouth as he pulled my pants down. He pushed me down into a sitting position on the floor with my back up against the door and my legs spread as he fondled me. I'd never been touched there before and knew that it was wrong. I kept telling him to stop, but he would not listen to me. He ordered me to stand up on the edge of the tub so that he could lick and finger my vagina. Why was he doing this to me? I was his little sister. This was not right. Why was this happening to me? When would Mom be home?

I kept telling him to stop, but he would not listen to me. He was getting rough with me, and I lost my balance and fell and hit my head on the toilet. I started bawling. Jordan did not want Joshua or Theo to hear me crying. The bathroom window was open, and the boys were just outside, playing in the dirt in the backyard.

Jordan held me and rocked me and tried consoling me to get me to stop crying so the boys wouldn't hear. Once I stopped crying, he ran the bathwater and told me to get in, and he got undressed and got in after me. He began fondling me some more and made me lie on my back, and he got on top of me inside the tub and started humping me and grinding himself on me. He rolled me on top of him. He wanted me to hump him back, but I wouldn't, so he put his hands on my butt and tried thrusting me onto him. Then he would roll back on top of me.

All of a sudden, there was a knock on the door. Jordan and I both froze. It was Theo. He wanted to use the bathroom.

"What do you want?" Jordan yelled.

"I have to use the bathroom," Theo said.

"Go pee outside!" Jordan barked back.

"Where is Andrea?" Theo asked.

"How would I know?" Jordan yelled back.

Jordan quietly told me to hide behind the shower curtain, and I did. I did not want to be caught in the tub with him. Jordan carefully got out of the tub, making sure he didn't make too much noise with the water. He gathered my clothes and put them under the bathroom sink. Then he got back in the tub with me. I was hiding behind the curtain with my knees bent up and was holding my legs, trying to conceal my nakedness.

Theo opened the door and him, and Joshua peeked behind the shower curtain and saw us in the tub together.

"I'm gonna tell!" Theo said.

Jordan leaped out of the tub and slipped his pants on. The boys took off running outside.

"If you tell, you are both dead!" Jordan screamed.

I stayed in the tub for a few minutes, crying before I got out, put my clothes back on, and ran to my room, quietly shutting my door behind me and throwing myself in bed, crying into my pillow on my belly.

Why was this happening to me? *Daddy, come home! Mom? Where are you? Why aren't you home?* I screamed and cried into my pillow until I fell asleep.

The secret wasn't out right away. Although that was the only incident that was ever made known, eventually, it wasn't the only time I was molested by my brother. Nobody—I mean nobody—knows what I am about to reveal next. It has long been a secret I kept to myself. I don't even think the boys remember this since they were so young at the time.

My mother and Jenny were gone again, and Jordan was left in charge of me and Joshua and Theo. He made me and the two boys stand in a circle in the boys' room with our pants down. He had the boys take turns touching me. The boys were both smiling from ear to ear. I was eight, Joshua was seven, and Theo was six. Jordan was twelve.

Jordan made me lie down on the floor and had the boys take turns humping me. There were a few times where Jordan had to show them how. None of them penetrated me, but Jordan did try. He didn't know what he was doing, but he did know that what he was doing was wrong.

One day, Jordan and Theo were fighting. Theo blurted out in the living room, "I saw Jordan and Andrea in the tub together!"

Both me and Jordan immediately denied it. I was afraid that I would get in trouble. My mom sent us both to our own rooms and started questioning us individually. That is when Jenny told me about what Clayton did to her. She told me about what he did so that I would talk about what Jordan did to me. Jenny was thirteen at the time. I didn't want to believe those horrible lies about my daddy. My daddy wouldn't do that. *Not my daddy!* He was a good man, and I loved him! The people you love just wouldn't do those things. They wouldn't do things to cause them to be separated away from their family. I was very angry at Jenny for saying that my daddy did those horrible things to her. My daddy wouldn't do that.

The police were called. Jordan stayed in his room, and I was brought out to the kitchen table where they questioned me. I'm still taken aback and angry about the type of questions they asked me. Questions like, "Did it feel good? Did you enjoy it?" What kind of question is that to ask an eight-year-old sexual assault victim? It's sickening!

I was eight years old and was molested by my twelve-year-old brother, and those pigs wanted to ask me if it felt good and if I enjoyed it? Where did they get off? They kept asking me how many times he humped me like I was supposed to lie there and count like

I was to count sheep! I was very angry and still am about the cold, ridiculous questions they asked me. That to me, at the time, was just as traumatizing as the act itself. I was completely embarrassed. They made me feel disgusting, like I was in the wrong. How could they ask an eight-year-old child that question? Why was that relevant?

My mother had to choose between Jordan and I. Which one of us was she going to send away? I can't imagine the position my mother was in to have to choose between two of her kids, but what her son did to her daughter should have made her choice a little easier. She chose for Jordan to be sent away. He was placed into the foster care system. Since he was twelve years old and a minor, he served no jail time or time in juvy. Being removed from his home was his only punishment, far less than what I got: a lifetime of blame, alienation, and an uphill battle of depression, hospitalization, suicidal ideations, rejection, blame, self-harmful behavior, and a lifetime of misery. My childhood was stolen from me. All innocence was lost.

How was I supposed to recover from this? My future looked dim at best. What was I supposed to do now? How was this going to affect the rest of my life? What kind of person would this turn me into? Why did this have to happen to me? What did I do wrong? How did I deserve this? I had so many questions, and my future looked unknown and riddled with uncertainty.

That little curly red-haired girl died that day her daddy went to prison. She was bound and chained and imprisoned in her own hell, and her own brother took the key and served her a life sentence for *his* crimes and perversions.

Every day from here on out was going to be a gruesome battle, an uphill climb. She never felt so alone in her life. What did the future hold for little eight-year-old Andrea? She died that day, and a new creature emerged from her ashes, a creature full of hatred and bitterness and anger; a creature who kept little Andrea imprisoned in a deep dark cell far within her own soul. The new Andrea was reclusive and vengeful, full of pity, and set on self-destruct. Her mission? Terminate the very memory of the once little innocent girl because it was too painful to remember how things once were.

2

A New Creature Emerges from the Ashes of a Dead Little Girl

A pedophile father and perverted older brother was one thing. A cold, hardened mother was another villain altogether and far more brutal. In fact, if it were not for her, my life probably would have turned out differently and easier, in spite of what Jordan and Clayton did. My mother was hell-bent on preserving her image and keeping the deep dark family secrets hidden that she sacrificed her daughter's well-being and happiness for the sake of keeping the family together. We were one big happy family, and all five of her kids were going to be together.

Clayton was actually molesting my older sister, Jennifer, for years, and my mother never knew about it. She never worked outside the home. In fact, she spent most of her time napping on the couch throughout the day and loved to watch her soap operas.

I remember one day being a nosey little kid. I had my ear pressed up against my bedroom door. I overheard Jennifer crying in our bedroom. She kept saying, "No! No! Stop!" I heard Clayton in there too. I thought Jennifer was getting into trouble. I held my ear against the door and was laughing at her. Just like any annoying little sister, I thought I was laughing at my older sister for getting into trouble, but that's not what was really going on. What I actually heard was my sick, perverted father molesting my older sister.

One day, Jennifer went to school after years of abuse and told her school counselor what was going on. That was how it all came out and was the family's undoing. Sometimes I wonder why it took her years to tell. Was he going to molest me next? Is that why she told? To protect me?

My mother never worked outside of the home, and Clayton worked on a farm milking cows. To this day, I never understood how my mother didn't know what was going on under her own nose. My mother didn't do a lot with us kids growing up. She never took us anywhere. We went to school and came home. We didn't even go with her to the store. Home and school were our lives. She barely even cooked for us. Jennifer did most of the cooking. Our trailer was infested with cockroaches. My mother has always been obsessed with family photos and plastered every square inch of every wall, bookshelves covered with family photos and knickknacks but not dirty.

From what Jennifer has told me over the years, my mother blamed her for getting molested and called her a slut. She was the reason why her husband went to prison away from his family. She blamed my sister for what Clayton did to her. My mom did not want to believe Jennifer. The police had to make her choose between her daughter or her husband, even though no matter what choice she made, he was going to go to prison. If she picked her kids, that did not stop her from writing letters back and forth or calling him. There was a pay phone across the street in front of the Herman's restaurant. She walked over there all of the time to talk to him. We even went over to my Aunt Goldie's house on occasion and got to talk to him over the phone. I remember asking him every time I got to talk to him, "When are you coming home, Daddy? I miss you."

He would always say, "Soon. I miss you too and love you. Be a good girl for your mom." He would always say, "Soon" every time I asked him when he was coming home.

When I asked him why he wasn't home, he would tell me that it was all a mistake and that it would all get sorted out soon. He would tell me that he was innocent. When he wrote us letters, he would also draw us cartoons, and I would write him back and draw pictures too.

In spite of him being gone, I still loved him. He was my dad, and I didn't understand why exactly he was there. I knew what Jennifer told me, but he always told me he was innocent and did nothing wrong, and I believed him.

My mother even planned on reconciling her marriage to him when he got out. But the long wait and burning desire to have a man take care of her was too much for her, so she started to date. She started to date this guy named Ken who was a real creep. I always felt uncomfortable around him, though he never did anything to me. He sat me on his lap a lot, and we were over at his house quite a bit.

The main thing I remember about him is one morning, me and the boys were all eating cereal at his house for breakfast. We stayed the night there. We mistook the salt for sugar and put salt on our cereal, and he made us all eat it because he didn't want us to waste it; it was disgusting.

I also remember that his yard was junky and that he had a ton of wood pallets. His yard was full of them, and when we went over there, my brothers and I made forts out of them.

One night, our trailer was filled with carbon monoxide, and my mother gathered us up, and Ken had to come get us. We spent the night at his house, but we had to leave early and go back home because two young girls were coming over to visit him.

My mom did not see much of him after that. In fact, she met another guy through him named Dwayne. We only met him a few times, and before we knew it, we were moving in with him. He lived in a very small town called Kingston on a backcountry dirt road surrounded by farm fields and woods. He had three kids of his own. Molly was the oldest, Dwayne Jr, or DJ as we called him, and then Nora was the youngest. Nora still lived with her dad, and she and Jennifer were only days apart in age.

Dwayne had this three-bedroom, two-bathroom newer double-wide on an acre of land. There was a farm field on the left that also connected behind us too. That field also extended to the other side of the neighbors to their right. There was also a field and woods across from us, so we were pretty rural.

Jennifer and I had to share a room. Nora wasn't giving up her own room, so the boys had to sleep on a pull-out bed together in the living room.

*****

Jumping back to the day Jordan was taken away, it was summer. After the police talked to me, I was sent outside to the backyard. I was peeking around the house and watched Jordan get taken away in handcuffs and put in the back seat of a police car. I felt guilty. I felt like it was my fault that he was being taken away. It was all my fault that my mother was crying. It was all my fault that my family was messed up. I just remember feeling such sorrow and guilt over the family being split up.

Not long after that, I found myself up in a tree in the backyard with my jump rope. It was a large pine tree and it was sticky. I had one end tied around a branch of a tree and the other end around my neck. How does an eight-year-old know how to commit suicide? I'm not sure, but I lost all hope at a very young age. Life was good before we had to move to Michigan. Our whole family just fell apart after we moved here, and our lives got turned upside down. My brother stole my innocence and got sent away, and my beloved daddy went to prison. My mom was crying and upset, and I felt as though it was my fault.

My mom has never been one to hug or love on us kids. We never really had a heart to heart. I could never talk to her. She has always been distant. This was the time I needed her the most. I was all alone. At such a young, tender age, tragedy struck twice, and our family was in shambles, and I had no one to turn to. I was left to sort through this by myself. As an eight-year-old girl succumbed by tragic events and the guilt it brought, I didn't see any other way out of this.

I don't think I really wanted to die. I just wanted things to go back to the way things were. I blamed myself for the way things were. My daddy was gone because of me, and Jordan was gone because of me, and my mom was upset and crying because of me. That was the sort of logic I had, even though I know now that it wasn't true.

I took all of the guilt upon myself, and it was overwhelming for my eight-year-old self to process and take. Maybe if I was gone, then the family would be back together again. Clayton and Jordan could both come home, and they could all be together again and normal again and happy again. My mother wouldn't be sad anymore, and I just wanted to make her happy.

Just as I was about to jump, my mother called out the back window for dinner. I didn't want her to know what I was doing, so I hurried up and untied the rope from around my neck and then from around the tree and hurried up and climbed down. It was a big tree that I was in, and I could see the front yard from how high up I was. That was my first suicide attempt.

It was just a couple of years later when I found out exactly why my brother did what he did. He looked up to Clayton. Clayton was his stepdad, but he was the only dad he ever knew. Jordan thought that if he did the same thing to me that Clayton did to Jennifer, then he would be where Clayton was, and they would be together.

Looking back, I understand that Jordan was just a child himself, and I have forgiven him, but it still does not excuse the fact that what he did ruined my life, and I put myself through hell and made some really bad decisions because of what he did, regardless of him being a child at the time. He was still old enough to know better. He knew that what he was doing was wrong, and I paid for his sins with my life. His actions drastically altered my life more than he could ever know. What he did was the domino that affected every other decision I ever made in my life. What he did was like an invasive virus that infected every aspect of my brain, my thoughts, heart, reactions and inactions, and it became a cancer that took over my mental health, physical health, and sanity. The cancer spread into my future relationships, and it ultimately killed the person who I was *supposed* to be and put in its place a girl broken and damaged, far beyond repair. What he did was irreparable.

*****

When we moved in with Dwayne, we couldn't move all of our stuff in right away and had to get rid of so much. Dwayne didn't want us to move the cockroaches in with us, so everything had to go in the front yard to be combed through before bringing them in the house. All of the extra stuff we stored in an old camper trailer in the back. We had a few cats as well, but Mom and Dwayne got rid of them before we moved and dropped them off somewhere at a farm. I had this fat orange male cat that I loved. That was my cat. I got him from Aunt Franny (Clayton's other sister). She lived with my grandpa, and they were hoarders. You couldn't walk through their house. They just had a narrow pathway to get to each room, and everything was piled high. They had a ton of cats, goats, and chickens. She had a litter of kittens, and I picked out the fattest one.

My mom and dad took us over there often to visit grandpa. I always tried chasing the cats down so that I could pet them. I was an animal lover and especially loved cats. I never had a pet before we moved to Michigan, and being in the city, I didn't really come into contact with too many animals. When Aunt Franny told me that I could have a kitten, I chased down this tiny fat orange kitten myself. They were in an old shed close to the house with a bunch of junk and were feral. I saw that orange one, and it was the one I wanted.

Aunt Franny helped me chase him down. I remember catching him, and he was struggling to get a way. He was wild and hissed at me, but I had a grip on him, and he wasn't going anywhere. He was coming home with me. He was mine. I got a kick out of how fat and round his belly was. Aunt Franny told me that it was a boy and asked me what I was going to name him. The first thought that came to my mind was Chubby, so that is what I named him. He never grew out of that belly. He was always a fat cat.

I have pictures of myself putting on puppet shows. I was a chatterbox and loved to tell stories, and I remember making a puppet show out of a cardboard box, and I would draw my characters on paper and glue them on cardboard and cut them out and tied string to them and made like a puppet show inside this box. I would tell stories with them, and Chubby would crawl inside my puppet show and become part of the story. *Mr. Roger's Neighborhood* was one of my favorite shows growing up which inspired my puppet shows. I had a wild imagination as a kid.

I was pretty upset that I couldn't keep this cat. My mom and Dwayne just dropped them all off at a farm. Dwayne didn't like cats. I always worried about Chubby. Was he being taken care of? Was he being fed? Was he warm in the winter? He was my very first cat, and I loved him. He was wild at first, but it didn't take long to tame him, and we became best friends.

*****

We got enrolled into Kingston Schools, and I went into the fourth grade. Mrs. Gerhardt was my teacher.

One night on a school night, Dwayne and my mom had company over, and they were up late, drinking and playing cards. They put up a curtain separating the living room from the kitchen and dining room. The boys were trying to sleep on the pull-out couch in the living room. They were goofing off instead of going to sleep, and they kept getting yelled at to settle down and go to sleep. How were they supposed to sleep with them partying and drinking in the next room with just a curtain separating the noise?

I was on my hands and knees peeking around my bedroom door, watching the boys horse around. My bedroom was right off the living room. I saw Dwayne come barging in the living room, busting through the curtain, yelling and screaming at the boys to settle down and go to sleep. He picked up Theo by the neck and body-slammed him down onto the bed and barked at them to go to sleep. With a pull-out bed, the mattress is thin, and there is a bar that goes across it. Imagine being a little boy being body-slammed onto that.

Dwayne had always had a short fuse and became the disciplinarian over my mom. He was way out of bounds most of the time, and every time she did try and stick up for us, they would get into a heated argument over it. So my mom just gave up. Dwayne was the boss. She would come to us and tell us that Dwayne had a temper and that we needed to behave because it was his house. She made excuses for him. I wasn't the brunt of Dwayne's temper, but the boys were because they were always doing something to push his buttons. They did everything they could to make Dwayne's life miserable. Theo was the main one to push Dwayne's buttons. Theo was very bullheaded and mouthy which really lit Dwayne's fuse. Theo was the troublemaker.

I became more and more reclusive and just hibernated in my bedroom. I would spend all day in my room. When I came home from school, I would go to my room and only came out for dinner.

None of my siblings liked Dwayne very much. I remember in the summertime, he would lock us outside. He wanted us outside to play and didn't want us running in and out. There were locks on the upright freezer to keep us kids away from their ice cream. Dwayne was always sitting at the table, watching TV, playing his handheld Yahtzee game and rolling cigarettes. He always went around without a shirt on, and his big belly was always sticking out. He wore suspenders to keep his shorts up, but his butt crack would still hang out. Dwayne's butt crack was a pretty common sight growing up. He also always wore his hair in a mullet with a long ponytail. He would sometimes ask me to braid it for him after his shower.

Dwayne never worked as long as we had known him. He had a back injury from multiple motorcycle accidents in his younger years, and he had to walk with a cane because of his unsteady gait.

After my mom met Dwayne, she had a few short-term jobs. She worked in a factory and came home really dirty. That didn't last long. She also tried working at McDonald's, but that didn't last long either because she didn't like working with young kids that told her what to do. She worked at Wingert's grocery store which was the longest job she had, but mainly, she and Dwayne stayed home and collected welfare, and Dwayne had disability.

We never went hungry as kids. Dwayne always made us dinner and had it ready for us or it was in the process of cooking when we came home from school, but we didn't have a lot of money or nice clothes or very many clothes. We sometimes got an outfit for our birthday or Christmas and maybe two or three outfits for school, and that was it. I was already very self-conscious as a kid. My hair was very bright orange, and I had unruly frizzy curls that I didn't know how to tame, so I always wore my hair up in a ponytail. I was really thin and always wore these big glasses.

Before meeting Dwayne, my mom always kept my hair really short which made my curls cling to my head even more because there was no weight to them. Dwayne loved long hair, so I no longer had to have short haircuts. I was old enough to do my own hair, so my unruly curls became my own problem. My mom also grew her hair out as well. Besides the mullet, she and Dwayne always had the same hairstyle: a low ponytail with a bunch of hair ties going down the length.

We all had to do chores. Jennifer and Nora were gone a lot, hanging out with friends or whatever. I always had to do the dishes, and we didn't have a working dishwasher. I also had to dust the living room which was a huge job because my mom had a ton of knick-knacks and pictures. I also had to do the vacuuming and cleaning of our bathroom. The two boys only had to mow grass in the sum-mertime and shovel snow in the winter. I was literally the redheaded stepchild and had to do most of the chores.

My mom and Nora never got along. My Uncle Timmy, my mom's little brother, came up to Michigan from Erie and helped us move back down to Erie. My mom said that she wasn't going to make Dwayne choose between her and her kids and his daughter. So we moved in the middle of that same school year and went back to Erie. It had been a few years since we came to Michigan, and a lot had changed. My mom would be leaving behind Jordan who was in fos-ter care. She wouldn't be able to see him once a week at Teen Ranch.

It was my father's side of the family that was from Michigan. All of my mom's family lived in Erie, so she decided to move us all back. Our first night there, we stayed with my Grandma Phyllis. I've been told that I looked and acted just like her, except she had dark black hair. I called her Mee-maw. We stayed with her for at least a week. Her apartment was so neat and clean, and she had this little Pomeranian.

Mee-maw always loved to play the lottery and always had to watch *Wheel of Fortune* and *Jeopardy*. One night, it was just me and Mee-maw sitting on the couch watching the *Wheel of Fortune*, and we were alone. She put her arm around me and hugged me tight. She told me that she was sorry about what Jordan did to me and that she was sorry about my dad. She told me that she never really liked my dad and that he was too old for my mom and that she didn't deem him a real man. She asked me if my dad ever touched me. I told her no. She told me to never let anyone touch me in my privates and that I needed to scream and run away and tell someone if they do.

This was never a conversation my mother had with me. She told me that she loved me but that she loved Jordan too because he was her grandson. She said my mom made the right decision by sending him away and that what happened was not my fault. I needed to hear someone say that to me: that it wasn't my fault. I'd felt like it was my fault for far too long.

Even though I heard those words, "It's not your fault," and it was something I desperately needed to hear, I still felt guilty and dirty and ashamed when Mee-maw was talking to me about this. I just sat there like a statue and froze up, not saying anything. I felt this tightening in my chest, and my stomach was in knots. That is how I get still to this day when someone confronts me or talks to me about something painful. The conversations are usually one-sided with me just sitting there, looking down in silence, listening and responding in my head but never verbally speaking what I wanted to say.

We moved in with my mom's longtime friend, Rose. Rose was Theo's godmother. Rose's sister, JoAnn, lived with her as well and she was my godmother. Rose's and JoAnn's mom, Brenda, who passed away a few years before that, was Joshua's godmother. JoAnn had a lot of health issues. She was in a wheelchair and had a catheter bag.

Rose had four kids. Alisha was the oldest, then Georgey, John Boy, and Felix. Alisha was a few years older than me. John Boy and Georgey were the boys' age, and Felix was a couple years younger than them.

They gave us the whole upstairs of the house. It had two bedrooms upstairs and a landing we used as our living room. We got enrolled in school. It was a huge school, and I was in the fourth grade. It was the same school I went to before we moved to Michigan, but I didn't really remember it. I went there for kindergarten and first grade. Boy, did I feel out of place. When we lived in Erie before, we lived in the projects in a primarily Black neighborhood which made our bright orange hair stick out even more. When we moved to Michigan, there weren't any Black people that lived around us or that went to my school.

Moving back to Erie was a culture shock. Even though I came from Erie and lived that city life, I became accustomed to that country lifestyle and small town. Erie was a whole brand-new world. We couldn't really play outside. There was no yard to play in, and all of the houses were pretty much on top of each other. There were a lot of rundown houses. I saw a family of kids holding up a sign to do a carwash to earn extra money. They were very poor. There was graffiti everywhere. It was a very sad, depressing place with so much poverty. We were now the minority. Most of my class was Black, and it didn't help that my bright orange hair made me stick out even more. I had such a hard time making friends. I was the new white girl. Being shy never made it any easier. It took me a while to be able to even talk to anybody, let alone make friends.

Recess was a lot different than in Kingston, Michigan. One day, the girls would go outside for recess, and the boys would all stay in the cafeteria to hang out. Then the next day, the boys would go outside, and the girls had to stay in the cafeteria. It's because the school was so large and there were so many kids. That system worked to help manage the number of kids, especially since the playground wasn't big enough to accommodate that many. There really wasn't a playground. There was just a cement slab that was fenced in, and we got to play four square, tag, jump rope, or just hang out. We had to entertain ourselves.

One day in class, it was my turn to be the leader in line to collect our fluoride tablets and go to the drinking fountain. This bigger Black girl named Cedrice, who never liked me, was standing behind me in line. Cedrice kept kicking the back of my legs. I ignored her at first. It takes me awhile to get worked up, and I'll let my anger build up before I lash out.

I told her to stop, but she kept doing it. So like a switch that went off, I turned around and grabbed her hair, dragged her out of line, and kept banging her head on the desk, breaking her glasses. The teacher split us up and yelled at Cedrice. She was the class bully, and the teacher called her out on it and told her that she needed to stop being so mean to everyone. After that incident, I built up enough courage to at least talk to my classmates. I never made any real friends, but at least people talked to me after that, and Cedrice never bothered me again.

Alisha and I became close. She loved the band NSYNC and loved Justin Timberlake. Alisha and I would jam to their music. She also loved the movie *Titanic*, and I watched it for the first time with her. Her favorite part of the movie was when Rose and Jack were dancing and spinning around in circles really fast, laughing. She and I did that too. Alisha was like the cool big sister I never had, but she wasn't the best influence either. She had cool clothes and dressed like a city girl. Her hair was always done with a pound of hair spray, and she always wore dark lipstick with painted on eyebrows. She wore huge hoop earrings, and her pants were always baggy with her belly showing. She dressed really hip, and I wanted to be just like her. She did my hair and makeup for me and gave me some of her clothes.

My mom would never let me wear makeup to school or wear any of Alisha's clothes. My mom had to pick us up from school and drop us off. There was no school bus.

Alisha went to school for troubled kids. She got kicked out of all the other public schools, mainly from fighting. She was trouble, and I looked up to her. She was also the one who taught me how to shave my legs for the first time. My mom was never really there for all of the girl milestones, not for my period, shaving, or anything like that. I had to figure out all of that stuff on my own.

I didn't really care for the younger brother, Felix, though. That kid was out of control. He was a kindergartener, and his mom let him smoke cigarettes. John Boy and Georgey were always wrestling and fighting too. There was a WWE wrestling match there every day between the boys. There wasn't any discipline in that house, and the kids were basically allowed to do whatever they wanted.

One day, Felix was upstairs, and I headed downstairs when Felix, unprovoked, pushed me down the stairs. They were long, narrow, uncarpeted wooden stairs. Once I hit the bottom, I was madder than a hornet, and my adrenaline was pumping. Felix came down the stairs, and I did a football tackle on him and tackled him to the floor, sitting on top of him, punching him in the stomach, in the face, and grabbing his hair and banging his head into the floor over and over again until my mom pried me off of him. That kid was going to get what he deserved. Neither of us got into trouble for fighting. Like I said, that house was a madhouse, and there were fights between the kids every day. Felix got what he deserved for pushing me down the stairs.

I don't know what happened, but years later, when we went back to visit, Felix was actually autistic and had a lot of mental issues and could barely talk. When I saw him again, I actually felt guilty and thought I was the cause of his condition after banging his head on the floor, possibly giving him brain damage.

My sister, Jennifer, searched for her real dad after we moved back to Erie, and she did end up tracking him down. He lived in a small studio apartment not far from where we were staying. He was an alcoholic. Jennifer had a lot of questions and wanted some answers. We went to see him as a whole family and gathered around his small table. Jennifer asked him why he left her and Jordan. He said that my mom took them and ran off and wouldn't let him see them and then moved them to Michigan and that he lost track of them. Jennifer asked him why he didn't come and look for them, and he said that he couldn't find them, especially after they moved out of state.

My understanding is he turned into an alcoholic because he was separated from his kids and didn't know where they were and just gave up and started drinking.

We didn't stay in Erie for very long. One good thing my mom did for us kids was realizing that the city was not a good place to raise children. In spite of her mom and all of her family being there, she had to get out of there. She had to move us back to the country and back to Michigan. We were only in Erie for maybe a little more than a month.

Before we left, my mom and Jennifer got into a fight. Jennifer wanted to stay in Erie and live with her newly found dad. She wanted to get to know him, but she and Mom didn't get along, especially after what happened between her and Clayton. She didn't want to move back to Michigan. She didn't get along with Dwayne either. She just wanted to stay in Erie, so she refused to get in the car when it was time for us to leave.

I remember Jennifer was trying to run out the back door in Rose's kitchen. Her dad was only a few blocks away, and she wanted to run to his house. My mom had her pinned down up against the back door with her arm on the door, and they were nose to nose, arguing back and forth. My mom told her that he couldn't take care of her. He didn't have a bedroom for her and lived in a tiny studio apartment and was an alcoholic. I think Jennifer was sixteen at the time, which made me eleven because she kept saying she was old enough to decide who she wanted to live with.

Needless to say, Jennifer got in the car and moved back to Michigan with us, and we all moved back in with Dwayne and Nora, which did not go over so well with Nora because she liked being an only child, and her dad's girlfriend and kids were intruding on her home and space.

I was glad to be back in Michigan and back in Kingston schools. I missed all my friends. When I first walked in the door of my school, my best friend, Jody, ran up to me and gave me a big hug. She told me that she had a dream the night before that I moved back to Kingston, and then she came to school, and here I was.

I was an honor student, but because of the move in the middle of the school year and then moving back, I didn't make the honor roll that semester, but I was close. Mrs. Gerhardt, my fourth-grade teacher, worked with me and let me do the makeup work to try and catch up.

Not only was I an honor student, but I also always won first place in the Young Author's Competition, not only for just our school but all the schools in the district who competed in the contest. I loved to write and always dreamed of becoming a published author one day. I had a wild imagination ever since I was a little girl and was always making up stories and conversations with my Barbie dolls. When I went to Marlette schools, I was always winning first place there too. I mainly wrote stories about my fat orange cat named Chubby. Chubby had a lot of adventures in my stories. Writing has always been an outlet for me, and I also love to read. I would finish a whole chapter book within a day or two. It was a great way for me to get lost in another story to take my mind off my own.

Although I was glad to be back in Michigan and have my old friends back, things were not going well at home. I started going to counseling in Caro, Michigan. This was the first time in three years since Clayton went to prison, and Jordan stole my innocence that I was finally able to go talk to somebody. For those three years, I was forced to deal with it all on my own with no one to talk to or help me process it. My counselor's name was Denae, and I really liked her. She was an older lady. I could not talk to my mom about anything, and it was even hard for me to talk to Denae. I found that it was much easier to write everything out on paper and give it to her to read during our session and then discuss it.

Before all of this happened to me, I never had a problem verbalizing my thoughts or speaking my mind. In fact, you couldn't get me to shut up half of the time. I wasn't shy and had no issues talking an ear off a fly. It seemed as though when Jordan took my innocence that day, he took my voice with it. I changed that day and became someone entirely different. This Andrea couldn't talk to someone while looking them in the eyes. Eye contact was a struggle, right up into adulthood. I always felt awkward looking at someone in the eye and always hung my head down in shame, afraid of them seeing through all of the brokenness and sadness and secrets I buried deep down in my soul. Talking about feelings and hard subjects has never come easy. I always knew what I wanted to say, but the inability to verbalize them overcame me.

There were times when my sessions were particularly difficult, and Denae just sat there next to me on her sofa with a tab of paper. The session would be almost completely silent, and she would just write out a question, and then I would write out my answer and go back and forth. Writing it out was much easier than trying to form the words on my tongue to speak them. During counseling, I would always talk to Denae by myself, and then she would call my mom back, and Denae would bring up issues that needed to be addressed.

I isolated myself in my bedroom most of the time, and the reason for that was because my mom was a picture freak. She plastered every wall in the house and bookshelves with family photos which included pictures of Jordan. There was a lot of pictures of Jordan. My bedroom was right off the living room. The wall right next to my bedroom door, my mom had eight-by-ten pictures of all five of her kids in order from oldest to youngest. I was always the middle right after Jordan. Under those pictures was a small bookshelf filled with more pictures of us kids and knickknacks. It was also my job to dust all of those pictures and knickknacks, so I spent a lot of time looking at them. That was right in front of my bedroom door. Every time I came in and out of my room, I saw his face. After all of the hell he put me through, why would I want to see his face and be reminded of what he did to me and the pain he caused me?

That wasn't the only place she had pictures of him. There were pictures of him on every wall in every room. Everywhere I turned, there he was, staring back at me, reminding me of the pain he caused and the life he stole from me. The only safe place I had where Jordan wasn't staring at me was my bedroom. My bedroom walls were covered in crosses and artwork. It was my safe place. I didn't know God at the time, but the crosses on my walls made me feel safe. What victim would want to stare at the face of the monster who hurt them and be reminded of what they did day in and day out? I can understand that it was my mom's son. Any mother should have the right to hang their kid's picture with pride. Was I being selfish for feeling this way?

Denae brought this issue up with my mother one day at counseling. My mom was highly offended by Denae, asking her to remove Jordan's pictures from the walls and asked her to only display them in her own bedroom. She wasn't mum about her displeasure in taking down every picture of her son. I presume she felt like she was removing the memory of one of her children. There isn't a thing your child can do to make you stop loving them, even if it includes hurting one of your other children, and I think she felt like she wasn't honoring her son by taking down all of his pictures and essentially removing him from the family. But should a son like that deserve honor when they have disgraced the family like he did?

I tried so hard to put myself in my mother's shoes. I was asking her to take down all of the pictures of one of her kids. Asking her to do this was very difficult for me to do. I felt like I was being selfish. It's bad enough he wasn't home and was being raised in the foster care system. Now I was asking her to remove him altogether. Was I being fair? But seeing his face every day really bothered me. I was stuck between my mother's happiness and my own psychological well-being. Was I really asking a mother to choose between two of her kids? Was I asking her to choose *me* over her son?

My mother did feel like she had every right to hang pictures loud and proud just like the rest of her kids. What he did didn't make him any less her son. He should be up on the walls just like the rest of us. She was not happy about taking them down and really made a show of it.

I remember my mom bringing me a baby picture of Jordan and asking me if it bothered me if she left it out. She had it displayed on the bookshelf by my bedroom door and had every intention to leave it there. I could tell that she was disgusted by her tone and choice of words. She was very angry, and it killed her to take them down, and she was set on making me feel guilty about it because it was my fault that she was put into this position in the first place. I was being selfish for asking her to do this, and I should have just swallowed my feelings and dealt with it.

Of course, it bothers me that *any* picture of Jordan was within my sight, even a baby picture. I see that baby picture, and it makes me think of Jordan and what he did to me. It didn't matter that it was a baby picture or a recent picture. It was still a picture of him. I just told my mom that it was okay to keep that baby picture out. She made me feel so guilty about it, and I have never been able to stand up to my mom and tell her how I really feel or think.

My mother hated that I went to counseling because Denae always brought things up to her that bothered me and was questioned about it. To my mom, I always made her look like a bad mother, and she didn't like that. Things were never her fault, and she never liked to take responsibility for anything.

One day, I decided I wanted to confront Jordan and just ask him why he did what he did. With the help of my counselor, Denae, we set up a meeting between me and Jordan, both mine and his counselor, and my mom. I wrote a long letter to read out loud in the meeting. In the letter, I described in every detail of what Jordan did to me except for the part about my two younger brothers. I wanted Jordan to *hear* all of the disgusting things he did and what pain and torment he caused me and wanted my mom to hear it too. I wanted Jordan to feel disgusting and guilty, which is why I spared no gory detail. Then, at the end, I asked him questions, and he would have to respond to each one.

My mom left as soon as I started to describe what he did to me. She just got up and walked out when I needed her the most. I needed her to be there for me, but she just couldn't listen to the horrible things her son did. It was not easy for me to sit there across from him and read everything out like that. It was extremely hard for me, and my mother couldn't sit through it and be there for me. She didn't hold my hand or hug me or support me in any way. I've always had to deal with it on my own. She ran out, crying. I wanted her to hear it just as much if not more than Jordan because then maybe she would understand what I went through and how I feel.

This was when Jordan told me that he thought that if he did the same thing to me as Clayton did to Jennifer, then he would be with Clayton. Jordan apologized to me for what he did.

Yeah! He better be sorry! I thought. Aside from knowing the why, I really wanted to make him feel horrible for what he did. I wanted to make him feel like the scum of the earth. I wanted him to be sorry. It was like I was this different person. I was vindictive with a heart boiling with rage and hatred and anger, and I took great pleasure in him crying at the meeting. I shed a lot of tears over what he did. It was about time that he did too.

My mom didn't say a word to me the rest of the day. The car ride home was nothing but awkward silence. My mother still does not know the extent or any detail of what her son did to me to this day. She refuses to hear it and chooses to remain ignorant to it.

Not long after that meeting, my mother persuaded me to go to Teen Ranch with the rest of the family to visit Jordan. I most certainly did *not* want to go and see Jordan, but I could not stand up to my mother and wanted to make her happy, especially after the whole picture incident. I wanted to make it up to her somehow, so I begrudgingly tagged along on these most dreaded family visits. My mom had a talent for guilting me into doing things I didn't want to do.

So once a week, I went to Teen Ranch in Marlette, Michigan, to visit the very person responsible for ruining my life. We mainly just played Skip-Bo or just talked. I hardly ever said two words. I avoided looking at Jordan at all cost. I always looked down. I found myself counting the wood grains in the big round table we sat at. I tried keeping my mind somewhere else.

Sometimes I caught myself going back to the pain that Jordan put me through. I tried so hard to block it out. I didn't want to be there. I just wanted to be home, locked away in my bedroom.

My mom was so happy that I was there, though. She made comments like, "I'm so glad to see all five of my kids together again" or "You all are brothers and sisters. You need to get along and be there for each other." My mom made comments like that a lot.

I always felt so guilty for not wanting to be there and for not wanting to make my mom happy. I felt so guilty that we all had to go to Teen Ranch once a week to visit him in the first place. Why couldn't I just forgive Jordan and put the past behind me so that my mom could have her family back together again? That would have made her happy. I tried so hard to put my own feelings and well-being aside to make her happy. I always felt like my mom blamed me for Jordan being sent away. A mother should not have to choose between her kids, but I made her choose between me and her son. Even though it was Jordan that she sent away, I always felt like she chose him.

In my head, I knew I had every right to be angry. I had every right to not want to see Jordan. I knew that in my head that none of this was my fault. It wasn't my fault that he was in foster care and separated from the family. I knew in my head that Jordan was to blame for everything. But my mom had a way of making me feel guilty and stamping the blame all over my forehead.

During one of the visits at Teen Ranch, Jordan's counselor called me into a separate room. He read right through me and knew I didn't want to be there. I barely talked and always hung my head. He came right out and asked if it was my choice that I was there. I had to tell him that I didn't want to be there. I told him that I only came to make my mom happy. He called my mom into the room and told her I didn't want to be there and that the only reason I came was to make her happy.

My mother sure did play it up. She cried. She said, "Andrea, you know you didn't have to come if you didn't want to. I don't want you to be miserable. Don't worry about making me happy. I want you to be happy. Why can't you come and talk to me and tell me what bothers you?"

My mother sure did know how to put on a show. It made her so happy that I was going to Teen Ranch with the rest of the family to visit Jordan. She really pressured me to go and see him. If I didn't want to see his face plastered all over the wall, then what made her think that I wanted to see him once a week in person?

Not long after I quit going to those family visits, my mom confronted me about going to counseling. She always grumbled about having to take me, and she cancelled them on me quite a few times. She asked me if I really needed counseling. I did really need it, but I couldn't tell her that. She said she didn't always have the gas money to take me all the way to Caro to go to counseling, but she sure was able to go to Marlette every week to see Jordan. It was the same distance either way. They were both a twenty-minute drive, just in opposite directions.

My mother just didn't want me to make her look bad. It was all about her image. She didn't want me to tell the counselor anything. She wanted to do anything she wanted without anybody saying anything about it. That is the way my mother was. She wasn't worried about her daughter needing anyone to talk to. She didn't seem to care that her daughter was miserable. She didn't care that her daughter bottled everything up inside as long as she kept her mouth shut and didn't make her look bad as a mother. That is why I couldn't go to counseling anymore.

At my last counseling appointment, I told Denae that I didn't need counseling anymore. I told her that I was doing better and that I was happy. I wanted to scream inside. I don't think she believed me. Denae called my mom in and asked my mom how I was doing. My mother really played it up.

"Andrea is doing a lot better. She's not in her room as much. She's smiling a lot more. I don't think she needs counseling anymore."

I wanted to *scream* inside! I *needed* counseling! I needed someone to talk to. I had no one. I was miserable inside. Who was I going to talk to now? I couldn't talk to my mother about anything. I wanted to die.

3

The Darkness Grows

Since my mother made me give up counseling, I had to find some other way to talk to someone without my mother knowing about it. If she didn't know about it, then she couldn't take it away. It felt good talking about things and getting them out of me instead of keeping it all in. I needed that validation that it was okay to feel the way I did because my mother made me feel like how I was feeling was wrong, and I felt guilty about it. The more I trapped them inside, the more the darkness within me grew and consumed me from the inside out. My mother couldn't understand that because she was more worried about preserving her own image, but mainly, I think it was because she wanted to suppress the truth and remain ignorant because if she did that, then she didn't have to come to terms with it, and it would be like it never happened. If she ignored it, it would just go away. That is how she dealt with it.

I imagine it was hard for my mom to have to deal with all of this in her own way, and her way was to just shove it under a rug and carry on as if it never happened because it was much easier than to have to face it. But she was selfish about it and never considered how I felt and had to process it.

I wrote down all of my feelings. I wrote down what Jordan did to me and about how my mother made me quit going to counseling and that I was so depressed. I wrote it down in a long letter and shoved it under Mrs. Henry's office door. She was the school coun-

36

selor. She came and got me from class later that day. I had butterflies in my stomach. I didn't know what to expect. That was a long walk back to her office. For a moment, I regretted giving her that letter because I said I wanted to die and didn't know what she would do with that. By this time, I was in the fifth grade and had Mr. Bruce for a teacher who was young and good-looking.

Mrs. Henry was finally someone I could talk to. I kept writing her letters and shoving them under her door when I first got there in the morning. She was someone I could talk to, and my mom didn't know about it and couldn't take it away from me.

When I was in the sixth grade, my depression continually got worse. This is also when I first developed an eating disorder. I felt like I had no control over my life, but what I did to my own body I was going to have control over. I could control *this one thing!* All I could think about was making myself suffer. I didn't want to live. All I could feel and see was just pain surrounding me with no way out. I just wanted to starve to death and die. I would not eat breakfast in the morning before school. I sat with my friends at school but did not get lunch. My excuse was that I didn't like school lunches and would just wait to eat when I got home.

Occasionally, I did eat lunch if it was something that I liked, like pizza. When I did eat, I would go to the bathroom and shove my fingers down my throat and throw it up. Yes, I was hungry. My stomach and body were screaming for food, and I was miserable, but in a way, I took pleasure in my physical suffering because it took my mind off my mental anguish. I welcomed the pain. The emptiness I felt in my stomach masked the emptiness I felt in my soul.

About the time we got home from school, I was starving and always came home to the smell of Dwayne's cooking. He wasn't a very good cook, and I always ate very little. Even though I was still hungry, I would never go back for seconds. I went straight to my room afterward. Sometimes I went straight to the bathroom to throw up everything I just ate and ran the water in the sink to drown out the sound of it. Sometimes I had to go outside to throw up in the cornfield or out back behind the camper.

At first, it was never about weight because I was already really thin, but the more I starved myself and threw up what little I did eat, it morphed into a full-blown eating disorder, and every time I did look in the mirror, I did see a fat ugly pig. It was always about *control* for me, though, because there wasn't anything else in my life that I had control over.

One downfall I had was sweets, and I would get to the point where I was so hungry that I would break down and sneak to the kitchen and grab Debbie's snacks and junk food, anything sweet, and take them to my room and gorge myself on them and then puke it all up. I was always starving but would never let myself eat.

My eating disorder started out as something I could control, but it soon transformed into something that controlled me. I cried myself to sleep sometimes because I was so hungry. I was miserable.

One day in the sixth grade, I missed the bus on purpose. I watched all of the buses leave without me. I walked up town to the main street in town which was M-46. I wanted to die so desperately. I was tired of being miserable. I was depressed and hopeless and felt utterly alone in the world with no way out. I was so blinded by my own pain that I could only see the darkness that I was in. My family was broken. My mother wasn't there for me emotionally nor was she supportive in any way. I wasn't going to counseling anymore. I mean, I talked to Mrs. Henry, the school counselor, but I was going into the high school next year and couldn't talk to her during the summer and just felt like such a burden to her. I thought I was better off dead. I would remove myself out of the equation so that my family could move on without me and be happier with me out of the way. I was tired of being hungry and hurting myself.

Was my entire life going to be this way? I couldn't bear the thought of spending my whole life miserable like this. That wasn't living but simply just existing. I didn't want to exist. I just wanted the pain to end. My mother made me miserable most of all. I couldn't please her nor make her happy. I never felt like she loved me. She would never sit on my bed and hold me while I cried. She never comforted me. I didn't get any of that from her. No "Everything is going to be okay." No reassurance. I never got anything of the sort from her. I needed that so desperately, and I think that if I would have gotten that from her, things would have turned out so much differently.

I didn't feel wanted or loved or important. I felt like my feelings were invalid and that I was the one being selfish for not forgetting about what happened and moving on so that the family could be back together. My mother made me feel like I was wrong for feeling the way I did, yet I couldn't help but feel the way I did. Was I the monster for keeping the family apart? Why couldn't I just forgive Jordan and forget about what he did to me? Why couldn't we just be one big happy family again? It was *me* getting in the way of that. Everyone else was willing to move on, but I could not. It's not that I didn't want to. I wish I could just forget about what happened so that I could move on. It would have made my life so much easier. But I just *couldn't*.

My plan was to jump out in front of a semitruck. M-46 was a pretty busy highway, and semis went through there all the time. I saw a semitruck coming to my left. This was it. I was finally going to be out of this hell I was in. This semitruck was going to release me from this hell I was in, this mental anguish and total despair and torment. Was it going to hurt? Would it be an instantaneous death? I didn't want it to hurt. I just wanted the pain to end. I wanted to be put out of my misery. I wanted that semi to hurry up so I could run out in front of it before I changed my mind.

Just as I was about to step out in front of that semi and stepped one foot toward my pain-free nonexistence, I looked across the street and saw my sister coming out of Beigeos. Beigeos was a pizza place, and they had arcade with games and pool tables in there. A lot of kids loved to hang out there. She saw me, so she was coming out of Beigeos to see why I missed the bus.

I didn't want my brains splattered all over the road in front of my sister no matter how badly I wanted to die. I remember thinking that I couldn't let that be the last image she saw of me in her head. I couldn't do that to her. So I took a step back and let the semi pass and then safely crossed the street to my sister. I acted like nothing was wrong and told her that I missed the bus and was walking home.

Mrs. Chris, who worked in the office at the elementary school, pulled up and saw me. She told me that there were a lot of people out looking for me and that my mom was on her way to come and get me. I went with her, and she drove me back up to the school. She told me that I needed to be careful. "There are a lot of crazy people in the world, and a young girl like you should not wander off alone like that again."

Mrs. Henry pulled me aside when I got to the school, and I told her that I just missed the bus. I was scared to tell her the real reason why I missed the bus.

When my mom got to the school, she was pretty mad about me missing the bus, but I got in the car with her and went home.

When I got home, I went to my room and wrote a letter to Mrs. Henry, telling her the real reason why I missed the bus. A couple of hours after school started, Mrs. Henry came and got me from class. We had a long talk about me wanting to kill myself. She asked me how I thought the driver of that semitruck would feel if he killed a young girl and that he would have had to live with that for the rest of his life. I never thought about that, but I didn't care. I just wanted to end my own suffering. I didn't want to live the life I was living anymore, and the only way I saw to get out of it was to take my own life.

I never went back to class that day and had to leave school early. Mrs. Henry was a mandated reporter, so she had to report that I was suicidal and had these thoughts of killing myself and tried jumping out in front of a semi. My mother was called up to the school, and she had to take me back up to Caro to see my old counselor, Denae. I was happy to see Denae again. I missed talking with her, but then she told me that I had to go to the hospital for my own protection, and I wasn't so happy to see her after that. I was pretty angry. My mom took me home to get some clothes and then drove me up to the psych ward in Saginaw where I was hospitalized.

At this point, I was very angry about what was happening to me. All I wanted was to be able to talk to someone about anything and about my feelings. I just wanted to be cared about and validated. I felt like Mrs. Henry and Denae both betrayed me. How was I supposed to talk to them now? If I couldn't trust them with my deepest darkest feelings of feeling like I wanted to die, then what else couldn't I trust them with?

I was so terrified. I wish I would have jumped out in front of that semi, even though my sister was standing there. I wouldn't be locked up in this crazy place if I had. *Why do I always put everyone else's feelings and well-being above my own? This is why I'm in this situation.* It was crazy to me that I was being punished for my depression. Jordan was the one who hurt me. Clayton was the child molester. My mother was a horrible mother and blamed me and made me feel guilty about Jordan not being a part of the family. But I was the one being locked up and punished. It just didn't seem fair. There was something wrong with this picture.

The psych ward was a horrible place to be. When I arrived, I had to go into this small room and talk to this guy about why I had to be there. He told me about all my legal rights and all of the rules I had to go by. What rights did I have anyway? They were allowed to keep me for three days, and I would be under twenty-four-hour surveillance. I wasn't allowed to leave. I was a minor. So what rights did I really have? I committed the horrible crime of depression.

After I went through the process of being admitted, I was led down this long hallway. There were doors at the end of it. The lady punched in a code, and the doors opened and then locked behind us. I flinched at the sound of those doors. This was it. This is what prison felt like.

We went through two more locked doors, and each time the doors opened and then clicked behind us, I flinched. I was really going to be locked in this place, and there was no way out. I wasn't ever going to get out of here. I was a crazy person, and they don't let crazy people out, do they?

When I got to where I was supposed to be, I was led to my room. I was made to strip all of my clothes off in front of this lady, and she had to examine each article of clothing and go through my pockets to make sure I wasn't hiding anything that could be used as a weapon to hurt myself or someone else. I was so shy and embarrassed. I felt like I was being traumatized all over again, standing there in front of a stranger in my nakedness. How was this supposed to help me?

After she checked my clothes and patted me down, I was able to get dressed, but then she moved on to searching through my bag. She took the drawstring out of my pajama pants in case I decided to hang myself with it. She also took the drawstring out of my sweatshirt. I hoped she knew those weren't so easy to put back in there. She also took my pencils and notebook away. Apparently, I wasn't allowed to have those either because sharp pencils could be used as a weapon or a tool for self-harm, and the notebook had a spiral binder on it which could also be used as a sharp object that people could cut themselves with. I also had to wear shoes without shoelaces. I guess people can be pretty creative and ingenious when it comes to wanting to hurt themselves. This place was nuts.

I wanted to die so desperately that I went to the extreme of almost getting splattered by a semitruck, and this treatment was supposed to make me feel better? I didn't get it. It just did not make any sense to me. I felt so invaded and humiliated by the strip search. I never had to be naked in front of a woman before. I never even undressed in front of my own sister.

After the search, the lady led me out to the main common area where there were at least twelve other kids along with a woman worker. They were all sitting around the table, doing group therapy. I was introduced to everyone, and everyone went around the table, introducing themselves. There were kids of all ages, most of them teens, and most of them were boys. There were only a few girls, but they were all older than me. When they all introduced themselves, they all had to say why they were there.

One girl had nasty scars all over her arms. She had long sleeves on, but she rolled them up to show me why she was there. One person tried to hang themselves. One boy threatened to shoot himself. They were all there because they were suicidal. When I had to tell them why I was there and told them I tried jumping out in front of a semi, they were shocked and started asking me a bunch of questions. They didn't understand why I was still here in one piece if I tried jumping out in front of a semi. I had to explain to them that my sister was across the street and that I didn't want to do it in front of her. They asked me how people found out what I was going to do. I told them that I told my school counselor. They all told me that next time I shouldn't tell anybody because I would just end up back here, locked up in the nuthouse, and they would just try and stop me from hurting myself.

The group counselor ended that conversation and scolded everyone for those comments. One girl told me that I looked really young and innocent. Jumping out in front of a semi seemed a bit drastic to her.

I hated being there. I didn't understand how being there was supposed to help me. That night, I couldn't sleep. People kept opening the door throughout the night to check on us.

Really early in the morning, I got woken up for blood work, vitals, and meds. I didn't even have to get out of bed or sit up for it. One of the nurses commented on how beautiful my curly red hair was and asked if it was natural. I'd been told that a lot. It seemed like not long after that, I had to get up. I got up and got ready for a shower and asked one of the nurses if I could have a razor to shave. They told me I could, but not without supervision.

Forget that. I wasn't going to have someone watch me take a shower just so I could shave. This place was so traumatizing. I had already been through so much and just couldn't understand how this place was supposed to make me better. They kept telling me that they wouldn't let me out unless I showed signs of improvement. I had to give them a reason to believe that I wouldn't hurt myself once I got out. How was I going to do that? I was miserable.

I refused all three meals that day. I felt so hollow inside. I was in hell. I felt abandoned and worthless. I was locked up in a nuthouse and was never going to get out of there because this place could not make me better, and I had to be better in order to leave.

After breakfast, we had to walk around the unit for exercise for ten minutes. There were four short hallways that went around in a square. I was speed walking around the unit but got yelled at to slow down. They were watching me more closely because I had been refusing all of my meals.

We had group therapy twice a day and one-on-one counseling once a day, and participation was mandatory.

That day, a really young girl arrived who was about six or seven years old. I don't remember why she was there, but she cried the entire time. I felt really bad for her. Why would a really young girl like that be here? What could she have possibly done to be put in a psych ward at such a young age?

In the common area, there was a foosball table, ping-pong table, bookshelves loaded with books and games, a big screen TV—but we were only allowed to watch the History Channel—and a couch and chairs to sit on. There was a big table in the center where we had our meals and did our group therapy.

There was this seventeen-year-old boy there. He kept flirting with me. He sat beside me on the couch and picked me up and put me on his lap. I tried getting off his lap, but he wrestled me and tickled me to make me stay on his lap.

There was a woman who stayed in the common area at all times to supervise us. I kept expecting her to say something to break it up and rescue me. It seemed like it was forever before she finally did say something, and I was able to sit by him instead of on his lap which made me feel very uncomfortable. He held my hand pretty tightly too, and my hand became sweaty. Why did he stake his claim on me so heavily? I barely said anything to him. I was very shy. I never flirted with him. I was too vulnerable to speak up for myself.

What Jordan did to me paralyzed me in a way. I was easily taken advantage of. I couldn't speak up when I was uncomfortable, and my body would just tense right up and become weak with no willpower, no voice, and just excrete every bit of vulnerable pheromones which attracted guys looking for an easy target.

When this boy asked me for my address and phone number, I gave him a fake one. He was seventeen, and I was twelve. He was in the ward because he threatened to shoot himself with his dad's gun.

I did manage to get away from him and go to the far corner of the common area to sit with the girls. One of the girls warned me about him. She said that he just wanted in my pants and that he was going to try and sneak in my room that night.

They did fifteen-minute bed checks, so I knew he wouldn't be able to get too far. Also, my room was right next to the nurse's station, and girls were on one end, and the boys were on the other end of the hall.

The boy came up to me, picked me up, and started spinning me around in circles. I was screaming at him to put me down.

The woman left in charge to supervise us finally yelled at him to put me down and told him that he needed to keep his hands to himself.

I spent three long days in that hell. The first two days, I didn't eat anything at all. Then I realized that in order for me to get out of there, I had to show some signs of improvement. So on the third day, I ate all three meals, got more involved in group, and acted like I was getting better so that they would release me and let me go home. I was released the very next morning and was able to go home to my own bedroom and my own bed. I was so happy to be home and out of that place.

Since I skipped the bus to run out in front of a semi, Mrs. Henry made sure to pick me up from class to escort me to the bus every day when it was time to go home to make sure I got on it. She did that for the longest time. She still pulled me out of class to talk to me, and I still wrote her letters. The first one I wrote after I got out of the psych ward wasn't very nice. I was very angry at her for turning me in and causing me to go to that place. I was careful of what I told her after that.

I was also very angry at Denae for sending me there. I spent a few sessions not saying anything to her and giving her the silent treatment. One time, I even brought in a handheld Yahtzee game to play instead of talking to her, and she got mad and told me to put it away. I didn't see her for very long after that. Counseling services got cancelled again, but this time, it was me that cancelled. I was so angry about being put in the psych ward and couldn't fully trust her or Mrs. Henry anymore with my feelings.

*****

Kingston schools were divided up between two schools. The elementary school went from grades K–6, and the high school went from grades seven to twelve. I was going into the seventh grade this year. I was excited to finally be in the high school.

The day before my first day in high school, I was sitting up on my bed, writing. Jennifer was also sitting on her bed doing something. Her bed was right up against the window. When I looked out the window, I saw this strange-looking man outside in our yard, leaning against the BBQ grill. I couldn't see his face, and he was dressed rather oddly. It was August, and he was dressed in a trench coat and wore a top hat.

I pointed him out and asked Jennifer if she knew who that was. She couldn't see who I was talking about.

"Right there! He's leaning up against the grill," I said.

"There isn't anybody there," she said.

I dropped it and didn't say anything more about it, but I knew what I saw. I wasn't crazy.

Later that night, I went to bed early because the next day was my first day of high school. I couldn't sleep because I was excited and anxious about the first day of school. I was wondering about what it was going to be like going from two classes a day to seven.

Since Jennifer and Nora were older, they got to stay up later. I kept tossing and turning. I couldn't go to sleep. All of a sudden, the man I saw earlier leaning against the grill emerged from my closed bedroom door. He stood over me, and I stared at him, trying to see his face, but it was too dark. He came over and sat at the foot of my bed.

"What do you want?" I asked.

"I could take you to Africa, far, far away from here," he said. His voice was deep, and he was almost whispering to me.

I always wanted to go to Africa. I loved animals, and seeing them in their natural environment in Africa was a dream of mine.

"I know what your father and brother did. Your mom isn't very understanding and doesn't treat you very nice. If you go with me to Africa, I will get revenge on every person that has ever hurt you. They will pay for what they have done to you. In order for me to do that, you have to sign this piece of paper, giving me permission to seek out revenge on your behalf and to take you away to Africa where these people will never be able to hurt you again."

He had this old looking scroll and a feather pen.

Revenge sounded so sweet at that moment. I started to imagine all the things I wanted done to Jordan, my father, and my mother and I took the feather pen in my hand. I was getting ready to sign it. How cool would it be to disappear in Africa? I didn't feel loved or wanted here anyway, and I desperately wanted out of this house and away from my mother.

All of a sudden, I heard this voice in my head that said, "Vengeance is mine! I will repay!"

I knew God was speaking to me at that moment and that I heard that verse in the Bible before.

> Beloved, never avenge yourselves, but leave
> it to the wrath of God. "Vengeance is mine, I will
> repay," says the Lord. (Romans 12:1–9)

I gave the man back his feather pen. As sweet as the sound of revenge was, I didn't trust this man. How did he know so much about me anyway? Something didn't feel right.

I kept asking him what his name was, but he just kept saying that he was a friend. When I told him to leave, he got really upset and kept urging me to sign this paper. I rolled over in bed and tried ignoring him, but he wouldn't go away.

Finally, I got up and went out to the kitchen. My mom, Dwayne, Nora, and Jennifer were out there.

"Mom, this guy won't leave me alone."

"What guy?" she asked.

I pointed to where he was standing, but apparently, no one else was able to see him.

My mom left and went in to her bedroom to talk to Dwayne. It was just me, Jennifer, and Nora out in the kitchen with this strange man.

"So who is this guy?" asked Nora.

"He won't tell me," I said.

"Ask him again," she said.

"What is your name?" I asked, looking directly at the man with no face.

"I'm the Devil," he said in a very malicious creepy voice.

"He said he is the Devil," I replied in a slow quiet voice.

Nora got a little creeped out, and her whole body shuddered.

"Where is he?" Nora asked.

I looked at Nora and got really scared. "He is standing right beside you and has his arm around you," I said in a very slow scared voice.

Nora started freaking out and jumped away.

My mom went outside to the car and came back in and called me into her bedroom with her and Dwayne. She had me sit on the bed next to her and showed me this silver cross necklace.

"This was Grandpa Francis's necklace that he wore in WWII. Where is that guy at?"

I pointed to where he was standing a few feet in front of me. My mom waved the cross in front of him.

The devil screamed, "I will be back for you! But next time, I won't be so nice!" He got sucked into the ground like a genie getting sucked into a lamp.

My mom put the necklace around my neck, and I never ever took it off.

One good thing about my stepsister, Nora, was that she introduced me to the Kingston Wesleyan Church. I was in the fifth grade when I first started going to church on Wednesday nights. It was the first time ever going to church, and I loved it right from the start.

Kingston Wesleyan Church was a phenomenal church. They had an excellent youth program. They had Clubhouse on Wednesday nights for kids from grades K–6. It was separated into age groups. I was in the fifth and sixth grade age group class, and Mr. and Mrs. Rye were our teachers. All of the kids from K–6 would meet in one room for praise and worship. We also rehearsed the pledge of allegiance to the American and Christian flags along with reciting the books of the Bible. Mr. Montei was the head of Clubhouse, and he always did a short Bible lesson before we all split up into our separate classes. I had these small pocket-size poetry books that had Christian poems in them. Every Wednesday, I got up in front of everyone in Clubhouse and read off a poem in front of my peers. I was the only one that did that, so it made me feel special and important.

I was in the sixth grade when I got saved and asked Jesus into my heart. Mr. and Mrs. Rye lead us into a salvation prayer. My stomach was in knots, and my chest was heavy, but as soon as I said yes to Jesus and accepted him into my heart, it felt like the weight of the world was lifted off of me. I felt at peace for the first time since I was eight years old. I knew things were tough in my life, but for the first time, I felt as though things were going to be okay because God was going to see me through. I was no longer fighting these battles by myself. My God was on my side, and He was going to see me through the valley.

> I will lift up mine eyes unto the hills, from whence cometh my help. My help cometh from the Lord, which made heaven and earth. (Psalm 121:1–2)

> Be of good courage, and he shall strengthen your heart, all ye that hope in the Lord. (Psalm 31:24)

I think that is why the Devil paid me a visit. I accepted Christ, and he wasn't too happy about that. He was trying to prey on my vulnerabilities and weakness to get me to stumble and fall back into his hands. He wanted me to sign my soul over to him and used my humanity against me by enticing me with revenge against my enemies. He wanted to use my body to possess me to carry out this revenge against my mother, brother, and father.

I was already a troubled girl. I was molested as a little girl by my own brother. My innocence was stolen from me. My father was a pedophile and molested my older sister over a period of years. I was in and out of counseling. I had a very dysfunctional family. I suffered from depression, an eating disorder, suicidal thoughts and attempts, showed self-harm behavior, and had a history of running away. My mother was alienating and unsupportive or unsympathetic toward me and even blamed me for the condition of the family. I was angry and bitter. I was in the psych ward. I was a perfect candidate for a girl gone crazy.

I probably would have been added to that list on E-News of child killers if I would have said yes to the Devil. The scary thing was I held that feather pen in my hand and was going to sign my name. I was going to do it. Revenge sounded so sweet to me. It was about time that those people suffered like they made me suffer. They deserved a taste of their own medicine. But then this voice came into my head: "Vengeance is mine! I will repay!"

Jesus saved me when he was knocking on the door of my heart in Mr. Rye's class, and Jesus saved me again when the Devil paid me a visit and tried slithering himself into my soul like the sneaky snake that he is, wrapped up in sweet revenge and a trip to Africa.

As if my life wasn't hard enough as it was, the moment I accepted Christ into my life, my life got even harder. I came to the conclusion that God was fighting hard for my soul, and the forces of darkness were piled against me. The darkness surrounded me and overwhelmed me, and the Devil used my traumatic past as leverage against me and as a stronghold. Being a Christian is not an easy road to travel because the world is a dark place and hates God. It is much easier to live off the world than it is to live separate from the world.

> If the world hate you, ye know that it hated
> me before it hated you. If ye were of the world,
> the world would love his own: but because ye are
> not of the world, but I have chosen you out of
> the world, therefore the world hateth you. (John
> 15:18–19)

Life kept throwing me hurdles to test my faith in God, and I failed time and time again all throughout my life. The more hurt and turmoil was thrown my way, the more I questioned God and His love for me. If I was a child of God, then why did I have to go through this? Why had God forsaken me? Did God really love a wretch like me? I thought God was supposed to protect His children. How come He doesn't answer my prayers? I must not be good enough or worthy enough.

The more pain and heartache I had to endure, the more I shook my fist at God and cursed God for the way my life was. That was the kind of tactic that the Devil used, and I will be the first to admit that it had worked on me time and time again. It was so easy to blame God for my problems because He was God and had the power to fix it. I didn't understand why He wouldn't wave his magic wand and make all the pain go away. I didn't understand why He wouldn't wash my tears all away and take away my fears.

When I went into the seventh grade, I graduated from Clubhouse and went into the WTFC (Winning Teens for Christ) youth group. WTFC was for the teens from seventh to twelfth grade. Youth Pastor Len Wyatt was in charge of WTFC.

WTFC was a lot of fun. We had a live band where the teens played the guitar, drums, and some were singing on microphones, and they led the praise and worship. I eventually became one of the kids singing on the microphone. I didn't have the best voice in the world, but I could carry a tune. I forced myself to put myself out there, such as reading poems in Clubhouse and singing in WTFC because I was so shy and wanted to try and overcome that.

I loved church. It was a way for me to escape my home situation for a couple of hours. My mother wouldn't always take me, though, and I was really devastated when I couldn't go. Sometimes the church van would come and pick me up, but not always. Pastor Len was usually the one who picked kids up in the church van. There were a few times where I either walked or rode my bike to church, and it was 2.3 miles.

There were a few times where I had to walk home because my mother forgot to pick me up. When I got home, my mom would say, "Oh, s—t! I forgot about you! I'm sorry, Andrea."

I was fuming. How could she forget to pick up her own daughter? What actually happened was that she fell asleep on the couch and didn't wake up in time to come and get me and had me figure out my own way home because she didn't feel like coming to get me.

My mother was a very inactive person. She didn't really work outside of the home and didn't do a whole lot around the house either. Dwayne did most of the cooking, and she napped on the couch many times throughout the day and snored very loudly. The rare times I did come out of my room to watch TV, I ended up storming back to my room because I couldn't hear the TV over her snoring. I got so mad, especially if there was a good show or movie on. I couldn't understand why she couldn't go to sleep in her bed in her room. There were times where I just tried turning the TV up to drown out her snoring, but she would either snore even louder, or Dwayne would turn his TV up in the kitchen or yell at me to turn mine down. It got very irritating most times, and they wondered why I spent most of my time in my bedroom.

4

Stuck in the Mud

One day in the seventh grade, I decided that I wasn't going to get on the bus to go home. I filled my backpack with a couple of outfits the night before. When the bell rang to leave, I grabbed my backpack and went to the bathroom and hid in a stall until everyone left. When the coast was clear, I snuck out and went down the hallway that led out to the football field.

It was the end of winter, and the snow had pretty much melted away with just a few patches of snow left here and there. Everywhere I looked, there was mud.

I went around the track and football field and hid in the patch of woods behind it. I went deep enough into the woods where no one could see me but to where I could also see the field and school. I found a spot up against a tree that wasn't muddy and sat down.

I got butterflies in my stomach and became really nervous when I heard Richard—the maintenance guy who was also in charge of the buses—circling the school grounds, yelling my name.

"Andrea! Andrea!" he hollered. "Andrea, you have a ton of people out looking for you!"

They sure didn't waste any time, did they? I wasn't even missing that long.

"Andrea! Where are you?" Richard hollered out.

I froze. I dared not move lest I be discovered. I slowly hid behind a tree to disguise myself even more.

"I don't know where she is at! I looked everywhere around the school. I don't know where she could have gone," Richard said over his walkie-talkie. He continued talking on his walkie-talkie about me as he headed back into the school.

I stayed there and watched and waited until it was all clear. I stayed in the woods but traveled west. I didn't want to come out of the woods in case someone found me. I couldn't travel down the roads. I had to stay where nobody would be looking for me and stay out of sight.

The woods came to an end not too far away from the school and opened up into this big muddy field. I didn't realize exactly how muddy it was until I started walking through it. I tried stepping around the really muddy spots, but sometimes it was much muddier than it looked. I kept getting my feet stuck in the mud. I lost my shoe a couple of times and had to stick my foot back in my shoe and curl my toes under to pull my shoe out. I started sobbing because I had so much more field ahead of me, and it was so muddy. I didn't think I could make it through this muddy field. My shoes were caked with mud, which made them heavy and made them get stuck even more. I couldn't travel down the road because they would find me. I didn't know where I was going. I just knew that I wasn't going back home.

Sobbing, I decided to continue on through the muddy field until I got myself really stuck. My left foot became really stuck this time and was completely immersed and buried in mud. I tried pulling it out but couldn't. I became even more upset and started bawling. I was freezing cold, but my face was burning up. I cried out to God.

"God, please help me," I said with tears rolling down my cheeks looking up to the sky. "I'm stuck, Lord. I just want to get out of here, Lord God. Please, God! Help me get out of here! Guide me, Lord! What do you want me to do? Where do you want me to go? I can't go back home! My mother doesn't want me there. She wants Jordan. I can't go back home. I don't want them to find me. Please get me out of this stupid mud, Lord! Please help me!"

I was sobbing uncontrollably. I tugged and tugged and pulled and pulled. The mud was just too heavy. The longer I remained stuck, the more I became stuck. I felt so weak and cold. I didn't eat anything all day. My feet were turning numb from being stuck in the freezing cold mud.

After what seemed like forever, I managed to pull my foot out of my very stuck shoe. I rested my sock-covered foot on top of my other foot and bent down and dug my shoe out of the mud. I was so thankful that I didn't get any mud inside my shoe. I tried shaking my shoe to get some of the mud off, but it didn't do any good. This was wet and heavy mud. I put my shoe down in a not so muddy spot and stepped back into it. I decided to turn around and head back toward the woods. I couldn't continue on in that field and risk getting stuck in the mud again.

When I got out of the muddy field and back into the woods, I took my muddy shoe off and banged it up against a tree. I found a stick and used it to scrape off most of the mud. I cleaned it off the best I could and slipped my foot back into it.

I went back to the tree I was hiding behind when Richard was looking for me. I stopped and looked back at the school to see if Richard or anyone was in sight. There was no one.

I don't know why, but I decided to walk toward the elementary school. There was a trail from the high school to the elementary school that I took. When I got to the elementary school, I went in a side door that nobody really used that much, and once I got inside the school, I went straight to the bathrooms but peeked around the corner of each hall to make sure I didn't run into anyone looking for me. The coast was clear. The bathrooms were in the corners from Mrs. Henry's office and down the hall from the office. I approached as quickly and cautiously as I could and hurried inside the bathroom. I went straight to the big stall and locked the door and cried.

I didn't know where I was headed or where I wanted to go. All I knew was where I didn't want to go and where I didn't want to be and who I didn't want to be with. I didn't want to go home to my mother where I didn't feel wanted, loved, or cherished in any way. She blamed me for Jordan not being home. She blamed me for having to take the pictures down of her son. I didn't want to be where I was not wanted. Anywhere was better than going back there with her. Would anyone want to be where they were not wanted? I was not going back home. I'd rather live on the streets and fend for myself. I couldn't depend on anyone but myself anyway. Everyone that I depended on had let me down so far.

What kind of environment was I in with my mom, anyway? I was so unhappy in that unhealthy toxic environment. It was a breeding ground for depression, self-harm, hopelessness, crushed dreams, isolation, anguish, and total despair. I hibernated in my bedroom even in the summertime and became very familiar with those four walls. It was my prison, even though that is where I felt most comfortable.

My mother and Dwayne both smoked weed. They never did it in front of us kids, but we could smell it, and it was definitely obvious what they were doing when they came out of their bedroom with red glassy eyes. Every time their buddies came over or Dwayne's oldest daughter, Molly, and her husband came over, they would all go into my mom and Dwayne's bedroom and smoke weed. The smell of it filled the whole house. The smell of marijuana always gave me a headache. I definitely had to stay in my room and shut the door. Sometimes I had to even put a towel under my door to keep the smell out and crack a window, but even then, I could still smell it. They smoked it every day and multiple times a day.

My mom talked about Jordan in front of me. Sometimes, she was a little more discreet about it. I overheard her tell Dwayne on quite a few occasions when they were talking about Jordan while I was within earshot, "I can't talk about Jordan in front of Andrea." When she did slip up and say something about Jordan in front of me, she would get awkward and apologize but then excuse herself and say, "He's my son too, and I have a right to talk about him."

My mother didn't make it very easy on me. Every day, she reminded me that it was my fault that the family wasn't together. She never came out and said that, but she also never tried to not make me feel otherwise. My mother was the main reason why I ran away from home.

I prayed to God in that bathroom stall. I cried and prayed and asked God why I felt this way. I was desperate. I hated my life and tried everything I could to escape it.

"God, why do I feel this way? Why couldn't I have been born into a different family who loved and appreciated me? Why have you chosen this life for me? If you love me, Lord, then please help me get out of this situation that I'm in. Please provide me a way out of that house. I can't go back there. I can't go back to my mother. She would rather have Jordan over me. Please make a way for me to get out of that house and away from my family. I'd rather die than go back there.

"My life is so terrible, Lord. I am so miserable! I just don't want to be here anymore. Can you please just strike me dead and take me home? I'd rather be up there with you where there is no more pain, no more crying, no more heartache or rejection. If I'm with you, Lord, no one can ever hurt me again, especially my mother. I'm tired of being hungry and hurting myself. Just take me home to be with you. I want to go to heaven. I want you to hold me and tell me everything is going to be okay. I want you to wipe away my tears. Please, Lord, help me."

When I finally calmed down and stopped crying, I came out of the stall and went to the mirror and looked at myself. I was in rough shape. My eyes were all red, and it looked like I had been crying long and hard. I had dirt and small twigs in my hair and dirt on my cheek. I washed my hands and then picked the dirt and twigs out of my hair the best I could. Then I took some paper towels and got it wet to wash my shoes off the best I could. I made a huge mess of mud on the bathroom floor and all over the bathroom sink.

Oops! The janitor will have fun cleaning this up, I thought to myself.

All of a sudden, I heard Richard and Mrs. Henry out in the hallway, and they were talking about me. I froze. I thought I was going to be discovered any minute. I went back to the big stall and listened very hard to what they were saying.

They said that they searched both schools and all of the bathrooms and I was nowhere to be found. They must have searched this bathroom just before I got there.

I waited until I didn't hear them talking anymore and waited just a few more minutes more to be sure they weren't out there. I slowly opened the stall door to make sure no one was in the bathroom with me. Then I walked slowly to the door and peeked into the hall to make sure no one was out there. The coast was clear, so I walked out of the bathroom really fast and headed for the front door to exit the school. Richard came around the corner and saw me.

"Andrea! There are people out looking for you!" Richard yelled as I took off running out of the school at full speed. I was a pretty fast runner. When we had track and field day in elementary school, I always got first or second place in running.

I ran to the road and made a right, away from town. I couldn't go through town because it would be easier for people to find me there, and I didn't want to be found. I took off running down the road. I stole a quick glance behind me and saw Richard coming to a stop just outside the school doors. He wasn't running after me. He stopped to say something on his walkie-talkie.

My thought was he was old and had a big belly and couldn't keep up with me. I kept running as hard and as fast as I could. My backpack slowed me down a little bit, and it kept flopping around on my back.

I ran until I saw some woods on my right, and I dodged right into them. My thought was to stay in the woods and hide until nighttime and then start walking again, but that plan didn't work out so well. It seemed like as soon as I got into the woods a little way, Richard pulled over on the side of the road in the van, and he and Mrs. Henry got out and started calling out to me. Mrs. Henry came into the woods after me.

"Andrea, you have a lot of people out looking for you!" she said as she walked towards me. I was sitting on the ground on my knees with my back facing her and was crying.

"Go away! Leave me alone!" I said in a sobbing voice.

"Andrea, what's wrong? Why are you doing this? It's cold out here," said Mrs. Henry.

"I don't care! Just leave me alone!" I cried.

"You will freeze to death out here. You have been out here for hours. I don't want you getting sick," she said in a caring but annoyed voice. She pulled on my arm and tried pulling me to my feet.

"Leave me alone and pretend that you never saw me!" I said as I shrugged her off of me.

All of a sudden, I saw red and blue flashing lights.

"Dave is here," Mrs. Henry said. Dave was the town cop.

"I'm not going back home!" I sobbed.

"Why not?" asked Mrs. Henry.

"My mother! She always talks about Jordan in front of me! My mom hates me because her son ain't home with her. Plus, her and Dwayne smokes weed. I don't want to be around that crap! It gives me a headache! I'm not going back home!"

"Andrea, at least come out of the woods and come back to the school to get warmed up. You are shaking," she said as she pulled on my arm, trying to pull me to my feet. I shrugged her off. "Andrea, I can't stay out here all day! I am freezing!"

"Well, then go!" I said.

Dave came in the woods. Mrs. Henry turned and walked toward him. They walked out of the woods together and left me alone. Mrs. Henry came back a minute or two later.

"Andrea, come on! Let's go!" she said as she tugged on my arm. She was clearly getting annoyed and was tired of being out in the woods in the cold.

"Just leave me alone! Don't touch me!" I snapped.

Mrs. Henry grabbed my arm and tried tugging me to my feet, but I wouldn't budge.

"Andrea, you either walk out of here willingly or we're going to have to drag you out of here!" she said in a stern voice, trying to scare me.

Dave came walking up. "Andrea, let's go. You can't be here," he said.

Mrs. Henry grabbed one arm, and Dave grabbed the other, and they pulled me to my feet. Dave let go of my arm, but Mrs. Henry held onto me. I guess she wanted to make sure I was leaving that woods, and she walked me out, holding onto my arm the entire time with Dave following close behind. I got into Richard's van in the back seat, and Mrs. Henry got in after me. My whole body was shaking uncontrollably. I couldn't feel my toes. Richard took his coat off and gave it to Mrs. Henry to wrap around my shoulders. We made the short trip back to the elementary school. We all got out of the van and went in and sat in the office.

Mrs. Henry went to the thermostat on the wall and turned the heat up to warm us up. I still had Richard's coat wrapped around my shoulders. I was shaking really bad to the point where it looked like I was having seizures. I was more nervous than I was cold, and I tended to shake like that when I get nervous. I was scared of what my mom's reaction would be. I knew they called her, and she was on her way up here. I was also scared because Dave was here. I didn't know what was going to happen. I was hoping and praying that they wouldn't think that I was trying to commit suicide again and send me back to the psych ward. I did not want to go back there. I was just trying to run away from home. I didn't want to be at home under the same roof as my mother. Why didn't she send me away to foster care instead of Jordan? My mom would have been happier to have me out of the way and have her son home with her instead. Then she could hang his pictures up on the walls and talk about him all she wanted without having to worry about upsetting me and running to my counselor to complain about it. Why did they have to come looking for me? Why wouldn't they just let me stay gone?

My mom showed up, but Dave didn't let her come in the office. They went out in the hallway and shut the door. I knew my mom was crying and probably putting on a sob show, telling them that she was worried sick about me and didn't understand why I was doing this and blah, blah, blah.

Me, my mom, and Dave all walked across the street to Dave's office. I gave Mrs. Henry Richard's coat to give back to him.

When we got to his office and sat down across from his desk, my mom asked me why I took off.

"Because of Jordan," I said. "You talk about him in front of me all the time and because you and Dwayne smoke weed," I said, loud enough so that Dave could hear.

"What? What are you talking about? We don't smoke weed," she said.

Dave chimed in and told her that he knew that she did it and that they would get caught eventually. Then he raised his voice and started telling my mom that she wasn't a very good mom and that she needed to get all of her kids taken away. He said that he also talked to the boys, and they both said that my mom and Dwayne smoked weed. Dave really lit into her, and I could hardly contain my satisfaction in it. It was about time somebody yelled at my mom.

Dave also told us that this running away was going on my record and that if I got two more, then I would be removed from the home and placed into a foster home. He kept saying that like he was trying to tell me that all I would have to do is run away two more times, and I would get my wish and be out from under my mother and go live in foster care. Anywhere was better than being at home with my mother. I didn't feel as though she wanted me anyway.

I think my mother caught on to that, too, because when I did run away after that, she never called the cops on me again. She went out looking for me instead. She couldn't have another one of her kids taken away from her. What would that do to her already broken family?

I hated the ride home with my mother. She yelled at me the entire time. She told me that she didn't smoke weed, Dwayne did, and he did it to help his back. Yeah, that's why she came out of the bedroom all glassy-eyed too. Why go in there at all if she didn't smoke it?

5

The Pain Cuts Deep

Jennifer and Nora both moved out at the age of seventeen. Jennifer moved in with her boyfriend, Anthony, and his mother. I got my own room, and the boys got Nora's old bedroom. I loved getting my own room. Jennifer was such a sloppy roommate, and now I could have my room all to myself. Getting my own room, though, with a lot more privacy came at a cost.

I was in seventh grade when I started cutting myself. I was so depressed and tormented within myself that I sought out ways to release the pain. I wasn't going to counseling anymore. I had to find some way of coping with the deep pain bubbling beneath the surface. I used knives from the kitchen, blades from utility knives, sharp pencils, broken glass, nails—anything sharp. I even tore razors apart and used the blades to cut myself. My favorite spots to cut myself were my legs and stomach, and my favorite weapon was utility knife blades.

My eating disorder also progressively got worse and more intense. What started out as a way for me to control this one thing in my life soon morphed into something that controlled me. Every time I looked at myself in my full-length mirror hanging on my closet door, I saw a fat girl staring back at me. One night, I went to my closet and shut the door and carved "FAT PIG" into my stomach and lower left calf. It also didn't help that my last name was Wilber, and everyone associated that name with the pig on *Charlotte's Web*.

Cutting was like an addictive drug to me. It was like getting high. I had so much pain stored within myself that I didn't know how to release or manage it. Cutting made me forget about the excruciating pain on the inside. Yes, it did hurt, immensely, but the physical pain masked the mental and emotional pain that I was in and made me feel better for that short period of time. I called it my pain transplant.

My mind went silent when I cut. All I could focus on was the blade up against my skin and seeing the blood. The blood symbolized the release of pain escaping my body. I forgot about all my inner pain and troubles, and my mind went blank and unable to think about anything except the physical pain that I was inflicting on myself. So many people close to me hurt me. They were the cause of so much of my suffering. If anyone else was going to hurt me, it was going to be *me*. I was going to be the author of my own pain. I wanted control over my own pain and suffering.

I had a pretty decent-sized walk-in closet. At night, while everyone else was asleep, I would go into my closet, turn the light on, and shut my door. Sometimes I would put a towel under the crack of the door so that no one would see the light on. I would sit in the corner of my closet and cut.

Cutting was very physically exhausting for me. When I was done, I would just curl up into a ball on the floor and just lay there for a while until I built up enough energy to move. When I laid there, the pain was intense. My body was weak and felt like jelly. It was always a throbbing and burning pain that sometimes took my breath away. It was a pain that I embraced, and I was addicted to that feeling. It was a feeling of euphoria, a high. Cutting my body was therapy for me. Even if it only masked my pain on the inside for ten minutes, it was well worth the little bit of time where my world didn't exist, and I didn't have to face reality.

After the high wore off, I went into deep regret and remorse over the cuts and scars that I had caused myself but also embarrassment and fear that someone may find out. But just like any drug, the addiction brings you right back to it during a time of desperation, and the need to numb the pain once more returned.

I didn't cut myself every day. After I cut myself, I would just keep picking my scab to make myself bleed. The blood symbolized the release of inward pain. When there was no more scab to pick, I would cut again. Sometimes, I would just slap my cut or press really hard on it to make it hurt.

I spent a lot of time in my closet. Sometimes I even fell asleep in there, curled up on the floor. I went in there to hide from the rest of the world. I went in there to cut and to self-destruct.

My eating disorder and cutting wasn't my only source of self-destructive behavior. I also tried hanging myself in my closet. I tied a rope around my neck really tight and tied the other end around my rack I got on my knees and hung there. I felt the blood rush to my face. It was hard to breathe, and I felt lightheaded. I embraced this feeling as I hung there. It felt like I was being set free. As I felt like the life was being squeezed out of me, it also felt like the pain was leaving with it.

Something always stopped me from finishing the job, though. That is what upset me the most. I couldn't just die. No matter how hard I tried or how bad I wanted it, I couldn't and wouldn't just die. I cried out to God on a regular basis and begged him to just take me home. I cried myself to sleep a lot because I was still here, alive and breathing, and barely hanging on to the end of my rope. This life was far too painful and too much for me to bear, and I felt like I was forgotten and abandoned in the midst of it. There was no one I could turn to and there was no way out.

I felt like a dog chained up outside. As a puppy, I was cute, and everyone wanted to play with me, but as I got older, I became more of an inconvenience, so I became isolated, not really a part of the family, with no social interaction, just an afterthought, an obligation you are stuck with that you have to water and feed or face the law. I felt unloved, unappreciated, and unwanted which is the worst feeling in the world that cuts deeper than you can ever imagine.

I couldn't bear the thought of waking up every morning to the same hell I was in the day before. There were times where I would put a pillowcase over my head and tie a rope around my neck and lay in bed with my head under the covers and just pray to God that

I would suffocate and die from a lack of oxygen. I would lie there on my back with both hands under my butt to try and resist setting myself free. It was very hard to breathe. With the pillowcase over my head, I was breathing in my own carbon monoxide and had poor air quality, making it difficult to breathe. But with God's innate self-preservation gene he gave to every human being to ensure the population of humanity, I set myself free and gasped for air and then became angry with myself for giving in and not letting myself die. I hated myself every time.

I did this quite a few times and even held a pillow over my face along with a pillowcase over my head and under the covers. I wanted to die so badly and put myself out of my own misery. I was just so tired of this life.

In spite of all that I had been through, if my mother would have had more compassion and understanding and had been supportive, things would have been different. I wasn't so much depressed because of what Jordan did to me but how my mom reacted and treated me for it. That is what did the most damage. She hurt me way beyond what Jordan did. My mother left me to my own devices. I couldn't go to counseling. I couldn't talk to her or anyone else. She isolated me in my own pain and then made me feel guilty for it, and as a young girl, I was forced to deal with it on my own, which is why I turned to self-destructive behavior, and that sort of negative coping skill that I learned followed me into adulthood.

One day, in gym class, we had to play crab soccer. I did like that game, but this time was different. This time I had "FAT PIG" carved into my lower left calf. We were required to wear red shorts and white t-shirts for gym class. I tried hiding it. I tried crossing my legs together to hide it, but when you play crab soccer, it is impossible to hide something like that on your leg.

I had to do the toss up, and Mrs. Smith, my gym teacher, was right there standing over us to toss us the ball, and she saw my leg.

"Andrea, nice tattoo!" she said, pointing to my leg.

I thought I was in trouble now. I was busted. Mrs. Smith was going to go tell the school counselor, and he was going to call my mother.

At the end of gym class, Mrs. Smith pulled me aside in the locker room. She pulled up her pant leg and showed me her tattoo on her ankle. She told me that if I wanted a tattoo, then I needed to go get it professionally done. She really didn't lecture me or give me too much of a hard time about it. She just told me to make sure that I cleaned it good with peroxide, and that was the end of it. I was quite surprised that I didn't hear a big lecture and that she didn't report me.

6

Unwanted Visits

I was in the eighth grade when Clayton was released from prison. I had mixed feelings about Clayton. I mean, he was my father. I went so long without a father. He went away for about six years. That was a big chunk of my childhood that he wasn't around, and a lot had happened in that time. Maybe prison changed him. Maybe he learned his lesson. I wanted a dad so badly. I remember what it was like when he was home, before he went away. I was a big daddy's girl and looked up to him as my hero. I missed those days. I wished we could go back to the way things were.

I was always so jealous of other girls who had a dad. I hated it when other girls talked about their dads. It made me feel so awkward and uncomfortable because I couldn't talk about mine. He was locked away in prison for a horrible crime. He was a pedophile. I hated Father's Day in elementary school when we had to make Father's Day gifts, and I didn't have a dad to give mine to. I missed out on so much by not having a dad, and it really complicated things for me in school.

I was really nervous when Clayton first got out of prison. I knew what he did, and part of me wanted nothing to do with him, but part of me wanted him to be my dad. Part of me wanted to give him a chance to prove himself to me and sort of put what he did in the past and try and move on and make things work. I felt like if I did try and have a relationship with him that I would be betraying

67

my sister because of what he did to her. But she had a relationship with Jordan, so was it okay to test the waters and see where things went with Clayton.

Seeing Clayton for the first time was very awkward. He came to the house and brought his girlfriend, Gladys, with him. He had to have supervised visits with us. My mom and Dwayne stayed in the kitchen while Clayton and Gladys visited us in the living room. I couldn't remember the conversation because I was so nervous with him being there. I just kept thinking about what he did for him to go to prison away from us kids in the first place. Jordan did what he did to me because of what he did to Jennifer.

I felt very uncomfortable with Clayton hugging me. I really paid attention to where he put his hands. He liked little girls. Would he try and do anything to me? I didn't trust him. It also felt weird to hear him tell me that he loved me. I couldn't believe that to be true. How could this man who is supposed to be my father love me? What dad who truly loved his kids would do anything to get himself separated from his kids? How could he love his daughter when he had the capacity to hurt someone else's daughter who he raised as his own? When he told me that he loved me, his words did not seem genuine but rather empty and hollow.

I tried so hard to put it behind me and forget about what he did. I wanted a dad so badly, and Dwayne wasn't going to be it. Looking back now, Dwayne was more of a dad to me than Clayton ever could have been.

The first few visits were really hard. I never felt comfortable around him, and he always wanted to hug me at the start and end of each visit. When it got warmer, we visited outside on the front porch while my mom and Dwayne stayed in the house. Jennifer was there a few times while Clayton was there. After what Clayton did to her, I don't understand how my mother could allow him to be there when Jennifer was there. Clayton molested her for years, and not just fondling, but he had actual intercourse with her. How could she let this man near her daughter again? How could she let him near her other daughter or any of her kids, for that matter? Just because my mother was there didn't mean nothing would happen. She failed to protect her for years while it was going on right under her nose while she was home. To think that just her mere presence would protect her girls from this man was absurd.

During our visits with Clayton, Clayton started making snide remarks about Jennifer. He would ask about her all the time. The boys were always forthcoming with information. At the time, Jennifer was dating a mixed Black man named Anthony and had two girls by him. Clayton would make comments like, "Once you go Black, you can't go back." He would also call her a slut and say things like she sleeps around and other derogatory remarks. It made me really angry hearing him talk about my sister like that whom he victimized over and over again.

If prison changed him and he was really sorry about what he did, then he wouldn't be saying things like that. If he wasn't sorry, then who's to say that he wouldn't do it again? What if he tried to do it to me? What if Clayton tried to molest me if Jennifer didn't report him when she did? Was that why she reported him? To protect me?

I had so many mixed feelings about this whole situation. I wanted a dad. I had this void, this emptiness inside of me that a dad could fill, but this man was a bad man. What he did was unforgivable and unforgettable. What he did was a permanent roadblock in any father-daughter relationship. It wasn't anything that I could move past and move forward to have a relationship with him.

I was in band and played the clarinet. I started playing in the band when I was in the fifth grade. I invited Clayton to my Christmas and spring band concerts. He told me that he would be there. He promised me that he would be there. Throughout the whole concert, I would search the stands for him. I couldn't find him. He never showed up to a single concert. I don't know why I expected him to be there when my mother never went to a single concert either. I knew he wouldn't come, but I always hoped that he would and was always disappointed when he didn't fulfill his promise to be there for me.

The next time I saw him, I asked why he didn't come, and he always offered up some lame excuse as to why he couldn't come to his daughter's band concert. You would think that after missing six years of his daughter's life that he would make it a number one priority to make it to all of her school events so that he wouldn't miss out on anything else in her life. It seemed as though I wasn't that important to him.

During the summer, my mom allowed us to go with Clayton and Gladys to Vasser at his sister Goldie's house for a visit. The only reason why I agreed to go was because two of my sisters were going to be there that I hadn't seen since I was a baby—Karen and Julie—and I wanted to meet them.

Clayton had many children by a handful of different women. My mom's three by him were his last ones. I am one of his twelve. That does not include my mom's two from a previous relationship, plus Dwayne's three who became my stepsiblings. I didn't grow up knowing any of my siblings from Clayton. They were all much older than me, but I wished more than anything that I could have gotten to know them, even now. I have all of these siblings, yet I feel so alone because I don't know any of them. I don't even know all of their names.

My mom didn't feel a need to have them a part of our lives, especially after Clayton went to prison. I feel like she did us such a grave injustice. Those were our siblings despite who their mother was. I feel like adults tend to be selfish in thinking of their own feelings when it comes to their kids. It is not like they lived far away either. Vasser and Mayville were only twenty to thirty minutes away. She could have arranged for Aunt Goldie to come and get us for the weekend so that our other siblings could come over and spend time with us. My mom didn't have to be a part of it.

My mother isolated us from our family. After she met Dwayne, it became just us and Dwayne's family. We lost contact with my mom's side of the family in Erie since we moved to Michigan. Then after Clayton went away, we lost contact with that side of the family as well. Now, today, with really no family to speak of, I am suffering the consequences of her decision to isolate us from both sides of the family. I don't think she realizes the gravity of the decisions she has made for her kids and I don't believe she ever will because she would never read my story due to the conviction it would lay on her. The truth would cut too deep and be too much for her to handle, especially knowing that she couldn't even sit through the meeting I had with my counselor, Jordan, and his counselor when I went into great detail of what Jordan did to me. She walked out of the room, crying. So I know my mom would never read my story, even though I feel like she needs to hear it the most, not because I want her to feel the pain I went through—I never want her to go through the pain I had to go through—but because I want her to *understand* why I did the things I did and why I *had* to make the decision to move on with my life without her being a part of it. She left me with absolutely no support system with not even her to turn to, so I had to build my own support system without her being a part of it which was her choice, not mine.

I did regret going with Clayton and Gladys to Aunt Goldie's, even though I did get to meet my sisters, Karen and Julie. I felt as though I put myself in danger by going with him. What if he decided not to take us home but took us to his house in Onoway, Michigan, instead or ran off with us? If a pedophile was capable of hurting a little girl he raised as his own daughter, then he was fully capable of anything. He was capable of hurting his own daughter. My mother didn't have very good judgment and didn't do everything in her power to keep us safe, in my opinion. She should not have let Clayton take any of us, especially me, her other daughter who she put into the hands of a pedophile. Anything could have happened.

During our visit with Clayton at my Aunt Goldie's house, we sat in the front yard quite a way from the house under a patch of trees by a camper and a tent that they stayed in while they were down, visiting. Most of the time, there was no supervision of our visit with Clayton. We were alone with him half of the time we were there. My sisters, Karen and Julie, sat with us part of the time, but there was the other part of the time where we were alone with him when he was supposed to be supervised.

During those times where we were alone with him, he bad-mouthed my mom to us. He kept telling us to act up and keep running away and make my mom and Dwayne's life a living hell so that she would give up and let us move in with him. Then she would be the one paying child support. Onoway was three hours north of

Kingston, and he had to drive that every two weeks to come and visit us for a couple of hours. My two brothers loved having their dad back in their lives and really fed off of what Clayton told them. They wanted to live with him.

That is exactly what the boys did too. They were hell on wheels. They kept mouthing back to Dwayne. Dwayne had a temper and yelled a lot, and the boys, especially Theo, loved to push his buttons. They broke into the neighbors and stole money, flashlights, *Playboys*, and a bunch of other small stuff. Dwayne's friend was storing his boat in the backyard, and it had a cover on it. The boys hid that stuff in this boat. They also rummaged through private nude photo albums that the neighbors made of themselves. They crawled into a basement window when they weren't home.

The boys did not get into trouble with the law because the neighbors were really good friends with my mom and Dwayne and smoked pot together on occasion. The boys also vandalized a big tractor, which included pooping on the seat. Their red hair gave them away. There weren't too many redheaded boys in the tiny town of Kingston. Theo kept getting kicked out of school and getting kicked off the bus for fighting. They were a handful, and I know that they caused my mom and Dwayne quite a bit of stress which took a lot of attention off of me.

In my sophomore year of high school, I wanted a class ring. My mom said that she would pay for half of it if Clayton paid the other half. Clayton would not pay for half, so my mom wouldn't either. I guess they both got each other off the hook for paying for my class ring. My mom made a big deal out of it and told everyone she came into contact with what a piece a crap he was for not helping her pay for my class ring and that she couldn't afford to pay for it on her own. Clayton was the bad guy, and she made sure everyone knew about it.

I had to pay for my own class ring. Patricia was a paraprofessional at Kingston elementary school and high school. I confided in her quite a bit, so she knew my situation. I spent the night at her house on a few occasions and spent a lot of time with her. She got me out of the house and got my mind off my home situation.

Patricia is the most positive person I know. She looks at everything as a blessing. She always saw the silver lining in every grey sky. I don't ever remember her saying anything negative. Sometimes she was frustrating to talk to because misery likes company, and every time I tried to complain about my situation to her, she would always come back with something positive and try to point out something good in every bad situation. If I complained about my mother, Patricia would tell me to forgive her and love her because she was the only mother I was ever going to have and that I needed to show her that nothing was going to ruin my spirits or bring me down. She tried really hard to get me to always think positive. She was the kindest person I knew and never had anything bad to say about anybody.

Patricia always tried to teach me that too much negativity was never good for anyone. The more negative you are, the more depressed you will be. Your outlook reflects your outcome. A negative attitude leads to an unhappy, negative life, and that is what she was trying to teach me. Sometimes I envied her and coveted her positive outlook on life. I wished I could be that positive despite my current circumstances.

How could anyone love life so much when mine sucked so badly? Patricia was a mystery to me. Even people who had a good productive life and were seemingly happy didn't have such a positive attitude like Patricia. She never let anything drag her down.

When she got into a bad car accident and the jaws of life had to get her out and she was in a wheelchair for a while with pins sticking out of her leg, she was just happy to be alive. Even that didn't get her down. Even then, there was a silver lining because it could have been much worse. She could have died, but she lived, and that was something she rejoiced over—her silver lining. How could she love life so much when I tried so hard to end my life?

Patricia had amazing flower gardens that even Martha Stewart would be proud of. They were beautiful, and she had a beautiful home. She spent a lot of money, blood, sweat, and tears on her home and property.

During the summer, I worked for her in her gardens. She would get mulch by the pickup truckload, and I would help her shovel it out and spread it around in her garden. It was very hard, backbreaking work, and I loved doing it for her. I paid for my own class ring by working for her and also worked for her to buy my own school clothes, and she would take me shopping.

Patricia and I have a few good memories together. She had a really long driveway, and at the end of it, there was a big rock on either side that she planted flowers around. She had this golf cart with a big water tank on the back end of it and a hose, and that is how she watered those flowers where her regular hose couldn't reach. She had me drive the golf cart to the end of the driveway, and she was riding beside me. When I backed up to try and turn it around, I ended up backing it into the ditch which was pretty deep. We were actually pretty lucky because there was this big truck coming, and we ended up going into the ditch instead of the road. We both almost ended up being roadkill. I was pretty upset and embarrassed that my lack of driving abilities might have hurt her golf cart and almost gotten us killed. Patricia made a big joke out of it and was laughing. I didn't think it was very funny. I was still upset about it.

Patricia made me drive the golf cart out of the ditch, and then we weeded the flowers, watered them, and she drove back up to the house. She tried to get me to drive it back up to the house, but I was still shaken up from going into the ditch. Looking back now, it was pretty funny, although I wasn't laughing at the time.

There was another time where I was helping her paint her little cottage in the backyard. It was a little garden shed that looked like a cute little house with a front porch. Part of the roof was glass, and she started her seeds in there. Patricia knew about my eating disorder and that I didn't eat very much, but she didn't want me working for her without something in my stomach, so she had me drink these SlimFast drinks. I love chocolate, so she gave me the chocolate flavored one. I had nowhere to really set it, so I sat it on top of the ladder that neither of us was using at the time.

When Patricia decided that she needed to use the ladder, she picked it up to move it, and the can of chocolate SlimFast came pouring down all over the top of her head. It was hot and muggy outside, so I guess a cold chocolate slim fast shower was a good way to cool off in the middle of a sultry afternoon. We both about died laughing. I tried not to laugh at first because I thought she would be mad, but Patricia always turned everything into a funny joke. There was never a dull moment with Patricia around. She called it her chocolate hair gel, and we just continued to paint her little cottage as if nothing ever happened but laughed hysterically about the little mishap with the ladder, cracking jokes every time we needed to move the ladder to paint. I love Patricia. She was so much fun to be around, and I still laugh and chuckle to this day when I think of chocolate SlimFast.

I worked with her quite a bit during the summer, earning money for school clothes. She always worked right alongside me, weeding and watering and planting flowers. I enjoyed the time I spent with her. She had so much positive energy, and her humor was contagious.

Patricia also really loved Christmas, and her house was always decorated so beautifully. She was in charge of the Christmas talent shows for school, and I can't even describe the amount of detail and extravagance that went into the decorating that even Bronner's, the largest Christmas store in the world—which is in Frankenmuth, Michigan—would be proud of. She spared no detail when it came to Christmas, right down to the cookie.

Patricia invited me over for a weekend of cookie baking and decorating. She had these gingerbread house cutouts that were the size of my hand, spread out. These cookies were a work of art and way too pretty to eat. I love art, so I especially enjoyed decorating these cookies. She had all different kinds of sprinkles in all shapes and sizes. She had silver ball sprinkles that we used for the doorknobs on the little gingerbread house doors. Not one cookie was the same, and they were all gorgeous right down to the fine detail.

Patricia was a joy to be around, and she got me away from my depressing environment at home as much as she could, and I am forever grateful for that.

There did come a point where I just did not want to see Clayton anymore. He didn't measure up to the high standards I wanted in a dad, not by a long shot. He was a creep and a pedophile that had no remorse whatsoever for what he did. I could not forgive him for

what he did to my sister and my family and I could not forgive him
for the example he set for Jordan to do the same thing to me. He was
the cause of our broken family and wasn't the least bit remorseful.
And because he wasn't sorry, I didn't trust that he wouldn't try to do
something like that again. I didn't want to put myself out there to get
hurt again. He had already done enough damage, and I didn't have
the energy or the strength to deal with the added anxiety that he
would put on my life. I built a wall around myself and my heart and
didn't let but a few select people inside. I'd been hurt way too much
far beyond repair and had to protect myself.

When Clayton and Gladys came to visit, my brothers would
come to my room and let me know that he was here, and I would
say, "Yeah, I know" and not come out. Gladys and Clayton both
came to my door a few times, asking me to come out and join them.
Sometimes I did just to avoid conflict because it was just easier. Most
of the time, I just waited and then came out at the last twenty to
thirty minutes of Clayton's two-hour visitation. Sometimes I just
didn't come out at all. Joshua and Theo got really mad at me when
I didn't come out to visit. They thought highly of their dad, despite
what he did. Their dad didn't hurt them, and they wanted to go live
with him.

My mom used me quite a bit as a spy. She talked me into visiting with Clayton, even though I didn't want to, just so that I could
go back and tell her everything that he was filling the boys' heads
with. Eventually, it got to the point where I just didn't come out at
all, and they got the hint and left me alone.

Clayton came one time a few days after my birthday when it
wasn't his day to visit. My mom met him at the door. I told her I
didn't want to see him, even though he came to give me a birthday
gift. I didn't want anything from him. He got really upset because
I didn't want to see him, and he drove a long way just to give me a
birthday present. I didn't listen to what all was said, but my mom and
Clayton stood there on the porch, arguing back and forth for a few
minutes until Clayton stormed off and backed out of the driveway,
squealing his tires. He was mad at me because I wouldn't come out
and accept the gift he bought me.

I could not be bought. He knew I didn't want to see him, and he couldn't entice me with a gift. I wanted nothing from him and wanted nothing to do with him. I did not want him to play any part in my life. I did not even like sharing the same DNA with him. That man wasn't my "dad." My "dad" died a long time ago. In fact, I never really had a dad. Anyone can father a child. Clayton had fathered many, but it takes someone pretty special to be a dad. Clayton was never that someone with me or any of his kids, for that matter.

7

God's Gift amongst the Darkness

Each day that I woke up was a struggle. It was a challenge to stifle back the pain, the misery, and depression. My mom never made it any easier with the added guilt she laid on my already burdened shoulders. I had a lot of anger boiling beneath the surface that worked its poison into every fiber of my being. Not only did I have a lot of anxiety, but I was also starving myself and cutting myself, which did not help the already stressful situation. I was trying to deal with this all on my own which did not prove successful. I was not equipped with the necessary tools I needed to handle this on my own and knew I needed help. I had to find someone that I could talk to, to help me sort through this mess I was in. I couldn't keep going on like this. I needed to find someone who had available resources and means to help me. I needed validation most of all.

I wanted someone to tell me that it was okay to be angry and to feel the way I did, especially since my mother made me feel like I didn't have that right, like I was in the wrong to think and feel the way I did. I was in the wrong for not being able to forget the past and move on and embrace Jordan with open arms as my brother. He was a kid himself when he did those things to me; therefore, I should just forget about it and move on. I needed someone to vent to.

My mother was a very cold and distant person. Every child growing up needs a mother that loves on them, holds them, spends time with them, and values them. Every child needs good, positive affection from their mother. Every child needs compassion and needs to be doted on by their mother. Every child thrives and grows on that, and it helps them to build positive relationships in the future.

My mother never gave that to me. She never hugged on me nor showed me any kind of love or affection. We never had positive heart to heart talks. She never tried to spend any time with me. We never even so much as touched hands or made any kind of physical contact with each other. My mother was very cold and distant and self-serving. I stayed in my room, and she napped and snored on the couch or spent all her time playing cards at the kitchen table with Dwayne. She spent a lot of time with Dwayne but never any time with her kids.

I had a hunger for that kind of relationship that my mother left a void in my life. I didn't know it at the time, but I was searching for a positive motherly and fatherly relationship.

Like a willow tree whose roots travel a far distance for water and food to thrive and grow, I had to look elsewhere for that type of human connection. I needed to get through this drought I was in. Trying to work through this on my own was not working out for me. The stagnant water that my mother offered me was riddled with decay that was only doing more harm than good. I had to spread my roots elsewhere.

It's amazing how God created willow trees to spread their roots, and they know exactly where to go to find water. God also gave me the same instinct to spread my roots and seek out the healthy relationship I needed to help me grow despite the lack of sunshine in my life. That is how I came across two amazing people who have stood by me, held me, prayed for me, cried with me, and stood by me from that point on. Their names are Pastor Ken and Regina Sandefur. Pastor Ken was the senior pastor at the Kingston Wesleyan church where I attended services on Wednesdays in the youth program.

I wrote a long letter describing my history and what I was dealing with at home and that I was looking for help. When I went to church on Wednesday night, I shoved my very thick long letter under the pastor's office door.

The following Wednesday night, after the service, Pastor Ken approached me and took me to his office, and he also brought along his wife, Regina. They introduced themselves to me and told me that they got my "book." They just talked to me and prayed with me and invited me to come to church on Sunday morning. I never in my life went to church on a Sunday before. My mom never took us to church. In fact, the first time I ever went to church was on a Wednesday night youth service at Kingston Wesleyan Church.

After that day, I went to church every Wednesday night, Sunday morning, and Sunday night. I always sat with Regina on Sundays. I also wrote the Sandefurs a letter once a week, venting to them about my home situation. It always felt good writing it out and sharing my feelings with them and getting feedback from them from a Christian standpoint.

I went to church an hour early on Wednesday nights and walked over to the parsonage to visit with the Sandefurs before church. Sometimes they were eating dinner during that time and they always offered me to eat with them, but I would always refuse. They knew I had an eating disorder and didn't like to eat but always encouraged me to eat with them anyway. I just sat with them and enjoyed their company. I felt so much love and peace from them and fed off of that because it was the complete opposite at home. I wished they were my parents and that I could live with them.

He was a pastor so they were close to God. I wanted to be close to God too. I wanted to learn how to live close to God like they did. God can make everything better, right? God can change my life for the better. I can be happy and learn how to move on with my life.

With the help from the Sandefurs, I could learn how to achieve that. They could teach me how to pray, and I could learn how to ask God to help me. The Sandefurs were my heroes, and I really looked up to them. I had something I didn't have before. I had something to look forward to. I went to church before and enjoyed going, but now it was really special to me because I really enjoyed spending time with the Sandefurs. They truly loved me and cared about me. I didn't get that at home. I didn't feel loved nor cared about at home, so the Sandefurs filled the need and void for me. I was able to escape from my horrible home situation and forget about it at least three times a week. At church, I felt accepted and welcomed and loved. I had a sense of belonging. It was something that I never had before.

Not only was I in the WTFC praise band, but I also joined the church choir, which Pastor Ken was also a part of, and I participated in the Christmas Cantata and Spring Cantata. Pastor Ken had a beautiful singing voice. The choir offered me more time away from home because I had to stay over for choir practice. I even sang a couple of solos in the Christmas Cantatas.

At first, church was just a fun place for me to go to escape my home situation, but as I continued to go, it became like a drug for me. I *needed* church. If for some reason I couldn't go because my mom wouldn't take me, I would get really depressed and have anxiety over it. I thrived at church, and it really helped me to have that time away from home. My four walls in my bedroom were suffocating. That is where my thoughts ran wild. That is where I locked myself in my closet and held a blade against my skin. That is where I isolated myself. That was my prison. Church provided me asylum, a sanctuary, a safe place away from myself and away from my mother.

I learned so much about God and how He died on the cross to save us from our sins. I learned how to talk to God which I did a lot of. I did read my Bible quite a bit. When I was down and depressed, I prayed to God to show me something in His word to uplift me. I closed my eyes and opened my Bible to a random page and pointed on the page and then opened my eyes to read what God directed me to. Most of the time, that worked. Most of the time, whatever God led me to did speak to me and was on point for that current moment. If I had a question about something, I would ask God to show me the answers in His Word.

My relationship with God grew, and I drew nearer to Him with each day. I really spent a lot of time in prayer. I talked to Him in the morning when I woke up, before getting out of bed. I prayed while I was in the shower. I prayed on the bus en route to school and on the way home from school. I prayed when I got home and before I went to bed each night. I was constantly talking to God. I asked God to help me forgive Jordan and my mom and to help me get through each day.

I still struggled on a daily basis with depression, suicidal thoughts, cutting, and with my eating disorder. None of that stuff went away. I didn't always pray for the right things. I prayed for death a lot. I prayed for God to just take me home. I prayed for a way out of my current situation.

I wanted God's loving guidance in my life because I did desire a better life and happiness, but most of the time I just couldn't see past the pain I was in. I found it hard to let go and let God take control. I wanted things to change in my life, but I was scared of it at the same time. The pain and the depression and the misery was what I was used to and all I've ever known. I didn't know anything different. Although I wanted to get out of that, I found it hard to step out of my comfort zone, regardless of how painful my comfort zone was. I couldn't get past what had happened to me. I couldn't move on from the past as long as I was stuck under the same roof as my mother who kept reminding me of it day in and day out. I didn't get any love or support from her, which made it very hard.

I ran away again in the eighth grade. I took off in the middle of the night and rode my bike to the Kingston Wesleyan Church. I didn't plan on going far. I just wanted to be missing long enough to get the cops called on me again. This would make strike two on my record for runaways.

The Kingston Wesleyan church had a tall wooden fence hiding the air-conditioning unit up against the backside of the church, facing the parsonage. I parked my bike behind that fence and sat up against the fence on the wood chips. It wasn't the most comfortable place to sleep, but I was determined to spend the night there and make my mom worry in the morning when she realized that I wasn't tucked away in my bed but was out in the darkness of the night where any psycho could pick up a young girl who was out all alone, wandering the streets at night, just to get away from her. I knew how dangerous it was to be out on the streets in the middle of the night, even if I was in a rural area. There are crazy perverts everywhere. But I didn't care. I couldn't just sit back and do nothing. I had to risk my life in order to save my life. I was going to kill myself if I didn't get out of there.

It wasn't cold outside. It was the end of spring, and we were just starting to get warmer temperatures at night. I had a backpack full of clothes that I tried to use as a pillow and laid on my side. I just couldn't get comfortable lying on the wood chips, although I did manage to doze off here and there. I was waiting for morning so that I could ask the Sandefurs if they could take me to Patricia's house. I thought she would take me in for a few days and help me figure something out.

When morning came, I had a hard time finding the courage to come out of hiding. There was an event going on that Saturday morning at the church. It was a cookie walk, and more and more cars started showing up at the church. The more cars that showed up, the more scared I got to come out from behind the fence and getting caught.

There was a door that went into the kitchen of the church right next to the fence where I was hiding. That was a pretty heavily used door because that is where the main part of the parking lot was. There were people coming in and out every few minutes.

I did eventually get caught. Someone spotted me and told Pastor Ken because he peeked around the fence and asked me what I was up to. I told him that I ran away and asked him to take me to Patricia's house so that I could stay with her for a few days.

He loaded my bike in the back of the church van. That's when he introduced me to his brother, Stan, from Indiana who was up visiting.

"Hey, Drea! This is Stan. He's my brother and is a police officer," said Pastor Ken as we were all getting inside the van and buckling up.

I got behind Stan who was in the passenger seat, and Pastor Ken was driving. I went by Drea in school, but it was mainly just Pastor Ken and Regina who called me that.

Upon hearing that his brother was a police officer, my chest filled up with instant knots. I thought I was going to be in some serious trouble. Stan rode with us to Patricia's house, but she wasn't home, so we came back to the church.

My mom showed up just a few minutes after we got back to the church as I was wheeling my bike back behind the fence. She began cussing and swearing at me in front of the pastor and his brother on church grounds. I was surprised that God didn't strike her down with a bolt of lightning talking like that on church grounds.

She told me to get into the dang car.

"What about my bike?" I asked.

"Forget that bike! I hope someone freaking steals it so that you don't freaking take off on it anymore!" she hollered. There was a lot of profanity coming out of her mouth. She was very angry, and Pastor Ken and his police officer brother, Stan, heard it all.

"I'm sick of you pulling this dang crap all the dang time! Jordan is my son too, and I'm going to freakin' talk about him. If you don't freaking like it, you're going to have to freaking deal with it," she shouted with a lot more profanity.

I looked at Pastor Ken, searching for an answer on what to do next. Do I get into the car and seal my fate? Do I refuse to get in the car and make my mom put her hands on me in front of a pastor and an out-of-state police officer? Was Pastor Ken going to rescue me? He knew what I had been through and what I went through on a daily basis. Was he going to stop her from whisking me away back into that hellhole I so desperately tried to run away from? His brother was a police officer. It was a little outside of his jurisdiction, but couldn't he do something to save me from my mother? I died a little each day under the same roof as my mother.

My plan to stay gone long enough for my mother to call the cops on me didn't go so well. She caught on to what Dave was saying the last time I ran away. He told me that if I ran away a total of three times and got the cops called on me each time that I would be removed from my mother's care and placed into a foster home. My mom knew that. The last time she called the cops on me for running away, she was the one who got chewed out. So she just had to go out looking for me now which is why she was so upset. Going out to look for me took her away from her naps on the couch and burned up her gas that she needed to go visit Jordan. I made her look bad when I ran away.

I knew she knew that I told the Sandefurs stuff. That is why she was so belligerent in front of the pastor. He was a threat to her because he knew the family secret. He knew the truth. I spent so much time at church. She knew that I confided in the Sandefurs. Anyone that I confided in and told the family secrets to was seen as a threat to her. Anything I say made her look like the crappiest mother on earth, even though it was the truth and I made her look bad, and she didn't like that. She didn't want me to talk to anyone, which is the main reason why she forced me to quit counseling. As far as she was concerned, those were the family's dark little secrets, and I didn't have the right to tell anyone about them. It had always been about her.

8

The Volcano Inside Me

My teen years were unbearable, and I did what I had to do to get through them. I had to cope with the pain and the depression somehow. Cutting was how I did that.

One time, I cut my wrist a little too deep. It was the worst cut I had ever inflicted on myself, and I still have a pretty noticeable scar from it. I went into my closet and sat down in the corner with a utility knife blade and pressed it hard against my wrist and dragged it across. I kept going over it and going over it, going back and forth. It hurt, but I wanted it to hurt. The physical pain felt so much better than the emotional and mental anguish bubbling inside of me. When I cut, I had this amazing feeling that would overcome my entire body. My body would get really hot, but my hands always remained freezing cold, and I would get an adrenaline rush like an amusement park ride, and it would make me feel so alive and so good. I was addicted to that feeling I got when I cut.

When I was done cutting, I put my ice-cold hands over my cut and lay on the floor in a ball in my closet. I was exhausted. Cutting really took a lot out of me. It made my arms and legs feel like a hundred pounds of jelly. My wrist was throbbing and burning, and the pain took my breath away, but I just lay there until the high wore off and I could build enough strength to pick myself up off the floor. With every high, there is a downside. You must come down from it.

When the high wore off, I got really down and depressed even more because of what I had done.

I probably should have gotten stitches that time because of how deep it was. You could probably stick a fat pointed pen in my cut and still have room on both sides. That is how deep it was, and it was because I kept going over it and going over it, causing it to be wider and deeper.

I had to hide it somehow. I couldn't let anyone see it because I didn't want them to hospitalize me. Back in the early 2000s, plastic jelly bracelets were all the rave, and they came in every color you could think of. I had a bunch of them and wore every single one of them. I had about two hundred of them going up each wrist, and they were all color-coordinated. I put them all on my left wrist to cover up the cut I inflicted on myself. Putting them all on one wrist covered up half of my lower left arm. I not only had all of those bracelets on one arm, but I also put a couple of hair ties over my cut to ensure that no one would be able to see it. I didn't put a Band-Aid on it either, so the bracelets and the hair ties sitting on it really irritated it and made it infected. I wore long sleeves as well, even though it was a little warm for long sleeves.

The high school counselor kind of knew my situation and knew something was up when he saw me wearing long sleeves when it was warm out and all of those bracelets up one arm. He pulled me into his office and asked me about it and asked to see my wrist, but I refused to talk about it or show him what I had done. So he called my mom later that day and told her to ask to see my wrist.

Later on that night, my mom came into my room. I was in my closet, getting ready to cut. When I heard my bedroom door open, I hurried up and hid my blade and jumped to my feet. I acted like I was reorganizing my closet. My mom opened my closet door and asked what I was doing. I told her that I was cleaning my closet, which was a stupid lie.

If you'd seen my room, that would be really hard to believe because my room was always spotless and nothing was out of place. Everything had a place and had to be perfectly symmetrical and col-or-coded and very neat. That went for my closet and dresser drawers and everything. My clothes were hung up, and they had to be color-coded with all of the hangers evenly spaced and not too close together. I knew exactly where everything was. I spent day in and day out in my room. What else did I have to do other than clean it? That was also an obsession of mine. I didn't have much control over anything else, but I had control over my bedroom. That was *my* space.

When my mom asked to see my wrist, my heart felt like it jumped out of my chest and took a few ribs with it in the process. *Damn that school counselor for ratting me out.* I couldn't trust anyone with my secrets. They always told on me.

I tried stalling. I showed her my right wrist.

"The other one," she said.

I showed her my left wrist with all of the bracelets on.

"Take all of them off," she demanded.

I slowly took each bracelet off, one by one, which took a while because there were a lot of them. When she finally did see my cut, she asked me why I did it, but I didn't answer her. She started crying and fed me a bunch of nonsense about how she loved me and didn't want to see me hurt. How could she tell me that she didn't want to see me hurt when she was the one who hurt me the most? How could she tell me that she loved me when she refused to let me go to counseling to get help, when she talked about Jordan in front of me, when she was so selfish and only cared about her own feelings? How could she say she didn't want to see me hurt when she let me suffer in my bedroom in silence without batting an eye? How could she begin to cry when she refused to console me and support me as I cried myself to sleep at night?

I was glad when she finally left me alone. I put all of my bracelets back on. My cut was pretty infected, but if my mom cared, she would have made me clean it with peroxide or taken me to the hospital to get stitches because of how deep and bad it looked. But if she would have done that, they probably would have hospitalized me and made her set me up with counseling again. She tried to keep me out of counseling for her own sake. I always made her look like a bad mother, and she didn't like that.

Dwayne took my door off its hinges that night so that they could keep a better eye on me. The next day, when I came home from school, I put up a blanket, and they never said anything to me about it.

Not having a door never stopped me from cutting. I didn't need to see in order to cut. I lay in bed and cut my leg under the covers at night. I mainly went into my closet to cut, and they never took that door away. My closet was my sanctuary where I went to hide from the rest of the world and where I went to self-destruct and to think. I felt safe in my closet. They should have taken that door away.

A couple of weeks later, they gave me my door back, but I had to leave it half open all the time, and my mom came and checked on me periodically. If I wanted to cut, I would just wait until she came to check on me, and then I would go into my closet to cut because I knew she wouldn't be back for a while to check on me. I learned to not cut in such obvious places where people could see. I cut my stomach, sides, thighs, and my back where I could reach. It got to where I was cutting every day. I got up in the middle of the night while everyone else was asleep and went into my closet to cut. I had to drag myself back to bed when I was done because cutting was that exhausting. I had to drag myself through school every day because I was getting up in the middle of the night to cut. I found myself sleeping a lot when I came home from school.

Cutting was the only way I had to escape from reality. The physical pain was more bearable than the emotional pain. Not only did it provide a way to cope with the raging storm within myself, but it was a way for me to punish myself. I hated myself and who I had become. The bubbling anger and hate I had stored in my heart and soul made me feel like such a monster. I just had a lot of evil thoughts and feelings toward everyone who ever hurt me.

I even prayed to God about it because the anger I held was like poison to my soul. I asked God to help me have a more forgiving heart and to forgive those who had wronged me. At the time, I really didn't grasp the concept of what it really meant to have biblical forgiveness. I didn't understand that forgiveness was for *me*, not for the person that was being forgiven. Forgiveness was what set me free. It was the hatred and the anger that kept me in bondage to the enemy. The act of forgiveness means that you are letting go and giving God the authority over it. We all have to answer to God for every act that we have done. Nothing goes unpunished. He is the Judge of all people and of all things. When we forgive someone, we are releasing ourselves from it and giving it to God.

I prayed for guidance so that God may lead me in the way I should go. I prayed for God to give me a still, quiet, receptive heart so that I may hear *his* still quiet voice. Most of the time, it was like somebody turned up the death metal music in my head on full blast as I sat there with my hands over my ears, unable to turn it down. That is how loud the hatred and the anger was screaming within me, like a volcano about ready to explode.

9

Trivialized Pain: Just Forget It and Move On

I was so devastated when I heard that Jordan fathered a child, especially a little girl. Her name was Ember. I was so scared for her. What kind of life would she have with a father like him? Would she grow up being molested by him? He doesn't deserve the right to procreate. What was the mother of that baby thinking? Did she even know what he did? Did she care? I was very upset by this and couldn't understand why God allowed this to happen.

Not only did Jordan have a little girl on the way, but so did my sister, Jennifer, who was having her second little girl. She also didn't deserve to have any children. She couldn't even take care of little MacKenzie, as it was, let alone another one. Jennifer and Anthony fought a lot. Their apartment was beyond disgusting and dirty with dirty diapers everywhere, the kitchen counters were full of dirty dishes, trash overflowing, and dirty clothes were all over the place and even lined the hallway. You could barely stand the smell. It stank so bad. Jennifer had never been a real clean person. She wasn't ready to grow up and be a mother. She didn't even finish high school. She moved in with her boyfriend at the age of seventeen, dropped out, and got pregnant and never got a job. She wasn't ready to grow up because all she wanted to do was go out and party and leave her kid with whoever would watch her.

I was a live-in babysitter on the weekends and most of the summer. When I was there, I tried to clean her apartment up some, but it would just be a complete waste of time because Jennifer would never keep it clean, and there was just so much laundry everywhere, and she had to pay to do laundry which never was a priority for her. I just tried to keep MacKenzie's room clean and the living room so that she would have a clean place to play.

Jennifer only paid me a handful of times to babysit. I spent so much time there that MacKenzie started calling me mom. Sometimes, Jennifer and Anthony would not come home until the next day, or if they did come home in the middle of the night, Jennifer would be drunk and stumbling around. I felt so used most times like she was just using me to watch her kid so that she could go out and party. She was my big sister. I wanted to spend time with her too, and she would promise to spend time with me but always broke her promises. She just wanted to hang out with her friends without her kid sister hanging around.

I took Kenzie uptown to the park a lot when the weather was nice. I would pack us lunch, and we would have a picnic at the park. Sometimes there would be no food in the apartment, so I would use my own money I earned working for Patti and bought us something to eat at the little mini mart on our way to the park. I spent so much time with that little girl and practically raised her the first few years of her life. I pushed her on the swing and spun her around on the merry-go-round. I dressed her, changed her, fed her, and did her hair. I was the one disciplining her. I even took her to church with me a few times and sent her to Clubhouse, which was the children's ministry on Wednesday nights, and even took her to church with me on Sunday mornings, and she went to Sunday school.

People would come up to me in the park and ask me if she was mine, and I always wanted to say that she might as well be, but I told them I was just her aunt.

MacKenzie was the cutest little girl. She was dark-complected because her daddy was half Black. She had chubby cheeks with the cutest dimples, and every time she smiled, it looked like her eyes smiled too. She had squinty smiling eyes. She also had a little curl to her hair. She was beautiful.

Jennifer named her next baby girl Kylie, and she was born around the same time as Ember. I already made up my mind that I didn't want anything to do with Jordan's baby. I was not going to be her aunt. It was nothing against Ember, a poor innocent child. I didn't want anything to do with Jordan or his family. I didn't want him to be a part of my life, which meant that Ember couldn't be a part of my life either. I felt sorry for her, but I had to protect myself. I just had to put up this wall to protect myself.

What if I did get attached to her and something happened to her? It would crush me. I couldn't put myself through that. Besides, how would I explain to a child why I didn't get along with her dad? It was in my best interest and hers to keep myself at a distance from her. It would have just made things a lot more complicated.

Jennifer brought Kylie over along with her big sister MacKenzie, and Jordan brought Ember over at the same time. My stepsisters, Nora and Molly, were also there along with Molly's husband, Jerry. Everyone had the babies in the living room, passing them around and making over them.

My room was off the living room, and I was on my bed, writing with my back up against the wall, sitting sideways on my bed. My bed was up against the wall that the living room was on, so I could hear everything that was going on. I knew Ember was out there, and so was Jordan, which was why I chose not to go out there, even though I hadn't seen Kylie yet. I would have plenty of opportunities to see Kylie since I was Jennifer's live-in babysitter anyway. I could wait to see Kylie.

My mom came into my bedroom and told me to come out and see the babies. I got up and went out to the living room and asked which one was Kylie. I knew something was up because I got two different answers. They were trying to trick me into holding Jordan's baby by telling me that Ember was Kylie. I wasn't stupid and figured out what they were trying to do. I studied both babies for a minute. Kylie was a little more dark-complected with dark hair, and Ember had blonde hair. I picked up Kylie and held her for a minute and then gave her back and went back to my room, ignoring baby Ember. While I was holding Kylie, they were trying to talk me into holding Ember next, and I kept telling them that I didn't want to hold her and that I was not her aunt.

They saw me as coldhearted and mean for not wanting anything to do with an innocent child, but I didn't care. I had to protect myself. I had no plans on ever having Jordan be a part of my life. How could I have a relationship with his daughter and not him? It just wasn't possible. The father of that child ruined my life. I didn't want any part of him. Why couldn't they understand that? I didn't want to be emotionally invested in that child. I didn't want to look at her. I didn't want to hold her. I didn't want her to melt my heart. I didn't want to fall in love with her. I didn't want to get attached to her. How do you not fall in love with a little baby? It's hard not to fall in love, which was why I chose to have nothing to do with her and to avoid her altogether. I felt that if her dad ever molested her, like he did me, it would be so much easier on me emotionally if I just wasn't attached to her.

Call me selfish if you want, but I had no choice but to build a wall around my heart to protect myself from getting hurt again since I'd already been hurt too many times as it was.

A few minutes later, Nora was knocking on my door and coming into my room with Ember in her arms. Leave it to Nora to force the issue. She was always an instigator.

"I want you to hold Ember," she said, walking over to me sitting on my bed.

"I don't want to," I said.

"You don't want to hold your niece?"

"She is not my niece," I proclaimed.

"She is your niece, just like MacKenzie and Kylie are your nieces, and you are her aunt just like you are their aunt."

"No because Jordan is not my brother, she is not my niece."

"Ember is an innocent little baby. She didn't hurt you. She did nothing wrong."

I knew that. I had no hard feelings against the baby and didn't hate her. I just wanted no part of Jordan, and she was a part of him.

It had nothing to do with her at all. Why couldn't they understand that?

"I want no part of Jordan's family," I said.

"Well, Jennifer, MacKenzie, Kylie, your mom, Joshua, Theo are all a part of Jordan's family, and me, Molly, DJ, and Dwayne are all a part of your mom's family. So does that mean you don't want any part of us either?"

Yeah, I thought to myself. I never realized until this very moment, writing this all out, how true that really was. Nora was right. They were *all* a part of Jordan's family, and it wasn't until later that I realized that I could never be a part of it because they would all choose Jordan over me. They always chose him over me every single time.

At that point, I was just getting angry. How could she possibly understand what I was going through? She never had to go through anything like I had. There was no point in wasting my breath, trying to explain to her about something she would never understand.

Nora got mad and frustrated with me and walked out of my room with the baby, leaving my bedroom door open. About a minute later, Molly came barging in and basically said the same thing her sister Nora did. They really laid on the guilt trip and made me feel like I was a monster for not wanting anything to do with an innocent baby.

Molly and Nora were both in my room now with baby Ember. Molly sat on my bed next to me, holding the baby, while Nora was standing in front of me. Molly kept trying to get me to look at the baby and how sweet and innocent she was and that she didn't have anything to do with what her dad did to me. I wouldn't look at her. I didn't want to look at her.

"Should Jennifer have anything to do with you, Joshua, or Theo because you are Clayton's kids, and he was the one who molested her?" said Molly.

I was flabbergasted when she said that.

"That's different!" I said.

"How is that different?" asked Molly and Nora both at the same time.

95

I didn't know how to respond to that. I was just getting very angry that these two were in my room and wouldn't leave me alone. I didn't want anything to do with the kid. Why couldn't they just accept it and leave me alone? Why did it matter to them so much? Why are they trying to force her on me? Weren't they worried that I would tell Ember what her daddy did when she got older? What would she think of her daddy then? Shouldn't they be grateful that I didn't want anything to do with her so that she wouldn't know the dark stain her daddy put on this family? Wouldn't the truth turn Ember away from her daddy? They were all mad at me for not wanting anything to do with Jordan, but how would they feel if Ember didn't want anything to do with him either after finding out what he did? Had they ever thought that me not having anything to do with Ember may not be a bad thing after all?

They did bring up one good point. I will give them that. One day, all of the kids will be over—MacKenzie, Kylie, and Ember and whoever else comes along—and they will all be playing together. Would I play with all of the other kids and not Ember? Ember would think her Aunt DeeDee hated her because Aunt DeeDee never played with her. Would it be fair to punish an innocent little girl for something her father did when he was just a kid himself? Should Ember ever wonder why her Aunt DeeDee didn't like her?

I never thought about it that way, and surely, this child made things more complicated for me. Jordan would be around a lot more now that Ember was in the picture, and I was right. Now that he gave my mother this grandchild, he was going to be around a lot more, and I was just going to have to deal with it.

I was not going to change my mind, though. I had to stand my ground on this no matter how difficult it was going to be. I could not be a part of this child's life. I had to protect myself, and that is exactly what I did. When all of the kids were over at the same time, I chose to stay in my room and not pay attention to any of them. I didn't want to be around Jordan anyway, so that worked out. I saw MacKenzie and Kylie a lot on the weekends and during the summer when I babysat them, so having Ember around didn't really affect my relationship with them.

My mom had made the comment to me before that I needed to forgive and move on and leave things in the past, which was easy for her to say. Nothing like that ever happened to her. But they all used this child as a way to try and soften my heart so that I would cave and *have* to let Jordan be in my life. If anyone was going to do that, then surely a small child could. That is why they tried so hard to get me to hold Jordan's child. They wanted me to cave. They wanted their perfect little family, and I was standing in the way of that. They wanted me to forgive and forget and embrace Jordan with open arms.

My mom complained a lot that her family was torn apart, and I know she blamed me because I refused to move on and put the past behind me. Jordan didn't have any problem moving on and put the past behind him. He didn't have the issue here. It was me that refused to move on. It was my fault the family was torn apart.

Ember was just the tool they were using to soften my heart so that I would have to have a relationship with Jordan. I knew what they were doing. It never really was about the baby nor making me hold her. My mom wanted her one big happy family, and they were trying to make that happen through a small child. I knew what they were up to and what they were trying to do. They weren't fooling me, and I wasn't going to allow them to push this child on me to get me to have anything to do with Jordan.

Molly and Nora were both getting frustrated with me. I knew they thought I was mean and cold for not wanting anything to do with an innocent baby. Molly sat closer to me and laid Ember on my lap and told me to hold her. I just put my hands up and told her to get her off of me. I wasn't going to hold her, and they were not going to make me. Why would you force someone to hold a baby? I would never hurt her, but they were not going to make me hold her. A newborn baby needed their head supported. Why would you lay a couple days' old baby on someone's lap that didn't want to hold it? They kept telling me to look at her and hold her, but I refused. I looked away and put my hands up and kept telling them to get her off of me. They got really angry with me and picked the baby up and walked out of my room. They were pretty disgusted with me.

I was so angry that they were trying to force her on me when I kept trying to tell them that I didn't want to hold her. Just leave it at that and leave me alone about it. I was the one who was coldhearted, mean, unloving, unforgiving, and a monster. I was taking it out on a small child for the sins of her father. I was worse than Jordan. I was unbelievable and out of line. I was hateful. That is how they made me feel.

When everyone was in my mom and Dwayne's room smoking weed, I snuck out to the kitchen. Ember was in her car seat on the table. I held her little hand and held her little feet and stroked her little cheek. I prayed for her as she held on to my finger. I prayed that God would protect her and keep her safe and that Jordan would never hurt this little girl like he hurt me. Then I hurried up and went back to my room before anyone saw me. I didn't want anyone getting the wrong idea. I still was not going to have anything to do with this child, but I was going to pray for safety over her. I still felt sorry for her and cared about her well-being. I didn't want Jordan to hurt that little girl like he hurt me and didn't trust that he wouldn't. In fact, I was very concerned that is what would happen to her. Once a pervert, always a pervert.

One day, I was lying on the couch, watching a Lifetime movie on the rare occasion that I did come out of my room. It was a movie about a ballerina that was suffering from anorexia. It was a movie that I could relate to because I too suffered from anorexia. In the middle of the movie, just when it was getting good, my mom came into the living room and sat on the loveseat across from me. She sat there for a minute without saying anything. I knew she was up to something, and the awkward silence was very distracting and deafening.

"We need to talk," she said, breaking the silence.

Oh, great. Here we go. I don't remember most of that conversation because she said one thing that really upset me and shattered every fiber of my pitiful, painful existence. Everything else she said after that I couldn't hear because that one thing kept replaying over and over again in my head, shattering me to the core each and every time.

The conversation was about Jordan. She wanted me to forgive and forget and move on. She told me that Jordan was my brother whether I liked it or not. She basically told me that it was wrong of me to hold a grudge against him for something he did when he was twelve years old. He didn't know what he was doing. She really trivialized what he did to me like it was no big deal. She made excuses for him and told me that Jordan was punished because he got sent away and had to go live with strangers. He'd learned his lesson. People changed, and I needed to give him a chance.

Then she said this one thing, and everything she said after that was a complete blank. What she said was a complete and utter shock to my system and leaves me in shock still to this day. I just can't get past it. It took my breath away! Did she actually say what I thought she just said? Was she serious? Did she actually say that to me?

"Back in the old days, incest was normal."

What? Did she actually say that to me?

"Back in the old days, incest was normal."

That kept playing over and over in my head.

"Back in the old days, incest was normal."

I still can't believe she said that. So what Jordan did to me was somehow okay since back in the old days, incest was normal? I just needed to forget it and carry on like nothing happened? Unbelievable!

Jordan knew very well what he was doing. When I had that meeting with him and both of our counselors and my mom (you know, the one my mother couldn't sit through and walked out on), I asked him why he did what he did. He said because if he did the same thing to me that Clayton did to Jennifer, then he would be in prison with Clayton, which is what he wanted. He knew that people who do bad things went to jail, so if he wanted to do something to put him in jail, then he had to do something bad. So he knew exactly what he was doing and that what he was doing was wrong. Twelve is old enough to know better. If my mother would have sat through that meeting instead of running out like she did, she would know exactly what she was trying to make me forget and forgive. She would know exactly what she was trivializing and what she was asking of me.

Still, to this day, she doesn't know all of the details of what her son did to her daughter because she refuses to hear it. She would rather remain ignorant because it is easier for her. It makes it easier for her to tell me to forget, forgive, and move on. It makes it easier for her to trivialize it. I really needed her there, and she ran out on me.

If incest was normal, then why all of the sudden was what Clayton did to Jennifer wrong? She turned her back to it for years while it was going on because I do not believe for a second that she didn't know what was going on. How can you not know? When Jennifer finally built up the courage to tell, and Clayton was hauled off to prison, she planned on staying with him and getting back together with him when he got out. When she started dating someone else because she couldn't wait any longer for Clayton, then all of a sudden, what he did was wrong. So if what Clayton did was wrong, then why wasn't what Jordan did wrong too? You can't pick and choose what you think is morally acceptable.

The reason why my mother wanted to have this conversation in the first place was because of what I did the night before. I found out that Jordan's real dad passed away. He drank himself to death. I wonder if it was because my mother took his two kids away and didn't tell him where they were that drove him to drinking.

Jordan called the house phone, and I happened to be the one to answer it. When he said it was Jordan after I asked who it was, I smiled from ear to ear and got an overwhelming feeling of satisfaction and butterflies in my stomach.

"Guess what?" I said. "Your daddy died," I said and hung up. I felt like skipping all the way back to my room. I was so proud of myself. I hurt him! Yes! I wanted to hurt him! I have to admit, I really enjoyed it at the time.

Not even a minute later, the phone rang again. Then a couple minutes later, my mom came barging in my room, yelling at me for telling her precious son over the phone that his daddy died.

"It's not something you tell somebody over the phone!" she barked.

I tried hard to hide the joy on my face for doing what I did, even when my mother was yelling at me for it. That was the first and only time that my mother ever told me that I was grounded, and it was because I hurt her son's feelings, not because of running away or anything like that but because I hurt Jordan's feelings. I didn't care. *Ground me!* What was she going to do? Ground me to my room? *Be my guest. I'm always in my room anyway.*

Jordan showed up at the house that night, crying. They were out on the front deck. My mom was hugging him and consoling him. I was sickened by that. What kind of comfort and compassion had she shown toward me? She never consoled me for what Jordan did. What was he crying about, anyway? He didn't even know his real dad.

I snuck glances out at Jordan crying about his dead daddy, and it brought me joy and satisfaction to see him on the receiving end of pain and suffering this time. Although that would never amount to the pain and suffering he caused me, it was still satisfying nonetheless.

10

Running for Anorexia

At the beginning of my sophomore year, my depression and anorexia kicked into high gear. I really felt like I needed someone to talk to at school. I had the Sandefurs, but I could only talk to them on Wednesdays and Sundays, and that was only if my mom dropped me off at church. I needed to be able to talk to someone whenever I needed to. I didn't trust the school counselor, so I decided to talk to a teacher. She was my English and Spanish teacher. Her name was Mrs. Robinson.

I wrote out a thirty-page letter describing my situation. I felt like all hope was lost and I was very depressed and wanted nothing more than for death to take me in the dark of night. Spanish was my last hour class, and I made sure that I was the last one out of class and left that letter behind on the floor but over a few spots. I prayed that it would be Mrs. Robinson who found that letter and that it wouldn't fall into the wrong hands.

The next day, Mrs. Robinson held me back after class. She told me that she found my letter and that she was there to talk to if I needed her. She also asked for my permission to give the letter to the school counselor. I really didn't want to. I didn't trust counselors anymore. Mrs. Henry and Denae both betrayed me and sent me to the psych ward. I told Mrs. Robinson in this letter that I wanted to die. I didn't want the school counselor to read it and send me back to the psych ward. Mrs. Robinson reassured me and told me that everything would be okay and that it would be confidential but that the school counselor would have a lot more resources where he could help me better. So I agreed to let him see the letter, even though I was leery about it.

That was the beginning of my secret relationship with Mrs. Robinson and the high school counselor. My mother didn't know about me telling them about the deep dark family secrets. I could tell them anything. I could vent, and my mother couldn't take it away because she had to let me go to school. She could take church away, but she couldn't take school away. I could work with them and try to brainstorm on how to get me out of that house without having to wait until I was eighteen. Running away wasn't working because my mom wouldn't call the cops on me. There had to be another way.

I had to write an essay for Mrs. Robinson's English class, and we could write about anything we wanted. I loved the sound of that assignment. I loved to write, but what was even better was that I could write about anything I wanted. I chose to write my essay on emancipation. Emancipation is where a minor can take their parents to court and essentially "divorce" them. The parents would no longer have a say, and if the courts saw it fit, the minor could live on their own and support themselves, essentially becoming an adult. It was common for child stars whose parents were embezzling their money.

I learned so much when I was writing this essay and really got the wheels turning in my head. What if I could get emancipated? I could get a job as a waitress in town. I wouldn't need to have a license or a car because I could walk to work and school. I could get an apartment across from the church, and my sister lived in those apartments too, so I wouldn't be completely alone. If I needed anything, she was right there, and the Sandefurs were across the street. I couldn't have better neighbors than them. I would not drop out of school. My mother and sister were high school dropouts. I wasn't going to be like them.

When I went over to my sister's, I imagined how my apartment would be. I wouldn't need a three-bedroom for just myself. My apartment would be really clean and organized, not filthy dirty like Jennifer's. My imagination went wild, and I had this whole design in my head for my own apartment. I fantasized about having my own apartment and what life would look like away from my mother. I would be so much happier.

I asked the school counselor about how I could go about getting emancipated. He didn't think I would be able to because of my unstable history with depression and suicide attempts and history of being hospitalized. But the reason for that was because of my mother. With my mother out of the picture, I could go to counseling and would be healthier and happier. I would be better. He also told me that I didn't have a job, so I wouldn't be able to support myself. Well, I could get a job. He punctured a lot of holes in the emancipation idea, and I didn't know how to go about that on my own. I was hoping that he would be able to help me with that but soon found that wasn't going to be the case.

My sister and Nora both moved out at the age of seventeen, so I knew that I could too. I was sixteen at the time and couldn't wait a whole other year. I was miserable, and it just seemed like hope was so far away.

I joined track that year, and Mrs. Robinson was also the track coach. Mrs. Robinson was a very young attractive woman. She had blonde hair and was short and thin with a very sharp, pointy nose. She was also very stylish, and I always loved her outfits. I wished I could dress like her. My mom couldn't afford to buy us nice clothes on welfare, and every job she had, she quit.

When I grew up, I was going to make sure that my kids had the best life I could give them. They were going to have nice clothes and anything they could ever want because I was going to make sure that I could provide for them. They would have the life my mother could never give to me. I was going to write books and become a famous author and have a lot of money, and my husband was going to be rich too.

In high school, I did write a pretty extensive novel called *The Road to Recovery*. It was about a little girl named Cayenne Catt. She was born into a rich family and had an older sister named Talia. Cayenne's mother died during labor with her. When Cayenne was just three years old, she was abducted during her father's annual

Valentine's Day party. Her abductor changed her name to Baraka and moved her far away to Maine to raise her as his own. Baraka's new dad was a photographer for a big-name magazine. When Baraka was old enough to start driver's training, she needed to have her birth certificate, so she started asking questions. Her dad would always change the subject or put it off.

Her dad became abusive and started keeping her from school. He was obsessed with taking pictures of her and made her model for him. The sessions became more and more sexualized, and he started dressing her in more and more revealing clothes until soon, he made her pose in the nude. He invited his partner over, and the two of them would take turns taking pictures of her.

Her dad then started molesting her and sold her virginity to his partner which turned into selling her to other customers who wanted to have sex with a minor.

One day, Baraka was cleaning and stumbled upon an old newspaper clipping of a missing three-year-old child who looked an awful lot like her. That is when she realized that she never really had any baby pictures of herself younger than three years old. She got out the old family photo albums to search for pictures of her three-year-old self. The resemblance was astounding. Could it be? Was she actually this little girl? Was her real name really Cayenne Catt?

Baraka went to the police station. She had to know for sure. Her life was hell, and if she was really Cayenne Catt, her real family would come and rescue her out of this hell away from these men who just wanted her body.

The police ran her fingerprints, and she was, indeed, Cayenne Catt. Cayenne's dad never stopped looking for her. He flew to Maine to get her, and her abductor not only went to prison for child abduction but also for child pornography, human trafficking of a minor, and child rape among other charges.

Even though Cayenne was now with her real family, she had an uphill battle of recovery. She grew up as Baraka, so becoming Cayenne was going to take some time. She was now in a totally different country. It was all a bit overwhelming for her to take in. Her older sister, Talia, resented her because now that the long-lost daughter had returned, she was getting all of the attention.

Cayenne suffered from major depression and was in counseling, but it wasn't helping. She couldn't handle the hatefulness from Talia, and Talia bullied her immensely and told her that she wished she would have stayed gone and that her little sister died a long time ago and that she needed to stay dead. Cayenne wondered if she would have been better off not finding those old newspaper clippings and if her real family would have been better off if she was never found. The guilt was too much for her, and what had happened to her in Maine with the man who raised her invaded her sleep and gave her nightmares and tormented her even more. She was really a tortured soul and tried to end her life by jumping off a tall city building. As fate would have it, a bad boy was there to stop her, a damsel in distress, which turned into a bad romance. The boy in leather had a motorcycle, smoked cigarettes, had tattoos, listened to rock and roll, and would lead her down an even darker path that helped her numb her pain.

Cayenne struggled to find her identity. Was she a little rich girl named Cayenne or was she Baraka, the play toy for older men?

I worked really hard on this novel, although I never got to complete it, and I had every intention of getting it published. I might have watched too many Lifetime movies, but it was a story that captivated you and kept you on the edge of your seat. It was a story that I got lost in and helped keep my mind off my own painful situation.

When I joined track, I was becoming more and more obsessed with my body. I didn't join track for the fun of it or for any other reason than to work out. Mrs. Robinson knew that I had an eating disorder, so she did keep a closer eye on me. At the beginning of the season, it was still pretty cold outside. For practice, we stretched in the cafeteria and ran laps through the hallways after school. I loved it. I enjoyed the exercise. This was the beginning of a new destructive behavior for me called overkill.

I dragged in my brother's weight set. I brought in all of the weights, the rod, and everything except the bench since the bench wouldn't fit in my room.

Every day after I got out of track practice, I went home and worked out some more in my room. I would work out for an hour when I got home and then another thirty minutes or so before I went to bed. And if I couldn't sleep, I would get up and do a hundred or more sit-ups and then go right to sleep. I pushed myself harder than I should have on top of being anorexic. I did over a hundred sit-ups at a time, a lot of push-ups, leg lifts, and arm exercises with and without weights. I utilized a lot of the exercises that I learned in gym class and track.

When it started getting nicer outside, I rode my bike down our dirt road and ran from the corner to the bridge, which was about a quarter of a mile. I did laps, back and forth. There weren't any houses right there, so I had my privacy as I was running back and forth. When I got tired of running, I would speed walk back and forth. I did this on top of all the other exercises I did, all while not eating or putting anything in my stomach.

No one knew just how much exercise I was doing and how little I was eating. There were times when I heard my mother coming while I was in the middle of exercising, and I would hurry up and put my weights away as quietly as I could and hurry up and jump in bed and acted like I was drawing or writing or doing homework. My mother liked to check on me every now and then because she never saw me since I was always in my room.

My room was very clean and spotless. Even my weights were organized, and each piece had a place. I was very careful to only get one thing out at a time so that if I had to, I could put it away really quick when I heard my mom coming. I also made sure that I had my radio on to drown out the noise while I was exercising. My mother never did catch me exercising. She was very clueless to a lot of things. Why didn't I want her to know? Because I already ate very little and didn't want her on my case about it.

There was a time that I was very sore and felt like I got hit by a bus. My whole body hurt, but especially my sides. It hurt so bad to move a muscle. It hurt to breathe, to yawn, and especially sneeze. It hurt to stand up and sit down. Every little movement killed me. All of this pain and suffering was from me overexercising. I went to school that morning and told Mrs. Robinson about it. She told me that when I got home, I needed to lie on my back on the floor and bend myself up into an upside down "U" position to stretch out all of my muscles or lay a pillow on the floor, lay on my stomach, and grab my feet behind me and bend myself into an "O" position.

When I got home, I did both of them, and it was extremely painful. It was very painful to make the slightest little movements, let alone do those. It felt like someone was kicking me in the ribs just to take a deep breath. I felt like that for about a week, but each day was a little better than the day before.

We were at a track meet in Akron Fairgrove, and Mrs. Robinson saw how sickly and weak I was. She pulled me to the side.

"Have you eaten anything at all today?" she asked.

"No," I replied.

"Here, I want you to eat this and show me the core when you are done or I'm not letting you run," she said, handing me an apple.

I took the apple and went and hid. I bit into the apple and spit out each bite. She said she wanted to see the core when I was done. I was going to show her the core, but I wasn't going to actually eat it. I didn't want this apple inside me. It would make me fatter than I was. I only weighed a hundred and ten pounds, and I was five feet, five inches, which was underweight. I should have been around a hundred and thirty pounds.

When I got down to the core, I showed Mrs. Robinson, and she agreed to let me run. I was in long distance and had to run the mile. Before I got to run, I went over to the pavilion where all of our stuff was. I got in my bag and took out two diet pills that I got from a friend.

Halfway through the second lap, I collapsed on the track and couldn't get up. I felt so dizzy and so sick. My head was spinning and my sight was blurry. I was scared. I was scared that they might call an ambulance and send me back to the psych ward. I couldn't go back there.

A couple of guys from the crowd picked me up and carried me over to the other end of the track by my coach. They sat me on the ground.

"What happened?" asked Mrs. Robinson.

"I twisted my ankle," I said.

I hoped that she believed me. I didn't want to tell her what really happened. She would blame it on me not eating, and I especially didn't want to tell her that I took those pills.

A little while later, Mrs. Robinson came up to me and told me that someone told her that they saw me coughing up blood. I knew exactly who it was that ratted me out. It was Maddie Clay. We were friends, but not all that close. I went to her house a few times to hang out, and her mother was my bus driver, the meanest one in town. Maddie was standing beside me when I started coughing. I looked at my hand, and it had a quarter size spot of blood in it. It scared me. I hurried up and closed my hand and walked fast to the bathroom to wash it off. I didn't think anyone saw it, but apparently, Maddie did.

It hurt to breathe. The cold air hurt my lungs, but I didn't care. I had to run. I needed the exercise. I was most unhappy with my thighs. I always had thunder thighs and hated them. I always envied the other girls who had skinny little legs and knobby little knees. I always thought that I had boyish looking legs with fat knees. I hated my legs. I even hated that they were so pale and paper white along with the rest of my body. Looking back at old pictures during that time, I looked grey and very sickly.

Mrs. Robinson told me that I was done. I wasn't healthy enough to run track, and she wasn't going to let me kill myself on her team when I wouldn't eat to sustain the energy I needed to run.

My mom only gave me five or six dollars to get something off the dollar menu after a track meet when we stopped to get something to eat. I never ate anything. I sat on the bus while everyone else went in to eat or I went in to sit because Mrs. Robinson made me. I always felt so sick sitting in there, smelling all of that food when I hadn't eaten all day. I always wanted to eat. I was always hungry, but I wouldn't allow myself to succumb to my hunger. I wanted to starve. I wanted to starve to death. Starving was just like cutting. I wanted to inflict pain on myself. If my body suffered physically, then my soul, my mind, and my heart wouldn't suffer so much. At least the physical pain would overpower the pain on the inside. The pain on the inside was so deafening and so unbearable I did what I had to do to drown that out, and making myself suffer physically was the only way I knew how to do that, short of death.

I actually did sprain my ankle when I collapsed on the track. I didn't fall because I sprained my ankle. I collapsed because I was weak, dizzy, and lightheaded and sprained my ankle on the way down.

My mother never knew anything about that because she was clueless. She never came to any of my track meets, band concerts, football games to see me march in the band, nor to hear me sing in the choir at church. She never came to anything of mine. But she went to Theo's parents' night for basketball. She went to his games. My mom always complained about having to take me to where I needed to go. She already had to take me to church two miles away, three times a week.

My mother didn't know about me getting kicked off of the track team. For the next couple of weeks, I stayed after school like I was at track practice. I walked to the park, which was next to the school with a bank in between. I stretched and ran laps around the tennis court. When track practice was over and it was time for my mom to pick me up, I walked back up to the high school and acted like I just got out of track practice.

My mother never asked too many questions, and I never offered up any information. We never really communicated unless it was her telling me that incest was normal or trying to tell me that I needed to get over it and move on. She never asked how my day went. I hardly got anything emotionally from her. We never spent any time together. She very rarely told me that she loved me. She never hugged me nor joked around or anything. It was a very cold, distant relationship with minimal communication. When we handed each other something, we did it without touching hands.

A couple of weeks after I got kicked off the team, I just told my mother that I quit. She was happy to not have to pick me up after practice anymore. She didn't encourage me not to quit anything. She didn't care. It benefited her because she didn't have to come and get me. Mrs. Robinson wouldn't let me tag along on track meets so I couldn't pretend anymore.

My mother didn't let me do a whole lot. I was mainly home-bound. My two brothers got to do whatever they wanted, and they got to go to their friend's houses all of the time. I very rarely got to get out of the house other than school, church, and my sister's.

I wasn't allowed to go over to a friend's house if she had an older brother. The only way that I could go over there if she did have an older brother was if he wasn't going to be home. Maddie was the only child at home, so I got to spend the night with her a few times. Meagan had two younger brothers, so I was able to spend the night with her on a few occasions too.

Alisha had an older brother, Darrel, and she was the one that lived closest to me. She lived right down the road from me a few miles down. I rode my bike to her house quite a few times, most of the time without my mother knowing. I just told her that I was riding my bike around the block, and she believed me. Every time I asked my mom if I could go to Alisha's, she always asked me if her brother was going to be there. I always told her no. She treated me like I was a slut and couldn't be trusted around older boys, like she was protecting them from me. I couldn't be around older boys because I might spread my legs for them and get pregnant. My mom had my older sister at the age of seventeen, and my sister got pregnant at the age of seventeen. It didn't mean I was like them. I wasn't even into boys and never had a boyfriend.

Why would any boy want me? I was nerdy looking. I had bright red, curly, frizzy hair. I wore glasses and was flat-chested. I thought I was fat at the time. I wore glasses. I was very shy and socially awkward and never found myself to be attractive. I never thought that any boy would like me, so I never bothered to ever be interested in them. I also knew that I had a lot of issues and was damaged goods. My mom always made comments like, "Girls can get pregnant, boys can't," even though it takes two to make a child, last time I checked.

My youngest brother, Theo, even had his girlfriend over quite a few times, but they weren't allowed in his room together. Theo went through quite a few girlfriends, and I knew they were having sex. He had told me about sneaking them through his bedroom window at night and having sex with them in the closet. My mom even found condoms in the boys' room and thought it was funny. She never found condoms in my room, yet I was a slut.

I hardly ever had any friends over, and they never stayed the night. I wasn't allowed to do a whole lot, and there was never anything to do. Also, they hated my mom and stepdad.

I didn't have much of a life outside of school. My mother never took us anywhere at all. She never made sure we had fun and never did any fun things with us. There wasn't a world outside of little old Kingston for me. I lived a very sheltered life. This is just another example of my mother's neglectful parenting. She made it so hard for me to grow up and experience new things. There was a whole lot more to this world than little tiny Kingston, but with her, I never got to experience it.

11

Running Away to Find Closure

When I was sixteen years old, I knew that I was approaching the age where I was soon able to move out from under my mother but didn't have any place to go. I thought about moving in with my sister, but I didn't think that I would be that much happier there. Then I would really be a live-in babysitter. My sister was also not the best influence. She tried to hook me up with a guy quite a bit older than me and was going to pay my way to go to a movie with him, but I refused. I wasn't ready for boys after all that I had been through, and I didn't trust them. I'd been hurt way too many times, and I knew that I was vulnerable and couldn't take another hit of trauma. This older boy would only be after one thing, and I didn't want to put myself in that position when I wasn't ready. My sister was very much in the party scene. She drank a lot, and all she did was go out and hang out with friends and drink. I couldn't move in with her. That was not an option.

Where else was I going to go when I turned seventeen? I wouldn't graduate from high school until I was nineteen. I didn't have any Internet at home to research any viable options. My mother pretty much cut us off from all of our family, so moving in with another family member was not an option either. I thought about asking the Sandefurs if they would take me in or even Patti, but I didn't want to be a burden to them and felt as though that would change the relationship that I had with them and not for the better. I really wished

113

that the Sandefurs were my parents, but I loved the friendship that I had with them and felt that would somehow change if I lived with them. If they would have asked me and offered, then it may have been different, but I felt really funny about asking.

I started spending my lunches in the library, researching teen shelters in my area, and I found one in Saginaw, Michigan. That was forty-five minutes away from me. They took in teen runaways and teens who were homeless and helped them get on their feet by finding them jobs and an apartment, getting their license and their GED.

This sounded like it would be my best option, but how would I get there? My mother wouldn't take me there for sure. I did as much research on that place as I could. I could go to that shelter at the age of sixteen, but only as a runaway.

I decided that this is what I was going to do. Saginaw was going to be my new home, and I was just going to get my GED, get a job, my license, my own car, and best of all, my own apartment. This place was going to help me achieve all of that. I was finally going to have control over my own life, and the sky was the limit. I was going to be in charge of my own happiness from here on out, and my mother was no longer going to have the ability to bring me down. She could have Jordan back, and I wasn't going to be in the way to stop her. I was going to move on and live my own life. But I didn't think that I could do that without first getting closure. I needed to be able to put the past behind me in order for me to move on; otherwise, the past would continue to haunt me into my new life, and I didn't want that.

How was I going to finally put my past to bed? I needed to visit where it all happened. I had to see the place where my life fell apart. I had to see the tree where I almost hung myself at eight years old. I had to see the yard that I played in. I wanted to sit on the front porch where my mother sat and watched us play. I had to visit the restaurant across the street where there was a pay phone out front, and I talked to Clayton in prison and asked him when he was coming home. I had to hold the phone in my hand and hold it up against my ear. I wanted to touch that phone booth. And if I could somehow break into that trailer, I wanted to go inside. I wanted to see my old bedroom. I wanted to see Jordan's old bedroom and the bathroom where it all happened. I wanted to see and touch everything to bring it all back to me in every detail.

I wanted to see my parent's old bedroom where I remember Clayton playing the guitar, and I sang, "Take Me Out to the Ball Game." I wanted to see the living room where Clayton chased me around and captured me and tickled me until I almost peed my pants. I knew it was going to be painful to do that. I wanted to see it all play out in front of me like the ghost of Christmas past. I wanted to go there so that I could scream and cry out to God and ask him why. Why did this have to happen to me? Why did this have to be my life?

Once I got it all out of my system, I wanted to give it to God once and for all. I no longer wanted it to control me. *I wanted to be happy and live a normal life!* I wanted this to be a healing experience for me, however painful it was going to be.

As far as I knew, no one moved into that trailer after we moved out. I knew exactly how to get there. I hadn't been there since we moved in with Dwayne, but I knew it wouldn't be hard to find my way there. I also planned on hiding out there as long as I could. No one would ever think to find me there. Who would think to find me where it all started? My mother would have to call the cops and report me missing. Then I could have the cops take me to that teen shelter in Saginaw and beg them not to take me back to my mother.

Yes! This was my plan. I was going to follow through with it. Friday night, I packed my backpack. I filled it full of clothes and bottled water. I put a few snacks in my bag too. I never ate much, anyway, but if I was going to try and stay gone as long as I could, I needed something to sustain me. Also, this was going to be a long walk. I decided not to take my bike because it would be easier to hide on foot if I needed to and not have to worry about a bike.

I had to stay gone for at least the weekend. I wanted to make my mom worry, let her drive around, trying to look for me, let her stay up all night, wondering where I was at, let her call the cops after I had been missing for twenty-four hours, let me rip her heart out, and let her feel just a tiny fraction of the pain she had caused me. This was going to get her attention. She would finally get that I wasn't happy here. Maybe she would wake up a little.

This was my cry for help. Maybe she would do the right thing by me and let me go and give me what I want, give me what I need and let this be the first right thing she could do for me as a mother. I wanted her to feel the pain of losing me. She had pushed me away and kept me at a distance. I wanted her to feel the reality of that.

That night, after everyone went to bed, I grabbed my backpack and slowly opened my bedroom door and peeked out to see if there was anyone out there. Everything was dark. Everyone was in bed. I hurried and walked to the front door off the living room. That was the door we never used. I didn't want to use the door off the dining room that was in the laundry room. My mom and Dwayne's bedroom was off that door.

The front door was locked, just as I expected. I was as quiet as a mouse. I didn't want to be busted, leaving in the dark of night. I unlocked both locks on that door and slowly opened the door. I relocked the doorknob. I wasn't giving myself the option to change my mind. I stepped out onto the front porch and shut the door quietly, locking myself out. This was it. There was no turning back now. There was only the darkness of night ahead of me now.

I hurried off the property and headed straight for the open road. I hurried and walked past the neighbors next to us. I didn't want them to see me escaping in the middle of the night on the off chance they looked out their window, even though all the lights were off in their houses as well. As soon as I got past their houses, I was pretty much home free. I was out of sight.

I was really doing this. I was terrified. I was traveling down an old dirt road with nothing but fields and woods all around me. What if a coyote saw me as a tasty midnight meal? That would be a terrible, painful way to go! I couldn't be eaten by coyotes. My mind was going wild, and I was scared by every sound the darkness made. Every hoot of the night owl, the sound of the crickets chirping their nighttime lullaby, the cows mooing in the distance, the neighbor dogs barking in the far-off distance, howls coming from the woods. Oh no! Were those coyotes? Were they lurking behind the trees, watching me, waiting for their opportunity to pounce? I could feel something staring at me. I felt like easy prey out in the open with no way to protect myself. What did I get myself into?

I could see the news headlines now. My mom would provide them with the ugliest picture she could find of me with my nerdy glasses, fake smile, and bright, frizzy, curly red hair up in a ponytail. My picture would be on the news, and the news anchor would say, "A troubled teenage girl from Kingston was mauled to death by a wild pack of coyotes in the middle of the night while she was running away from home. The girl's mother said she knew her daughter was missing when she went to check on her in the morning and she wasn't in her room. Her remains were found by a farmer who said he stumbled upon the half-eaten girl at the break of dawn when he went out to feed his cows and ran back to his house to call 911.

"The man said he was shocked because nothing happened in the quiet town of Kingston, and he didn't know what had happened to the poor young girl or how she ended up in his field. It was later discovered, during an autopsy, that the teenager was mauled to death by a pack of wild canines. The family asks for your prayers during this difficult time, and any donations to help with funeral arrangements is appreciated."

My mind was going crazy! I was very alert, and my ears were keen to every sound the night made. My adrenaline was pumping into high gear, and I was constantly looking in all directions—in front of me, beside me—and spun around to look behind me. I was looking for glowing eyes. I prayed the entire time, "Please, God, don't let anything eat me. Please look after me. Please send your angels to look after me. I'm so scared." I kept telling myself, "I'm not scared of the dark. I'm scared of the things *in* the dark."

Every crackling of leaves and sticks in the woods made me jump. I was walking so fast and even took off running as fast as I could part of the way. Then I thought maybe I shouldn't run because then something would really run after me, so I stopped running and decided that I would just walk really fast. I had to hurry up and get off these dirt roads and get to the main road. I would be safer. I would be less likely to become dinner on the main road.

I turned off Rossman Road and onto Clothier Road, another dirt road. I was almost to the main road of M-46. I walked as fast as I could, still looking in every direction. My ears picked up on every sound the night made. I'd never been so scared in my life! I had to keep pressing on. I had to do this. I had to make it to my destination. I had to go to that teen shelter in Saginaw. This was going to change my life for the better. I had an end goal. No coyote was going to keep me from getting there. God was protecting me. He was going to guide me there safely. All the times I tried killing myself, He wouldn't let me finish the job. He wasn't going to allow me to get eaten by coyotes. Not tonight. Death couldn't find me no matter how bad I tried to find it. I wasn't going to die. God wouldn't let me die. Believe me! I had begged him plenty of times to let me. He had some reason for keeping me around. I didn't know why, but I knew there had to be a reason.

As soon as I saw M-46 in the distance, I felt a little more at ease. The further away I got from home, the more I knew that there was no turning back. There was nowhere to go but forward. I was wearing all black so that I could blend into the darkness easier. I did not want to be found.

The late June air was a tad bit chilly. Was it possible to be both cold and hot at the same time? I took my black sweatshirt off and tied it around my waist as soon as I got to the corner of Clothier Road and M-46. The night air was cool against my skin, but I had a long walk ahead of me and knew that I would get too hot with it on and didn't want to stop until I got there.

I never realized just how long of a walk it was, and it seemed like it would take all night to reach my destination. I was praying that I would get there before it started to get light out because I wanted to sneak into that trailer while it was still dark. I needed this closure and had to go to that teen shelter. I had to do this. I was all out of options, and this was my only way out. I didn't have anywhere to go when I turned seventeen and didn't want to stay under my mother's roof longer than I had to. This plan had to work.

When I got to M-46, I turned left toward Scott's Quick Stop which was a gas station on the corner of M-46 and M-53. I knew that once I got to Scott's, the old trailer was three miles past that on M-53. I had to focus on making it to Scott's, and once I got there, I would focus on making it to my final destination. I had to break my journey up like that to trick my mind into thinking that I was almost there to keep myself going, to push myself further because I was getting tired.

A couple on a motorcycle stopped and pulled up beside me in the opposite lane going the opposite direction. I was on the left walking against traffic.

"Do you need a ride somewhere?" the man asked. The woman looked to be in her late thirties, and the man had a rough-looking salt and pepper beard.

Where are they going to put me? I thought. *On the handlebars?* There was no way that I was going to fit on that motorcycle with the two of them. Besides, I wouldn't go with them anyway. They were strangers, and I knew better than to go with strangers and I would never ride on a motorcycle.

One day, when I was walking MacKenzie up to the park in a stroller, I was coming off the side street headed toward the main road in town, which was M-46. I saw flashing lights up ahead. Her daddy's truck was involved, and I didn't want her to be exposed to that, especially if her daddy was hurt. So I turned around and took her back home, despite my burning curiosity that wanted to go up there and be nosey. A couple on a motorcycle T-boned Anthony in the passenger side of his truck, and the woman on the motorcycle had to be airlifted to the hospital. The man was hurt pretty bad too, but Anthony was okay. Motorcycles are dangerous, and I never wanted to get on one.

"No, thank you," I told the couple.

"Are you sure?" the man asked. "It's not a problem. Where are you headed?"

"I'm going to a friend's house," I lied. "It's just up there a little ways," I said, pointing ahead of me. "I'm almost there."

"Okay," he said as he nodded at me and rode away.

I thought I was scared of the coyotes. I was really scared now that some psycho was going to pick me up and do bad things to me.

119

For a moment, I thought that would be a better fate than staying with my mother. Anything was better than staying with my mother. Some guy kidnapping me and selling me into prostitution was better than being with my mother. At least then I would know what to expect. With my mother, she was so cold and distant, and I longed for a better relationship with her. I longed to feel loved and cared about by her. I had to be a terrible person if my own mother didn't love me. Jordan was more important to her. She could hug on him and be motherly toward him but not me.

I'd rather some psycho pick me up than to go back with her. They wouldn't take me back to my mother. I knew what to expect from a sexual deviant. I deserved it for putting myself in this situation in the first place, being a young girl out in the night, walking the streets alone. I knew better. I knew the risk I was taking. I was willing to risk my own safety and well-being to be away from my mother. That is how bad it was at home.

I continued toward Scott's Quick Stop. It was 4.2 miles from home. I was trying to walk as fast as I could without stopping. The faster I get off the road, the better, and the least likely I would be found.

Another man on a motorcycle pulled up alongside me.

"Where are you headed?" he asked.

"To my friend's house," I lied again. "I'm almost there."

"I can give you a ride. Hop on."

"I'm okay. I'm almost there."

"Are you sure? It's not a problem."

"I'm good. Thank you," I said as I continued to walk.

"Okay," he said as he drove off.

Just a few minutes later, a man in an old work van stopped alongside me. I was really scared this time. *This is a pervert in a rape van*, I thought.

"Hey! What's a young girl like you doing out, walking the streets alone at night?"

"I'm headed to my friend's house," I said sternly. "She lives just right up there."

"It is not safe for you to be out at night alone," the man said. "I'm not going to hurt you. Hop in. Let me take you there."

"Her house is just right there. I'm fine," I said. "I can walk."

"Are you sure? I wouldn't want anything bad to happen to you."

"I'll be fine. Thank you," I said as I walked away.

I turned down the first driveway I saw and started walking up toward the house and acted like I was going to my friend's house. The man drove off. I waited until he was out of sight and walked back up to the road and started walking as fast as I could.

Why won't people just be on their way and leave me alone? I don't want a ride from anyone. I just wanted to get to my destination without anyone stopping me to see if I needed a ride. I didn't trust anyone. I wouldn't get into a car nor on a motorcycle with strangers. I'm not that stupid to go with strangers.

From then on, every time there was a car coming, I walked up the nearest driveway and acted like I was going home so that no one would stop me and ask me if I needed a ride.

I was relieved when I saw Scott's Quick Stop in the distance. I was almost there. I started walking faster. The lights from the old busy gas station got closer and closer.

When I got there, I tried to walk past it as fast as I could, because even in the middle of the night, they were pretty busy. I had no idea what time it was. I just knew that I was tired and there couldn't be that much more time before it started to get light out, so I had to hurry and keep moving forward. There were a few semitrucks parked there for the night. Scott's was on the corner of two busy roads, and semitrucks frequented both of those roads pretty heavily.

I hoped and prayed that I could quickly walk past these semitrucks without anyone spotting me. I'd watched a few Lifetime movies and scary movies where young girls were picked up by truck drivers, and they turned out to be rapists and serial killers. Movies didn't portray truck drivers as very nice people. If I got picked up by a truck driver, they could take me anywhere, and no one would be able to find me.

I walked past them as fast as I could. I didn't want to run and draw more attention to myself. I was so tired. I knew that I had three more miles to go, but I didn't know exactly how far I had walked so far. I didn't think I was going to make it. I should have taken a nap earlier that day to prepare myself for this long journey in the middle of the night. I was determined to reach my destination. I had to keep going. I could do this.

I walked two more miles that night, not realizing that I was almost there, just one mile until I reached my destination. I couldn't go any further. I felt like I was going to collapse on the side of the road. I had to stop somewhere to rest. But where?

I prayed to God to help me find a safe place to rest. I prayed out loud, "Please, God! I'm getting so tired. I don't know how much further I can walk. Guide me, Lord. Provide a safe place for me to rest. Help me, Lord Jesus!"

When I looked up, I saw a lit-up sign. The closer I got to it, the more I saw that it was a church. I barely made out the tall white steeple piercing the lonely night sky. I had a renewed sense of energy and began to walk faster and faster toward this church. I would rest here for just a little while and then finish my journey back to where it all started where my life fell apart. I had to have closure. I had come too far not to make it back to my old house.

When I approached the church, I walked up the long driveway. I was hoping that it would be unlocked. In the movies, people go into a church to pray in the middle of the night. I could sleep on the pews in their sanctuary at the foot of the cross. Jesus guided me here. I prayed for a safe place to rest and looked up and saw the lit-up sign for this church. God answered my prayer. I prayed for protection when I was on the dirt roads and prayed for God to send His angels to watch over me so that I wouldn't get eaten by coyotes and God answered prayer. Three different people had stopped me and asked to take me where I needed to go. Three strangers. They could have been people who meant serious harm, and God protected me. I was a young teen girl walking the streets at night, wearing all black. Anything could have happened to me, and God protected me. He sent his angels to surround me that night and led me to this very church, a safe place, a place of rest.

Come unto me, all ye that labour and are heavy laden, and I will give you rest. (Matthew 11:28 KJV)

I traveled 6.2 miles that night on foot, and God protected me the whole way and brought me to this very church when I prayed for rest. When I didn't think I could go any further, He gave me the strength to make it that far. He provided a safe place, a refuge under this tall white steeple, a beacon of hope, a symbol of light piercing the dark lonely sky. God protected me in the darkest of night and led me to His house, a house of God.

The church doors were locked. I walked around the church, looking for a way in, but everything was all locked up. I walked the grounds. There was a parsonage next door, but it was dark, and all of the lights were off. I walked over to the parsonage. I peeked in the windows. There were boxes everywhere. Nobody lived there. They were either moving in or moving out. I wasn't sure which.

I saw that there was a playground on the church property and walked toward it. There was a little Noah's ark. I climbed inside it. It had a roof and everything on it. This was going to be my shelter for the rest of the night. I was going to rest here for a little while and then finish my journey from here. Just like God provided Noah a safe place in the ark amongst the storm, during the flood when the seas were raging, God provided me a safe place in the ark when the storm clouds of my life were closing in and the seas were raging. God provided me a safe place of rest in the midst of the storm and in my darkest hour.

I tried to get comfortable in the little ark, but the inside of it was filled with wood chips, and it wasn't the most comfortable place to lay. I tossed and turned. I used my bag as a pillow. I just couldn't get comfortable laying on these wood chips. I must flee the ark and find some other shelter to lay my head, even for just a couple of hours, and then I would be on my way.

I went back to the parsonage. I checked all of the doors, and it was locked. I thought since no one was living there that maybe I could go inside and lay down for a couple of hours. I was so exhausted from walking all those miles.

I went back up to the church to see where I could rest. There was an overhang over the main entrance and a ramp that went up to one of the doors on the second level. I decided to go under the ramp and lean up against the building to rest. The cold pavement wasn't very comfortable to sit on either, but at least it was smooth and not lumpy like the wood chips in the ark. I sat there for a few minutes. It was a little chilly, so I untied my sweatshirt from around my waist and draped it over the front of me.

My butt started to hurt after a while from sitting on the cold hard pavement. I tried lying on my side and using my backpack as a pillow, but it hurt my bony hips to lay on such a hard surface.

Oh, God, I wish I could get comfortable and get some rest. I fidgeted around for a while, trying to make the best of my situation and getting comfortable enough to rest. I needed to close my eyes, just for a little while.

It seemed like not long after I finally closed my eyes it was daylight, and a man was nudging my shoulders, trying to wake me. I got scared and flinched.

"It's okay," the man said with his hands up, "I'm not going to hurt you."

I immediately crawled out from under the ramp and stood to my feet.

"What brings you here?" the man asked.

"I'm sorry. I will be on my way," I said as I started to walk off.

"No, no, no," the man pleaded, "I'm Pastor Don, the senior pastor of this church. Is there something I can help you with? Can I take you somewhere? Do you need a ride somewhere?"

"I ran away from home," I said. "I don't want to go back there. Can you take me to Saginaw?"

"Okay, you look like you have had a rough night. Why don't we go into my office where it is more comfortable?"

I nodded.

"So what is your name?" Pastor Don asked while unlocking the door to the church and leading the way to his office.

"Andrea."

"Do you have a last name, Andrea?"

"Wilber."

"Where are you from, Andrea?"

"Kingston."

124

"You walked all the way from Kingston to here?" he asked, a little surprised.

"Yes," I replied, still unsure how this was going to play out.

When we reached his office, Pastor Don unlocked the door and turned on the lights and waved me in first. He followed me in but left the door cracked half open.

"Can I get you anything, Andrea? Something to eat or drink? You must be starving and thirsty after such a long walk," said Pastor Don.

I couldn't look at Pastor Don. I was staring at the floor and shook my head no.

"Are you sure?"

"No, thank you," I said quietly, looking at the floor.

"Okay. Let me try and get a hold of my wife, and we can talk. Okay?"

Pastor Don picked up his phone and called his wife and asked her to come to the church. "There is someone here for you to meet." He hung up. "So, Andrea, do you go to a church somewhere?"

"Yes, the Kingston Wesleyan Church."

"Oh, okay, I know where that is. So you know Jesus Christ as your personal Lord and Savior and have accepted Him into your heart?"

"Yes."

"Wonderful," said Pastor Don. He paused for a moment and looked at me, puzzled.

"So things are pretty rough at home?" he asked.

I nodded.

"I'm sorry to hear that. Want to talk about it?"

"My brother molested me when I was eight, and my mom wants me to forget about it and move on so she can have her big happy family back together. She won't stop talking about him in front of me and lets him come over."

"I'm sorry you had to go through that, Andrea, and that your mom is not very understanding of your feelings."

"She knows that it bothers me, but she doesn't care."

A woman knocked on the door and stepped in.

"Hey." Pastor Don stood up and introduced me. "Andrea, this is Julie, my wife. Julie, this is Andrea."

Julie and I exchanged smiles and shook hands. Julie was very thin and attractive. She had shoulder-length dark hair and big brown eyes and dressed very modestly in a long jean skirt with a button up white t-shirt and a pink blouse underneath.

"Julie, I found Andrea here sleeping underneath the ramp outside when I got here this morning. She walked here in the middle of the night, all the way from Kingston," Pastor Don said, filling her in.

"Oh," Julie said, looking at me, puzzled.

"Where in Saginaw do you want us to take you?" asked Pastor Don.

"It's called Innerlink. It's a teen shelter for runaways," I said.

"Do you have a number for them?" asked Pastor Don.

"You can look them up on the Internet," I said.

Pastor Don turned to his computer and looked them up. "Do you mind if I called them to see if they have a bed available for you since they are only an eight-bed facility?" he asked.

I nodded.

Pastor Don dialed the number and started talking to a lady on the other end for a few minutes and then hung up.

"Okay, there is a bed available, and we can take you there right now, but here is the deal. Your mom is probably really worried about you, and you need to let her know where you are at and that you are okay."

I didn't like the sound of that. *Let her worry about me? She is probably happy that I'm gone anyway.*

"Is it okay if we take you home first so that you can grab more clothes and let your mom know where you are going?"

"I don't want to go home. I packed a bag," I said, showing him my backpack.

"Well, I really think that we should take you home first so that your mom knows that you are okay, and then we will take you there. I promise."

"Okay," I said, nodding my head and looking at the floor.

I really did not want to go home. What if she kicked Pastor Don and Julie out of the house and wouldn't let them take me to Innerlink? He was being very persistent about talking to my mother. I guess I would just have to deal with my mother in order for me to have a chance at going to that shelter. My mom liked to put on a show for other people. Maybe with the pastor there, it wouldn't be so bad, but I still hated confrontation. I'd rather run and hide than to have to confront someone with my feelings, especially my mother. Running away was much easier than facing it head on.

I never made it to our old house. I never received that closure that I thought I needed at that time. I was only one mile away from my destination. God kept me safe that night. He was there every step of the way when I walked 6.2 miles in the middle of the night. He protected me, and each time I cried out to him because I was scared, He was right there with me. No coyotes got me. Three men tried picking me up that night, but they didn't grab me. God protected me all the way. I had planned on going back to that old house for closure I didn't make it there. God knew that I wasn't ready. I wasn't in a good place then. I wouldn't have been able to handle it, and it probably would have made things worse. I was a stubborn teenager, and when I had it in my head to do something, I was set on doing it. I was going to run away that night, and God said, "Okay, have it your way, but I'm going with you to make sure you don't get into more trouble." He gave me just enough strength to get to that church but not enough to walk that last mile to a place I was not yet ready to go to.

I can see it all so much more clearly now. That little Noah's ark boat symbolized a shelter in the storm. The white steeple represented a beacon of hope, safety, a refuge in the midst of the darkness. I can see how God was with me that night, protecting me each step of the way. Every time I got scared walking in the darkness of night all alone, I cried out to Him.

As children of God, sometimes we feel like we are all alone in this dark world. This world is full of sin and wickedness, and it seems like the darkness is closing in on us, but if we cry out to *Him*, He is faithful and He will be there every step of the way to guide us through. He is the light of the world, and if we look to Him, He will help us find our way with His protection over us. Sometimes our plans are not His plans, and things may not always work out the way that we want them to, but if we have faith and trust in Him, then things will work out just as they should and in His perfect time.

I followed Pastor Don and Julie out of the church and to their van. We stopped at Scott's Quick Stop gas station where I hurried past the big semitrucks the night before. I stayed out in the van with Julie while Pastor Don ran in to get drinks. He asked me what I liked to drink, but I told him that I didn't want anything. I didn't want them to spend any money on me when they were already spending the gas money to take me home and then to Saginaw. He knew that I had an eating disorder and didn't like to eat anything.

He came out with a fruity V8 drink for me. I took it and told him thank you. I had never had a V8 drink before and didn't think that I would like it, but they were doing me a huge favor, and I wanted to be polite. So I took it and took a small sip.

When we arrived back home, my mother was waiting for me in the dining room. Pastor Don and Julie followed behind me and kind of intercepted my mother. Pastor Don told my mother about the teen shelter in Saginaw and asked her if it was okay if they took me there. They told her that it would probably be a good idea for us both to take a break from each other for a little while. My mother agreed to let them take me to the shelter, and I went to my room and threw more clothes and a notebook in my bag.

Before we left, my mom did give me a hug and told me that she loved me, but it all seemed like a show for Pastor Don and his wife Julie. It never felt genuine. She would never do that if no one was around.

When we got to the shelter, we said our goodbyes, and I thanked them for all that they have done for me.

*****

The shelter was a lot smaller than I thought it was going to be. There were two sections. One side of the building was for the younger teens, and the other side was for older teens or pregnant teens, and the two sections were divided by a locked door. I was on the side with the younger teens.

There wasn't a whole lot to do there except to watch movies. We watched a lot of Madea movies.

One of the workers there who was a very nice black lady was very impressed by my hair. Before I ran away, I braided my hair into a bunch of tiny braids and did a basketball net hairstyle on the top half. I was a white girl with a Black girl's hairstyle. I did my hair like that because I was planning on hiding out for a few days at our old house and thought that it would be easier to manage my hair in tiny braids and not have to worry about it.

I didn't get to stay there very long due to my eating disorder. They were not equipped to handle that. Therefore, they sent a social worker to drive me back home. I was only there for six days. I was there during the Fourth of July and remember going into the bathroom during the fireworks to look at myself in the mirror. I was paper white and sick looking. I lifted up my shirt and could see every rib bone and hip bone, and my stomach caved in. It was at that moment that it really hit me that I had a problem, but at the same time, I was so fascinated by how skinny I was. I was proud of how I looked. I knew that I looked sick and knew that other people thought I was too skinny. I was so skinny my stomach caved in. I never thought I was pretty, but at least I could be skinny.

I finally felt like I was thin enough, but then I started to squeeze the skin on my arms and on my stomach. I must not be skinny enough if I was still able to grab fat. I was almost where I wanted to be. I caressed my stomach and admired how it caved in. If only I could lose just a few more pounds.

The entire six days that I was there, I didn't eat a bite of anything. That was why I could no longer stay there. They could not help me with an eating disorder. Those six days were the longest I went without eating anything at all.

12

Rescued by the Joneses

Every year during August, before we all went back to school, Kingston had a week-long celebration called Kingston Days. There were carnival rides, dunk tank, games and prizes, a parade, beer tent, arts and crafts, street dance, face painting, food vendors, and burnouts—You name it. It was a pretty big deal for the little town of Kingston.

This year was particularly special for me. It was the year 2005, and I was seventeen. I always had to march in the parade in the band, but after that, I walked around and did my own thing. I met up with friends, and we walked around, looking at everything. My favorite thing to do was watching the youth pastor get dunked in the dunk tank. When I got separated from my friends, I ran into the Joneses. They were lying on a blanket in the grass, enjoying all of the festivities. I was friends with their daughter, Bella, and they took me camping a few times with their family. They were really nice people and did a lot with their kids. Bella was also in the band and played the flute.

Betsy and Ronald Jones had three kids. Raegan was the oldest and was married and had a little boy at the time. Then there was Bella and their little brother, Ronnie, who was also in the band and played the trumpet. Ronald was a disabled vet from the Air Force and also a retired corrections officer from Michigan Corrections. Betsy worked as a phlebotomist and lab tech for a hospital and doctor's office. They also took in a boy named Tom who they never legally adopted. Tom was raised by a single father and was an only child. When his dad died, the Joneses mentored him and took him in as their own. Tom married a woman named Emily, and they had five kids together who all called Betsy and Ronald Grandma and Grandpa.

"Hi, Andrea," said Betsy from the blanket on the grass.

"Hey."

"How have you been?" asked Ronald.

"Okay," I said, even though things weren't. That was just the immediate response everyone says when someone asked you if you were okay.

"Bella is really worried about you. Are you sure things are okay at home?" asked Ronald.

I didn't say anything and just stared at the ground.

"You're seventeen now, right?" asked Betsy.

I nodded my head, still staring at the ground.

"Betsy and I already talked about it, and you are more than welcome to come and stay with us to get you away from your mother and your brother," said Ronald.

"We are used to taking in strays," joked Betsy. "Raegan moved out, so you will have your own room."

"We care about you and want to help you, and we will take you in and treat you like one of our own," said Ronald.

I was excited to hear this, but it all took me by surprise. I didn't want to be a burden to them. I also didn't want to stay under the same roof as my mother, and since I was seventeen, I could legally move out but didn't have anywhere else to go. I didn't have a job or a license. My mother never felt it was necessary to put me through driver's training. She never taught me how to cook nor prepared me for the real world at all. Also, I had two more years of high school left. The only option I had was to stay under her roof. But then, here were the Joneses providing me another way out. They offered up their home, their lives, and their family to me. It was like an answer to prayer, but what if it didn't work out? What if I became too much of a burden to them and had to find somewhere else to go? I would have to come crawling back to my mother and didn't want to do that. This was a big decision that I had to make.

"Take some time to think it over," said Ronald, "You are always welcome to come and stay with us. We would love to add another daughter to our family."

I did decide to move in with the Joneses. Betsy, Ronald, and Bella all came to my mom's and helped pack me up and moved me in with them. I got Raegan's old bedroom upstairs, and Bella's bedroom was next to mine, and Ronnie was next to her. Raegan still had some of her stuff there, and Bella and I packed it up and took it right over to her. She lived in a little house right around the corner, and there was a trail through a small patch of woods that connected the two properties.

This finally happened. I waited my whole life for this moment. I was finally away from my mother. I didn't have to see Jordan anymore nor hear his name nor see his face plastered on the walls. My mom could have her son back without me standing in her way. This was the moment I was waiting for, and I couldn't believe that this was happening.

My mom knew this day was coming. I was seventeen. Jennifer and Nora both moved out when they turned seventeen. I ran away so many times. Me moving out was inevitable. There was nothing she could do about it. What was even more ironic was my two younger brothers also moved out the very same day, but it was never planned that way. We didn't collaborate when we would all move out. That's just the way it happened. They were both old enough to decide who they wanted to live with, so they chose to move in with Clayton up in Onoway. My mom lost all three of her kids at the same time. I thought it was poetic justice in a way. Because Clayton paid child support and we no longer lived with my mother, my mother could no longer receive that child support payment on any of us.

I don't know what happened with the boys' portion, but I received my portion of it and used it to pay for school clothes and other things I needed. I could actually buy decent clothes and started to build up my wardrobe. I also used it to buy hygiene products as well and got away from using cheap VO5 shampoo on my hair and noticed a complete difference in the health and texture of my hair. I had so much fun trying different brands of shampoo and conditioner. I never knew there were so many choices. I could buy good razors and not cut myself with the cheap ones. I also no longer smelled like a chain-smoker. The Joneses didn't smoke, and the air quality in their home was so much better.

Because my mom lost the child support money for all three of us, and she and Dwayne didn't work outside of the home, the house eventually got foreclosed on, and they were the ones bouncing around for a while between Dwayne's oldest daughter Molly's, Dwayne's brother's, and Jordan's.

The Joneses had an older two-story house with a large downstairs addition where they added a large living room, office area, and master suite. The living room had a large football-shaped stained-glass window that came out of an old church that burnt down. It made it really unique, and it stood out.

When you first walked in the house, you entered into the dining room which was quite large to accommodate large family gatherings. Off the dining room was a decent-sized kitchen and laundry room on one side and a pair of glass French doors on the other side that led into a smaller room that they used as a library. There were wall-to-wall shelves from floor to ceiling which were covered in books and family albums. They kept an old antique couch in there as well. That used to be a bedroom that they converted into a library.

Next to the library, there was a very large bathroom with a corner shower and clawfoot tub with a big picture window between the two. That bathroom used to be a large bedroom that was converted, which was why it was so large. On the back of the dining room was the stairs that went up to the three bedrooms.

Since my bedroom was on the end upstairs, my room had slanted ceilings on two sides. I positioned my bed up against the slanted ceiling. There were built in shelves inside that wall that I put different trinkets on. The view outside my window overlooked the front yard, garage, and driveway. There were also built in shelves under the other slanted ceiling where I started my collection of shoes.

It was a fairly large house and became my home. I decorated my room and settled in nicely. I was still amazed and shocked that I actually made it out. I almost had to pinch myself to make sure this was real.

The Joneses got me a welcome gift with new bedding, pillow, hangers, laundry basket, and trash can for my room. They were really good to me and treated me like one of their own.

Every Saturday was clean house day, and all three of us kids split the downstairs up and had to clean the house which I didn't mind doing. I wanted to contribute and help out in any way that I could for them taking me in. I was so grateful that I didn't have to live with my mother anymore. After I moved out, I had little contact with my mother, and she never came to visit me at the Joneses.

Living with my best friend's family and her room being right next to mine took some time getting used to. After school, we hung out in her room. Her room wasn't the cleanest. Betsy didn't realize that a teenager's room could be clean until I moved in. Ronnie's bedroom was right by the stairs, and his room was always puking, and you couldn't see his bedroom floor at all. Bella and I were constantly shoving things back in his room that spilled out above the stairs.

The Joneses did a lot with their kids. It was nothing I was used to. They took them camping twice a year. They had a membership at a campground in Standish, Michigan, which was less than two hours north. This campground had a large clubhouse with an indoor pool and hot tub in one section with locker rooms and shower rooms and a big activities area in another section where there was karaoke, Bingo, crafts, and other activities. There was also a large outdoor pool with hot tubs. There was a nice playground area and putt-putt golf and a large pond with a nice sandy beach area where people also swam and played in the water. We built sandcastles and a turtle sculpture in the sand. There were even nature trails through the woods. There was plenty to do, and we always had so much fun.

Halloween was a big camping weekend. They had a haunted corn maze, hay ride, haunted house, and trick or treating. Everyone decorated their campsites and competed for the scariest campsite.

There was also a costume contest. They went all-out, and it was a pretty big deal that weekend, and we always had so much fun.

I never had food cooked over a campfire before the Joneses. They introduced me to banana boats and so many other new things. They were really big into camping and even had a camper with four bunks in the back.

I had my sister drop off Mackenzie to me one time to take her camping with us, and her mother only sent her with the clothes on her back. I had to go out and buy her clothes for the weekend. I didn't see my nieces as often after moving in with the Joneses, so I tried to get them for a weekend here and there.

Ronald recruited me into his CAP (Civil Air Patrol) cadet group. CAP is an auxiliary of the United States Air Force. It is a youth cadet program. Ronald and Betsy were in CAP when they were kids and started their own group when Ronnie got old enough to be in CAP. We met at the Sandusky airport once a week where we practiced marching, carrying the flags, folding the flag, and presenting the colors and gun-twirling. We also learned how to salute. Being in a marching band was a huge advantage because I already knew how to march.

Once a month, we had to run a mile and do some fitness exercises. We also had workbooks and tests we had to take in order to get promoted and earn rank and badges and ribbons for our uniforms.

There were two types of uniforms. One was a BDU uniform, which was basically camos, and the other one was blues. The blues were a dressier uniform with navy blue pants and a baby blue button-up shirt.

I was the one that carried the CAP flag. We marched in parades, presented the colors at air shows, and even went to a boot camp at an air force base in Grayling, Michigan. Boot camp was a lot of fun. They separated girls from guys, and we all had to stay in the military barracks. It was a week-long encampment. We had to run a mile every day, early in the morning, do marching drills, push-ups, sit-ups, and all kinds of different exercises. We had to learn how to make a bed with hospital corners, and it better be perfect or we would be doing it all over again.

We also had to run through an obstacle course where we had to crawl on our bellies under netted rope, climb over walls, run through old tires and the works. It was very physical which was up my alley because I loved doing that sort of thing.

Boot camp wasn't all work. We also got to fly in a small four-seater CAP plane over the base that took us over some pretty cool sinkholes. The pilot even let us take turns flying the plane. I loved to fly.

I remember the first time I got into a plane. I really didn't want to do it. I was so scared, but Ronald ordered me to get on that plane since he was the commander, and I had to obey orders. I was so glad I did because once I got over that fear and was able to see God's beautiful creation from the beautiful blue sky, I never wanted it to end. We also got to fly in a glider. A glider is a small two-seater aircraft with no motor. There were two ways to get a glider in the air. You were either catapulted up in the air or you were towed up by a small airplane, and then the cable released once you were in the air, and you just glided in the wind like a giant kite and slowly glided back down into a controlled landing. The pilot sat in the second seat. The cool thing about flying in a glider is that you are surrounded by glass from the waste up, so it truly felt like you were riding on a cloud, and the scenery was amazing since your view isn't obstructed in any way. We also got to fly in a glider during bootcamp. It was very memorable, and I had so much fun.

Not only did I experience flying for the first time in a small aircraft and in a glider, but I also got to fly in a very large KC-135, which is a very large military plane. Basically, it is a large gas station that refuels fighter jets up in the air. They lay on their bellies and pass gas. That was the running joke because the men would literally lay on their bellies and control the arm that extends out to connect to the other aircraft for them to get fuel. That was quite the experience, and not many people can say that they have ever been in one. It was a once in a lifetime opportunity for which I am forever grateful.

We also had competitions where all of the cadets from all over the state of Michigan would come and compete. We competed in the mile run, presenting the colors, which included raising the flag, taking the flag down, and folding it to perfection to present it to one of the judges. They also judged us on our uniforms and marching and everything. Everything had to be perfect, and we won first place in the state of Michigan.

I am forever grateful for that experience, and it was such a privilege to be a part of CAP because of all the new things I got to do that I wouldn't have experienced otherwise.

The Joneses invested so much time into their kids. Bella was in Girl Scouts, and Betsy was the leader of their small humble troop. Raegan was also a part of Girl Scouts when she was still at home. They sponsored blood drives at their church, and we all spent an entire weekend at the church, baking cookies for it. I wasn't a part of Girl Scouts, but they included me in any activities they did.

Betsy, Raegan, and Bella also loved to scrapbook, and they had a room at their church all set up for scrapbooking. They got me involved in scrapbooking, which I really loved because I love being artistic and loved the bonding time with them. Betsy included me in all of the group family photos and printed them off for me to add in my scrapbooks. I scrapbooked all the CAP pictures, camping pictures, and everything. I had so much fun with them. Although I still spent a lot of time in my room, I was getting out so much more and doing things and experiencing life outside of my four walls which I never got to do before.

We took a family trip to the African Safari Zoo in Ohio. The whole Jones clan went, including Raegan, her husband and little boy, Tom and his family, Ronald's elderly mother, and I got to take my niece, Mackenzie, as well. The Joneses had a minivan with a sunroof. Do you know how cool it is to drive through the field where they kept the animals, and we got to feed them through the windows of the van? The giraffes stuck their heads right through the sunroof to eat from the cups of food they provided us. It was such a neat experience.

They also took me to downtown Detroit during the winter time, and we got to see it all lit up for the holidays and ate at the Hard Rock Cafe. They took us out to eat a lot. My mom never took us out to eat. Their favorite place to eat was Chinese. I had never had

Chinese food before, and it became my favorite place to eat, even to this day.

The Joneses were also big into politics, and I learned so much from them regarding politics, especially from Betsy. My mom never cared about politics at all. Betsy and I had many discussions about politics. They were Republicans. They took us down to meet Terri Lynn Land one time, and we got to shake her hand and take a picture with her. She was the forty-first Secretary of State for Michigan.

After moving in with the Joneses, I started to eat more and no longer struggled with an eating disorder or cutting and didn't overexercise. We went out to eat a lot. It was a big part of what they did as a family. There was no way I could be anorexic and be a part of what they did as a family. I was much happier. I got to experience *life* with them. I truly felt like I was a part of their family. I never knew what that was like before. They taught me so much. They taught me what a real family was supposed to look like.

They never treated me any different than any of their kids. They pretty much adopted me and took me in as one of their own. I got to see more than just the little town of Kingston. They were always doing things with us and taking us places. They were a very active family. I wasn't used to that. My mom never did anything with us.

Thanksgiving and Christmas was a huge deal. Their dining room could handle a large family gathering comfortably. They lined three or four tables together to accommodate everyone. The whole Jones clan was there, including Ronald's sister, her husband, and two kids from out of state. There were nineteen of us. I was never a part of something like that before. We were a family that held hands and prayed before our meals, all gathered around one table, passing food back and forth, and enjoying a good meal in fellowship together. We all chipped in and helped clean up. We took a family photo afterward of the whole group with a timer on the camera so that everyone could be in the picture and then each individual family picture. The Joneses always included me in the pictures as one of their kids. They were so good to me, and I never felt left out.

For Christmas, they would buy me just as many gifts as their kids. I never expected it because I was never a person that liked to take or take advantage. Even though they always made me feel welcomed, I still felt like I was intruding in a way. The very first Christmas that I spent with them, I honestly didn't expect to get any gifts. I wasn't one of their kids. I was very surprised to receive anything, much less receive as much as everyone else. It made me feel a little uncomfortable because I didn't get anyone else anything.

We all went to Bronner's, which is the world's largest Christmas store in Frankenmuth, Michigan, and the Joneses had me pick out a bulb with my name on it and put it on the tree with the rest of their kids' bulbs. They always went out of their way to make me feel like I was welcomed and a part of their family, just like one of their kids.

Despite all of this, I still suffered from bouts of depression. I was so unhappy for so long I wasn't used to being happy. I didn't always know what to do with that or if it would last. Something was bound to happen to ruin all of this. I wasn't supposed to be happy. I didn't know how to be happy, but I did become good at pretending. This wasn't my happily ever after. Although I was happy that I was no longer living with my mother, it bothered me that we weren't close. It bothered me that she would never come to see me or call me. I was only ten to fifteen minutes away from her.

Witnessing firsthand what a loving family looks like and being a part of that also bothered me because I wanted more than anything to have that with my natural family. Why couldn't my family be like this? Betsy was really close with both of her girls, and they could come and talk to her about anything. I wanted that with my mother.

Although I was much happier with the Joneses, it was so hard for me to be on the outside looking in on a perfect family who was happy, close, who spent time together, and did things together and invested a lot of time in each other. It made me see what I missed out on my entire life. Bella had both her mother and father together in the same home. Ronald loved on his girls and even wrestled with Bella and horsed around. She had a dad that loved her. I didn't have that. They all teased each other and joked around.

Betsy and Ronald were involved in everything with their kids. The girls were in dance, and Ronnie and Bella were both in karate and band. Betsy and Ronald went to all of their concerts, competitions, parades, everything. Everything their kids were into, they were there cheering them on and supporting them. My mother never came to anything of mine, and it was a hassle for her to pick me up from track practice.

This was completely foreign to me, and I didn't always know how to process it. I didn't always know what my role was in all of this. I didn't grow up this way. I grew up isolating myself in my bedroom and not socializing with anybody. I was basically not a part of a family. Living with the Joneses, I had to learn how to be a part of a family. It really did take me awhile to warm up and get comfortable, but I always had those moments where I felt like I was a burden and intruding. It was nothing that the Joneses did to make me feel that way because they were always so generous and went out of their way to include me and make me feel like a part of their family.

I didn't feel loved for so long nor did I feel I was worth anything. It was hard for me to accept that anyone could love me. It was hard for me to accept that the Joneses did think of me as one of their own because how could anyone want me when my own mother didn't want me?

Every time they spent money on me and we went out to eat or they celebrated my birthday and bought me gifts, I felt uneasy. I just didn't know how to accept it. I was grateful, but it sort of made me feel uncomfortable because they did so much for me already, and I didn't know what I could do to repay them. I didn't feel worth it. I didn't feel like I deserved any of it. I didn't deserve to be happy. My mom made me feel responsible for basically destroying her family. Did I deserve to be a part of this one?

There were times where I felt like I was intruding on mother and daughter time. When Betsy, Bella, and Raegan went to church once a week to scrapbook, I felt like I was intruding on mother and daughter bonding time. I didn't want to take away from Bella and Raegan. I always went, but I couldn't help but feel like I was a burden in some way.

I knew they thought of me and accepted me as their own daughter and tried to make me feel that way, but I just couldn't help but feel like I was intruding on their family. I struggled daily with it within myself. I just couldn't accept that these people wanted me. I was always waiting for something to go wrong, just like they always did. There had to be a catch. When was this going to come crashing down? What was I going to do if this didn't work out? That thought was always in the back of my mind. What was plan B? There was no plan B.

Sometimes, all I wanted to do was stay isolated in my room and pretend like I wasn't there because that is what I knew how to do. I just tried to lay low because I didn't want to somehow mess up a good thing. I really struggled with the fact this family really did love me and really did adopt me as their own.

Even though I was removed from a toxic situation, I still struggled with depression and self-worth. It was hard for me to get out of that mindset, and in a way, it sabotaged my newfound freedom because my past and relationship with my family always affected me in the present time. My past always caught up to me no matter how hard I tried to run from it. It affected all of my relationships and any thought of happiness or normalcy. I didn't know how to form any kind of a normal relationship with anyone because every relationship I ever had wasn't normal, and I didn't know what normal actually looked like until I moved in with the Joneses. Everyone that was supposed to matter to me let me down in some way.

The Joneses really tore down a lot of walls for me, but I couldn't let them all down. I had to keep some walls up to protect myself. The Joneses were amazing people. Don't get me wrong. I just couldn't let my guard down completely just in case I got hurt. I was used to disappointment. I was used to getting hurt. I was used to family turning their backs on me. I wasn't their real daughter. There would come a day when all of this would come to a head. I couldn't totally devote myself to playing house with them. I always had that doubt that festered and spread like a cancer inside of me that always ruined any sense of real peace and happiness that came my way.

I could never have peace or total happiness. My past wouldn't allow it. My past sabotaged it every single time. I was broken and would forever remain broken until my last dying breath. I was a tortured soul, chained and bound by depression, broken relationships, and a slave to doubt and fear of anything remotely healthy or normal.

When I moved out, I thought that my mother couldn't "get me" anymore. I didn't think she would continue to have power over me. I didn't think Jordan or Clayton would still have power over me. I had an unrealistic expectation that just by simply moving out of my mother's that everything would instantly be a bed of roses and all hunky-dory. I struggled with that immensely. This is what I wanted. I was finally out of my mother's house. How come still wasn't happy? I couldn't understand that. I struggled with it daily. If moving out of my mom's didn't "fix" me, then what would? How can I ever be truly happy? Could I ever run far enough away from my past to find happiness? Would anything be enough? Would any amount of distance or time take the pain away and "fix" me? All hopelessness was setting in all over again.

13

Another Hit

I started dating when I was eighteen in my junior year of high school. I wasn't at all popular, but there was this boy who was popular and on the football team. His name was Craig. He had blonde hair and he was really tall and built. I only came up to his shoulders, and I was five-foot-five.

He used to date this girl named Robin who was super skinny and pretty but very shy and quiet, and she was popular. They were together a long time. They both went to the same church I did and were always sitting next to each other, holding hands. One day, they just weren't together anymore.

I was never interested in boys because I thought they were never interested in me, so I didn't bother drooling over any of them. I had bright frizzy red hair, glasses, uncool clothes and I was a band nerd. I always thought I was ugly. I was socially awkward and shy. I didn't think any boy would like me. I had enough of my own problems to worry about any boys. I never desired to have a boyfriend. I wasn't ready for boys because I thought they only wanted one thing, and I wasn't ready for that.

Most of my friends were having sex. They called me a Goody Two-shoes, but I didn't care. I didn't want to be that girl. I especially didn't want to date in high school. All the boys my age were so immature. I was a "good" girl and wanted to save myself for marriage. I was a Christian. That is what we were supposed to do.

One day, my friends and I were horsing around in the hallway at school and pushing each other. Craig was sitting on a bench in front of the office with some other guys, and I got pushed into him as we were walking by, and my hand landed in his lap. I was so embarrassed and my face turned beet red. I got up and caught up to my friends, and they were laughing at me, and I smacked the one who pushed me into him.

Apparently, falling into his lap like that got him to notice me, and he came up to me in the hallway a day or two later and asked me out. He was a popular football player. I was a dweeb. I had to say yes. It really took me by surprise that he was interested in me, but I wasn't going to pass this up. Craig was in a grade ahead of me, so I wasn't in any of his classes.

I started to see a lot more of Craig. I still went to the Kingston Wesleyan church, and one time, after Wednesday night church, I left with him. He was a foster kid that aged out of the system. He was nineteen and lived in the basement of a classmate of mine. His parents were the leaders of the clubhouse ministry in the church, and he was friends with their older boy, Cameron. I went to school with Cameron's younger brother, Jacob.

Craig took me over to where he was living and showed me around. He asked me if I would like to go swimming with them at a pond on M-46 behind a log cabin store. It was just going to be me and the three boys that were going.

Cameron drove his car, and Jacob sat up front, and Craig and I sat in the back seat. Craig was very handsy. He always had to sit really close to me and always had to hold my hand, which made me feel uncomfortable because I wasn't used to that close human contact. I never liked to be touched. I never even allowed my friends to play with my hair and hugs were uncomfortable for me. I always had to keep my distance from people because that close physical contact was painfully awkward for me.

I was also the type of person that could never speak up for myself. I knew what I wanted to say but could never speak the words. I had a hard time setting that boundary with Craig because I wanted him to like me, but he was already moving way too fast, and I thought this was how relationships worked. All my friends who dated were very affectionate with their boyfriends. They held hands and kissed and hugged. This was how boyfriends and girlfriends were supposed to be. I wasn't ready for this, but was I ever going to be ready? I was being lame. This boy actually took an interest in me. Who else would want to date me?

They took me home so that I could get my bathing suit. I changed into my bikini and put on a mini skirt and a pink tank top over the top. I didn't even own a bathing suit until I moved in with the Joneses. I never felt uncomfortable wearing a bikini before because the Joneses were basically my family. Ronnie was like a little brother to me. I only wore it when we went camping. This time was different. I was wearing a bikini in front of a boy that liked me and two of his guy friends, and I was going to be alone with them.

Craig followed me in the house and talked with Ronald and Betsy downstairs while I went upstairs to change. I grabbed a towel out of the bathroom and left with Craig and the other two boys to go swimming. I got back in the back seat with him and realized that a mini skirt was a bad idea. I just thought this would be easier to wear over a bathing suit. I also wanted to look nice for Craig.

Craig was holding my hand pretty tight, and we were sitting as close as we could to each other without sitting on his lap. He flipped my hand on top so that his hand was touching my thigh, and he kept inching his hand further and further up my thigh to see exactly what he could get away with. I knew exactly what he was doing, and it made me feel super uncomfortable. It gave me goosebumps, and the hairs on my arms were standing up. It took my breath away, and I froze like a statue. The other two boys were in the front seat. I didn't want to draw attention to what Craig was doing. I moved his hand down, and he slowly moved it back up.

When we arrived, we all walked back to the pond. There was a picnic table under a tree beside the pond. I went straight to the picnic table and sat down. I wasn't ready to strip down to my bikini and get in the water. I was very shy and felt very uncomfortable to be exposed like that in front of the guys. There was no one else around, and it was sort of secluded. You couldn't see the pond from the road, and it was behind a store that didn't get that much foot traffic, and there were woods behind us.

The three boys jumped right in the water and were horsing around, wrestling and splashing each other. Craig begged me to join them, but I didn't want to. I didn't want to be in a bikini in front of them. Craig got out of the water and threatened to pick me up and throw me in. I got up and ran. He chased me down and captured me. He picked me up and carried me toward the water and put me down in the water. He never got my clothes wet, and the water was up to my knees. I got out, and he followed me back to the picnic table.

"Come on!" he said.

"Okay," I said as I shyly took off my clothes and folded them up and put them on the picnic table. I wrapped my arms around my pale white nakedness and tried to hide. I was very nervous standing there, exposed. I hurried up and got in the pond so that I could hide my body under the water. I felt awkward being there with him—with all three of them. Cameron and Jacob went to the other side of the pond, leaving me alone with Craig. Craig pulled me close to him, facing him, and kissed me on the lips. I turned my head and could feel my face turn beet red.

"What's wrong?" asked Craig.

"I'm new to this," I said. "I've never been with anyone before."

"It's okay," he said.

I didn't know how to swim, but I turned and walked away from him and sat down in the shallow end with the water up to my neck. Craig came by and started splashing me, and I splashed him back. Then he tackled me, picked me up, and tossed me further in the water.

"I can't swim!" I yelled.

"Stand up," he said. "The water isn't that deep."

I stood up, and the water was up to my neck. He disappeared under the water and swam around me. When he surfaced, he grabbed me and pulled me back over to the shallow end. He sat down in the water and sat me on his lap. We were still hidden under the water, and the water came up to my shoulders. Craig wrapped his arms around me and held me close to him, and he started kissing on my neck. I looked at Cameron and Jacob to see what they were doing. They were floating on their backs off in the distance, not paying any attention to us. I moved off of his lap and moved away from him. I could feel him getting excited through his swim shorts with me on his lap, and I was very uncomfortable. He moved back over in front of me and grabbed me between the legs and kissed me, inserting his tongue into my mouth. I went stiff.

"Stop," I said, grabbing his hand and pushing him away.

"What?" he said, putting his hand back between my legs, moving my bikini bottom aside and inserting his finger.

I froze. All I could think about was what Jordan did to me, and it paralyzed me. I didn't know what to do. I wasn't ready for this, and he was moving way too fast. I didn't want to draw attention to what he was doing. The other two guys were within sight. I didn't want them to know what he was doing to me. I was very nervous and uncomfortable. I just wanted to go home at this point. I tried to pull his hand away, but he was way too strong. He kept fondling me. He took my hand and put it on his erect penis. I yanked my hand away. I tried moving away, but he spun me around and sat me on his lap under the water. He tried inserting himself into me.

"Stop," I said, "I'm not ready for this."

"Come on! Let me just stick it in and hold it there. I want to know what you feel like," he whispered.

"I can't," I whispered. "I'm a virgin." I didn't want the other two to hear.

"I know. I never had one. Let me be your first."

"Cameron and Jacob are right there! We can't do this in front of them," I pleaded.

I moved away from him, and he let me go. I got out of the pond and could feel his eyes staring at me as I walked toward the picnic table. I hurried up and wrapped myself in a towel to hide my body from his staring eyes.

He stayed in the water and swam around for a while. I was assuming he was trying to calm himself down so that he could get out of the water.

As soon as I dried off some, I hurried up and slipped my clothes back on over my bathing suit. There was no way that I was getting back into that water for him to try anything again.

The car ride home was much of the same. Craig sat extremely close to me in the back seat, holding my hand and stroking my thigh. I was like a frozen statue. I couldn't move and could barely breathe.

Why was this boy so into me? I never had a boy lust after me like this. What did he see in me? I wasn't as pretty as his ex, Robin. I was just skinny. I was flat-chested, unlike Robin. He could have any girl he wanted. Why was he after me? I was lame. Any other girl would have sex with him. Why was he wasting his time with me? I was damaged goods and came with a lot of baggage.

Craig walked me inside the house. Everyone was home, and Craig followed me upstairs to my room.

"When can I see you again?" Craig asked once inside my room.

"I don't know," I said. I didn't think he was that bold to follow me up to my room with everyone home, and the other two were waiting for him out in the car.

"Will you be at church on Wednesday?" he asked, hugging me tight and holding me there.

I was stiff and wondered if he felt like he was hugging a board. I tried to relax but couldn't. He made me too nervous, and he was way too hands-on for me. Was I ever going to get used to this? All I could think about was what Jordan did to me, and I was aware at the time that hindered me from fighting back and setting boundaries with Craig. I was like a wounded bird that fell prey to a cat and couldn't fly away.

I knew where this relationship was headed, but I felt obligated to stay. This boy liked me. He was popular. If I broke up with him because I wouldn't have sex with him, then what would that do for me at school? What would he tell his friends? He went to the same church as me. What the Sandefurs thought of me mattered more to me than anything. I was scared of what they would think of me if they found out that I had sex outside of marriage. I didn't want to be a disappointment to them. I would never be able to go to that church again. I was a Christian. What would they think of me?

148

I was scared that my reputation would be ruined both at school and at church. I had to stay with Craig. I had to make him slow down. I could build up the courage to set boundaries with him. He went to church too. I could make him understand. If I told him that my brother molested me when I was little, maybe that will make him understand why I was so nervous to have sex with him, and that would get him to back off a little bit.

*****

The following Wednesday, I went to church. I was not in the teen youth group anymore. Pastor Ken invited me to be in their adult prayer group on Wednesday nights with all the older people. After class, Craig met up with me, and I left with him, and he took me home with him. Pastor Ken saw me in the truck with him and stopped us as we were pulling out.

"Hey, Drea! Are you two a thing now?" Pastor Ken asked.

Uh-oh! I'm busted now.

I nodded my head.

"Where are you two headed off to?" asked Pastor Ken.

"We are going to go hang out at my place," said Craig.

Pastor Ken knew that he lived with the Monteis.

"You better be good to her," Pastor Ken said. "She has been through a lot, and I care about her."

"I will," Craig said.

"I'll see ya later, Drea, and we'll talk," said Pastor Ken.

Pastor Ken backed away from the truck, and I waved at him as we drove off. Craig didn't live too far from here, about a mile outside of town on M-46.

When we got there, he took me down to the finished basement where he was staying. He was sleeping on a couch, and there was a TV in front of it. It was a walkout basement with sliding glass doors, and it was carpeted. There were a couple of bedrooms and a bathroom down there, but he really didn't have a bedroom.

We sat on the couch and, of course, he had to sit as close as he could next to me. He turned the TV on and pulled me onto his lap.

Joel Montei came downstairs, and I hurried up and slid off his lap and sat next to him. I was very uncomfortable being alone with him, even though the Monteis were all upstairs. I didn't want to be seen sitting on his lap. I knew it wasn't appropriate.

After Joel went back upstairs, Craig laid down on the couch and had me lie in front of him to where he was spooning me. He wrapped his arms around me and kept feeling my stomach. He couldn't get over how thin I was and he told me so. When he was feeling my stomach, he inched his hand further up to my chest, but I grabbed his hand and moved it away. He started tickling me, trying to goof off. I kept trying to grab his hand to make him stop, but he was much stronger than me. I even told him to stop, but he wouldn't. He always pushed the boundaries to see how far he could go and what he could get away with.

Craig was on his side, lying on the couch, and he rolled me onto my back and stared into my eyes and told me that I was pretty. No one ever told me that before, especially a boy. He leaned over me and kissed me on the lips and worked into a French kiss. I was very nervous and very uncomfortable. I wanted him to like me, but I wasn't interested in having sex with him, and I knew that is what he wanted. I wasn't ready. I was too damaged. I didn't know how to kiss, and it was weird to me having his tongue in my mouth. I did not want to be making out with him, but he was very persistent. He kept feeling my stomach as he was kissing me and moved his hand further down between my legs. I immediately sat up. I couldn't do this.

"What's wrong?" asked Craig.

"You are moving way too fast for me. I'm new to all of this. I've never had a boyfriend before."

"I can teach you," he said as he pulled me back down to lie with him.

He started rubbing his hand on my stomach again and lifted my shirt up, exposing my bare stomach.

"You are so skinny," he said. "Your stomach is so flat, and I can see your ribs. It's so hot," he said, sitting up a little to get a better look at my stomach.

I could feel my face starting to turn red. He lifted my shirt further up, exposing the bottom of my bra. I got goosebumps all over. He made me so nervous. It was almost paralyzing.

"You are so pale and milky white. Do you ever tan?"

"Redheads don't tan," I said with a knot in my throat.

He slid his hand further up my shirt, reaching my breasts. I tried pulling his hand away, but he was too strong.

"Relax," he said.

"I can't do this," I said softly.

I heard Joel walk down the stairs and jumped to my feet. I didn't want to be seen lying on the couch with him. He would think that I was a slut. Craig sat up and looked at me.

After Joel went back upstairs, Craig grabbed my hand and pulled me onto his lap.

"Do I make you nervous?" he asked.

I nodded.

"Why did you get up when Joel walked down here?"

"I didn't want to be seen lying on the couch with you," I said.

"Why? We weren't doing anything," he said. "They know we are dating."

I looked outside. It was starting to get dark.

"Can you take me home? It is starting to get dark."

"Do you have a curfew? You're eighteen."

"No, but they don't know where I'm at, and I don't want them to get worried."

Craig walked me upstairs to say goodbye to everyone, and he took me home, holding my hand the entire time.

*****

School was out for the summer, and there was a KCQ country concert coming up on Ojibway Island in Saginaw. The Joneses tried to go to it every year. They invited Craig along to try and get to know him better. The whole family went. All of us kids were in one van, and Betsy, Ronald, Scott, and Raegan were in another van with little Tate. Bella's boyfriend, Christian, drove. Bella sat in the passenger seat. Stella was Bella's friend. She came along too, and she and Ronnie sat behind them, leaving Craig and I in the very back seat.

Craig held my hand and tried feeling up my leg.

"Stop," I said quietly, gritting my teeth and pushing his hand away.

He wouldn't stop. He knew he could get away with it in a van full of people because he knew that I wouldn't make a scene in front of everyone. Me telling him no and telling him to stop, made him want to touch me even more. It was a game for him to see how far he could go before I would crack and finally give in to him which he was counting on.

We arrived at the concert and all walked together as a group, trying to find a place to sit. We were pretty early so that we could get decent parking and a decent place to sit. We didn't want to sit in the fenced-in area of chairs in front of the stage because we had to pay for those. We all wanted to walk around anyway, so we set up blankets on the grass under a tree a little ways behind that so that we could still see the stage and were somewhat in the shade. We also had folding chairs that we brought along as well along with a cooler with drinks and snacks. After we were all set up, Craig and I walked off together, looking at everything.

It wasn't just a country concert. They had old classic cars there doing a car show. There were all sorts of food vendors and other vendors selling crafts, t-shirts, blankets, jewelry, and the works. There was a bounce house for the kids and a photo booth. There were all kinds of stuff there. Craig held my hand as we walked around. We spent a lot of time looking at the old classic cars. The photo booth was right there too, so we went and got our pictures taken together.

I wore my bathing suit under my clothes just in case we decided to go swimming because there was water there with a sandy beach. Bella and Stella both wore their bathing suits as well. I thought I was safe from Craig trying anything with me with all of those people there. It got crowded quickly.

I needed to get something out of the van, so we walked back to where we set up on the grass and got the keys from Betsy. Craig walked me to the van. It was sweltering hot in there. We left the side door open to let the heat out before we went in there. Craig climbed into the back and told me to come sit by him, and I did. We left the side door open for air. Anyone walking by wouldn't be able to see the third-row seat without poking their head in, and the windows were tinted. Craig pulled me on top of his lap and started kissing me. I just froze right up.

"Hey. Can I tell you something about me?" Craig asked.

I nodded.

"My dad walked out on me, and my mom got into drugs and couldn't take care of me, and I got taken away. That's why I was in foster care."

"I'm sorry to hear that," I said. "My mom wasn't a very good mother either."

"Why? What did she do?"

"My older brother molested me when I was little, and he had to be placed in foster care. My mother blamed me."

Craig hugged me close and pushed my head onto his shoulder. "Is that why you're so nervous around me?" he asked.

"A little," I said.

Actually, he made me so nervous because he wanted something I was not willing to give him. I thought that maybe he would be more understanding and back off some if he knew what had happened to me. It actually made him even more clingy and even more hands-on. We always had to be holding hands if we were together.

Craig grabbed my face and started French kissing me. I really didn't like this. I wasn't comfortable having any sort of physical contact with him at all. He didn't understand boundaries. Since we were dating, then my body was fair game to him, and he wanted it.

Was this how it was supposed to be when you had a boyfriend? Was I just being lame?

Craig slid his hand up between my legs, under my skirt, grazing his fingers across my crotch as he was kissing me. I couldn't breathe. I froze like a statue.

"It's way too hot in here," I said, mustering the strength to speak up. "Let's get out of here."

We both got out of the van and were about to lock up when Bella and Christian walked up.

"We thought you guys got lost," Bella said. "What were you guys doing? Making out?"

"No," I said defensively.

"Uh-huh! Sure!" she said.

"We just came out to the van to get something," I said reassuringly.

Craig grabbed my hand, and we walked away. He escorted me to the porta-potties so I could go to the bathroom. I needed that minute away from him to catch my breath and calm my nerves. We continued to walk around until it was time to leave.

It was dark on our ride home, and Craig and I sat in the very back again. He held my hand and tried sitting me on his lap, but I protested.

"Put her down and leave her alone!" Bella yelled back. "She can't be sitting on your lap driving down the road. Do you want us to get pulled over?"

Thank you, Bella.

Craig let me sit beside him, but he had my hand in his lap and always sat with his legs spread wide open. He rubbed my hand on his crotch to let me know how excited he was.

When we got home, Craig followed me up to my bedroom to tell me goodnight before he left and went home himself, but he had other ideas. Once he was in my room, he shut the door and held me and kissed me on the top of my head. He led me to my bed and pushed me onto it, climbing on beside me. He grabbed my face and started making out with me.

"Stop!" I said.

"Come on!" he said, still kissing me. "I love kissing."

"Stop!" I said, turning my head to avoid his kisses.

He forced my face back toward his to continue kissing me, and his hands started to wander down between my legs.

"Stop!" I pleaded. "I don't want to do this."

"It will feel good. I promise," he said, kissing me. "Just relax and let me do all the work."

"You need to leave! The Joneses are right downstairs!"

Craig sat up and unbuttoned my skirt and tore it off of me. Then he grabbed my bikini bottoms to pull them off of me as well, but I grabbed them, holding them up. He pried my hand off of them and pulled them down.

"Don't. I don't want to," I pleaded.

"You have been driving me crazy all day," he said. "I have been walking around with a boner all day because of you."

This was it. My fate was sealed. I froze. Why couldn't I fight back? How come I didn't scream? The Joneses would have made him leave. Ronald had a gun, and he was a big scary guy. He would have kicked him out of the house. Why was I so scared to make a scene? Why didn't I just run out of the room. Bella and Christian were in the room next to me. Why didn't I scream? They would have heard me.

Craig climbed on top of me.

"Stop!" I said.

"Relax," Craig said as he positioned himself between my legs and slammed himself into me. He wasn't even remotely gentle and wasn't wearing a condom.

"That hurts!" I said. "Stop!"

Craig didn't stop. He pinned my hands above my head and got more aggressive. His whole body was lying on top of me, pinning me down.

Scream! I kept telling myself. *Scream!* I just couldn't. My voice was paralyzed. I couldn't scream and couldn't move. I knew what I was supposed to do. I was supposed to fight and scream. But I was paralyzed. I was reliving what Jordan did to me when I was eight years old, and I couldn't move or scream. I became a helpless little girl again. I just laid there and waited for it to be over.

When he was done, he got up and said I was bleeding. He put his pants back on. I stood up and got dressed. He kissed me and he left. I went downstairs to take a shower. I balled up on the shower floor and cried. I cried until I couldn't cry anymore, and then I got up and turned the water off. I got dressed and went straight to bed to cry myself to sleep.

What just happened to me? It didn't fully hit me until a few days later. Craig took something from me that I wasn't ready to give to him. I was never going to get that back. Why do bad things always happen to me? How come I didn't break it off with him the first time he tried something with me? I knew this was what he wanted. I wasn't ready for a relationship, but I said yes to the first guy that paid me any interest. He was popular and wanted me. He saw me as weak and an easy target. He took advantage of my shyness and broken, wounded bird demeanor. He took advantage of my weakness. He was much bigger and stronger than me and used that to his advantage.

I blamed myself for the whole thing and kept playing the "What if" or "If I had done this" game. What if I had screamed? Would someone come running to my rescue? If I had made my *no* mean no, would it have made a difference? What if I fought back more and kicked him in the nuts? What if I broke it off when he first started laying hands on me? I shouldn't have gone to the van alone with him. I should never have come upstairs to my room for him to follow me up there. I was thinking that since there were people around, I was somehow safe from him going all the way with me. Having people around didn't seem to matter to him at all. He was going to take what he wanted, regardless. I was just a game to him. He loved the thrill of pushing the boundaries to see how far he could go.

This threw me into a deep depression. Not only did I have to deal with what Jordan did to me, but now this. I wasn't even remotely healed from the first traumatic experience, and this made the first one all the more real again. I was reliving the past and the present all at the same time.

*****

A few days later, I told Bella that I needed to talk to her in my room. She sat next to me on my bed, and I told her what had happened.

"When we came back from the concert, Craig followed me up to my room. He made me have sex with him, but I didn't want to.

I told him no, but he wouldn't listen to me." I said that in the most detached way with no emotion. I didn't want to feel anything. I was numb. I was still in shock.

"That's rape, Andrea. If you told him no and he did it, anyway, that is rape. He raped you," said Bella.

I didn't say anything. I didn't know if I should call it rape since I didn't try to stop him. I didn't fight back. I wore a bikini in front of him and a mini skirt. Wasn't that asking for it? It was my fault. I blamed myself. I put myself in this situation by being alone with him. I didn't scream nor try to run away. I didn't fight back. I should have kicked him in the nuts, but I didn't. I knew what I was supposed to do in that situation, but I froze. I became a traumatized eight-year-old girl again. Did Craig really rape me if I didn't fight back?

"Did you tell Mom?" asked Bella.

"No. I just told you because I didn't know what to do," I said.

"You need to tell Mom," she said.

"I don't want to." I was afraid to tell her. I was embarrassed.

"Do you want me to tell her?" asked Bella.

"I don't want her to know," I said.

"She needs to know. Dad will protect you and make sure he doesn't come here again. You need to call the cops so he doesn't do it to anyone else."

"I don't want to call the cops," I snapped.

"He raped you, Andrea! He needs to go to jail!"

"I don't want to go through all of that."

All I could think about was his lawyer putting me on the stand and making me out to be the slut that wanted it and then regretted it and cried rape. I've watched *Law and Order*. I didn't want to put myself through that. That would just traumatize me even more. I just wanted to forget about it.

Bella left, and I just curled up on my bed. A few minutes later, Betsy was knocking on my door and coming in. I sat up, and she sat down on my bed next to me.

"Hey, DeeDee." My nieces and nephews called me DeeDee, so she adopted that nickname for me. "Bella came downstairs to talk to me and told me what happened with Craig."

157

I was mad at Bella for telling her mom but relieved at the same time. I didn't want to carry this alone. I didn't fully understand what had happened to me yet. It didn't fully hit me yet. I wasn't ready to call it rape just yet because I had put so much blame on myself. It was my own fault for putting myself in that situation to begin with. I was stupid. Was it really rape if I didn't fight back? I let it happen. I was such a slut for dressing the way I did and letting him get away with pushing the boundaries. I kept going with him, knowing what he wanted. I deserved this. It was my own fault. I was so stupid and naive. How could I be so stupid? I should have broken it off with him after the pond incident.

My friends at school talked about their first time they lost their virginity. One girl said it really hurt at first, but then it felt good. I knew Bella was having sex. Christian lived with us too and shared a room with Bella. I was the only one that was a prude. I was the "good" girl. What if this got around school? If I called this rape and this got around, what would happen to me, especially if I reported it to the police? Craig was graduated now, but he was popular. He had friends in grades below him.

Betsy put her arm around me and held me. She was teary-eyed. "You know you can come and talk to me about anything. I love you like a daughter. If Craig shows up here, Ronald will have him leave. He's not welcome here. You don't have to worry about him anymore. Okay?"

I nodded. I didn't say anything. I didn't cry. I was just a blank statue with no emotion. I was all out of emotion and suppressed it as much as I could, so I didn't really have to deal with it. I was very empty and hollow and closed off. I sat there with my legs tight together and my arms tight together on my lap, staring off into space. I was very stiff. I couldn't wait for Betsy to leave the room. I never liked to cry nor show emotion in front of anyone. I liked to do that in private. As soon as she left the room, I curled up in a fetal position under my blankets and cried myself to sleep.

*****

The cops were called, and I had to make a report. They did go talk to Craig, but I dropped the charges. I didn't want to put myself through court and go through all of that. I went with Craig multiple times, knowing what he wanted. I didn't think any of the charges would stick and that he would just get off anyway. I didn't want the Monteis to be dragged into court as a witness to seeing me cuddled on the couch with him. I didn't want Cameron or Jacob on the stand, giving their account of what they saw at the pond. I just wanted it to be over so that I could pick up the pieces and move on with my life. I didn't want to think about it anymore.

The next Wednesday at church, I gave the Sandefurs a letter, telling them what happened. I sat in their living room on the couch, and Pastor Ken was sitting in his recliner, and Regina was sitting across from me on the other couch. Pastor Ken was reading the letter and handed off the pages to Regina to read as he was reading it.

I told him I didn't want to come to church anymore because I didn't want to run into Craig. Craig was in the men's Bible study, which was in the next room beside the prayer group that I was in.

Pastor Ken and Regina stood up with me. They both held me and cried with me and prayed over me. The three of us were huddled together in their living room for quite a while. I tried so hard not to cry. I didn't want to cry in front of them. I had this huge knot in my stomach. I knew that they loved me and really cared about me. I didn't like seeing them cry.

Shortly after that, there was an annual church picnic at a church member's house. They had a beautiful property with a pond and pavilions next to the pond. Everyone brought a dish to pass, and all of the kids went swimming. I did go, but so did Craig. That was the next time I saw him after what he did. He approached me and asked to talk to me. I looked at the Sandefurs, and I got up and walked away a little within sight of the Sandefurs but out of earshot. That is when I broke it off with Craig and told him that I didn't want to see him anymore. Then I went and sat next to the Sandefurs.

Pastor Ken did confront Craig about what happened, but Craig denied raping me and basically said it was consensual. Pastor Ken told him that he did not believe that I would have sex with him.

I slowly stopped going to church and then stopped going altogether. I started just going to church with the Joneses. They had a very small congregation, and there really wasn't a pastor. A few of the guys took turns preaching. Ronald was one of them. It was a much different pace than what I was used to, but at least I didn't have to see Craig.

I felt like the Monteis looked at me differently. The cops showed up at their house, wanting to talk to Craig. I was paranoid that other people in the church found out what happened. I just couldn't face them, so I just stopped going.

That is when my faith in God really started to falter. That is when my life started to spiral into more bad decisions and more dark times as if what I had been through up to this point wasn't enough.

14

My Brush with a Cult

My senior year of high school was the first time I ever got kicked out of school. Word got out about me and Craig. Maddie, who was supposed to be my friend, was spreading rumors about me crying rape against Craig. I went to Maddie's house a few times and spent the night. She was a bigger girl, and her mom used to be my bus driver. I was angry. I never felt so betrayed by a friend. I mean, we weren't that close, but she was still supposed to be my friend. Maddie had a lot of issues herself and was also a cutter and had thoughts of suicide and suffered from self-esteem issues. She was dating a guy at the time and was telling our group of friends that she was no longer a virgin and was proud of herself for it. She was telling everyone, right down to the details.

When I found out she was behind the rumors about me and Craig, I lost it. I had to get back at her. Since she was already telling everyone about her sex life, I decided to do her a favor and make a school announcement. What better way to do that than during lunch in the cafeteria?

I went into the cafeteria during lunchtime and pulled out a chair near where she was sitting. My other friends all gathered around. I stood up on that chair.

"Hey, everyone! Can I have your attention, please?" I shouted. You could hear a pin drop, and everyone froze right where they were and stared at me. The whole cafeteria went silent. I was a very shy girl that barely spoke to anyone, so I bet it took everyone by surprise. My adrenaline was pumping.

"Maddie here wants everyone to know about her sex life, and I decided to help her out. She had sex with this guy, and he fell asleep, and she was still going at it. She is no longer a virgin. I just thought everyone should know!"

I got off the chair, and Maddie confronted me. She was a big girl, and I stood up to her. We argued for a minute about who was going to throw the first punch, and then I just punched her in the face, giving her a black eye. She tried to punch me back, but a paraprofessional stepped in and split us up.

That paraprofessional gave me a disgusted look. She saw me get up on the chair, making that announcement. She didn't know the whole story. She just saw me being a bully. She didn't know why I did it. She didn't know what Maddie did, spreading rumors about my rape. What about that? What about me? I was defending myself and my honor. I was teaching her a lesson. I may be a shy little weak Andrea, but make me mad enough, and I will fight back. My redhead temper will come out.

Maddie went crying to the office, and I got sent to the principal's office. She was sitting in the office with an ice pack on her face, and her eye was already swollen and turning black. I was suspended for three days.

Maddie's mom called the cops on me, and I had to go down to the state police station for questioning. The cops came to the school that very same day before I even got a chance to leave. I snuck out of the school and walked to my sister's apartment. I knew they were there for me, and I panicked. I told my sister what happened and that the cops were looking for me. My mom called a couple of hours later and said that the cops were at her house, looking for me. I waited a couple more hours before I had my sister take me back home to the Joneses, and we got there just a few minutes after the cops left. I told Betsy and Ronald what happened, and Betsy told me that I had to turn myself in or I would just make it worse for myself and that they just wanted to ask me some questions.

*****

The next morning, Betsy and Ronald took me to the state police post. I told them who I was and said that they were looking for me.

A woman state trooper took me back to the interrogation room, but since I was eighteen, I wasn't allowed to take anyone back there with me. She questioned me and called me a bully and told me that I was going to go to jail for assault. She was pretty cutthroat and not the least bit understanding when I tried to tell her why that girl deserved to be punched in the face. She was behind the rumors going around school about me and Craig. The woman officer didn't care. She was especially mad about me announcing Maddie's sex life to the whole school. I was just a big mean bully picking on a poor fat girl. She was throwing the book at me and was yelling at me. She told me that since I was eighteen, I was an adult and would go to an adult jail for assaulting a minor.

When she was done yelling at me, I left with the Joneses and told them what she said. They took me straight to an attorney they knew in Caro, and I had to make payments to pay him off.

There was a school assembly in the gym. It was a guest speaker who was a one-man volleyball team. He was a motivational speaker that played volleyball. He would be on a team by himself against a whole bunch of people, and he kept increasing the number of opponents playing against him with volunteers, and he was able to hold his own and win every time. He was very good.

He was hosting another event after school but in Vasser, Michigan, at the high school gym. This one was more religion-based since it wasn't during school hours and opened to the public. We all went as a family. At the end, he passed out a questionnaire. There were three boxes to check: Are you saved? Do you want to be saved? And would you like to recommit yourself to Christ? There was also a box where you could write in a prayer request and you also had to fill out your name, phone number, and address.

I checked the box that I wanted to recommit myself to Christ and wrote in the prayer request section that I needed prayer to help get me through some traumatic experiences I had to go through in my life.

A few weeks went by, and I got a phone call from a lady from the one-man volleyball team assembly. She got my card about wanting to recommit my life to Christ and asked specifically about the trauma I wanted prayers for, and I told her.

That was the beginning of my relationship with Cassie Shuecraft. She set up a meet date with me where she would come to the house for a visit so that we could talk and meet in person. The following week, she came on a Wednesday, and I took her into the Joneses library. I gave her a letter of a brief description of what I went through so that she could better pray for me because I needed all the prayers I could get. She read it silently in front of me, and then we talked about it, and she prayed over me. She came to visit me once a week after that for a Bible study and prayer time. She also started calling me throughout the week, and my relationship with her grew more intense.

Cassie was a slender woman about my height. She had dirty blonde shoulder-length hair she kept in a half ponytail. She dressed very modestly with long ankle length skirts, and she was in her forties. She was a Baptist minister's wife. Her husband's name was Jerry, and they had three boys—Jeremiah, Joseph, and Steven.

Her beliefs were quite a bit different than what I was taught at the Kingston Wesleyan church. She believed that it was not biblical for a woman to wear pants and that they had to wear long dresses and keep their hair long. When she came for Bible studies with me on Wednesdays, I made sure to wear a long dress or skirt. I wanted to be respectful.

Betsy could see what was happening, and she told me that she didn't care for Cassie. She said she was brainwashing me. I told her what Cassie said about woman wearing dresses and how she justified it scripturally, and Betsy tried to unravel the web of misinterpretation of Scripture that she twisted to fit her beliefs.

I liked Cassie. She was a pastor's wife and meant well. She listened to me and prayed for me. It seemed like she had a really close relationship with God, and I was drawn to her. I wanted to be as close to God as she was. Maybe if I got my life right and started living close to God like she did, then nothing bad would happen to me, and I could finally be happy.

The Joneses were great Christian people, but I felt like Cassie knew better at the time. I stopped going to the Kingston Wesleyan church so I didn't get to see the Sandefurs as often anymore and needed someone to talk to. I knew that I could talk to Betsy but always felt like a burden. I didn't want to burden her with my problems and had a lot of them.

Cassie started calling me on the phone every day on Betsy's cell phone. The conversations grew longer and longer. Sometimes she would just keep me on the phone and not say anything, and we would be on the phone for hours. Talking with Cassie became something I *had* to do. She was the only one that got me and understood me.

I was suffering from very deep depression, and all I wanted to do was die. I knew Ronald kept a handgun in his closet. Everyone was gone, and I was home alone. I started isolating myself more and more and didn't do as much with the family. I grabbed the gun and took it out to the living room and sat in the recliner right in front of their bedroom door next to Bella's guinea pig cage. I looked at it in my hand for the longest time.

Was this something that I really wanted to do? I just wanted to die. I wanted the pain to end. I thought that moving in with the Joneses would magically make me better. If that didn't work, then nothing would. I couldn't imagine going through an entire lifetime feeling this way.

I started losing friends at school because I was too depressed. I started hanging out more in the library. I was very alone. I felt abandoned. It didn't feel like anybody liked me anymore. Betsy was getting mad about me tying up her phone but I felt like I had to talk to Cassie every day. She was the only friend that got me and listened to me. I didn't feel like a burden to her like I did everyone else. I can see now that she spoke to me in such a way to draw me in and made me feel like I needed her.

I was dwelling on what happened with Craig and how stupid I was. Why didn't I run? Why didn't I scream? Was it even rape since I didn't fight back? I put so much blame on myself. My mother never called me. Cassie, a complete stranger, cared more about me than my own mother did. I felt useless and worthless, like I wouldn't amount to anything. I was forever going to be depressed, and that's just how my life was going to be.

I put my mouth around the barrel of the gun with my finger on the trigger. I squeezed the trigger just a little bit with tears running down my face. I decided that I didn't want to blow my head off this way. Where else could I point this gun to do the job that wasn't as messy and horrific as putting it in my mouth?

I remember, as a small child, one of my earliest memories at five years old. I went to my uncle's funeral. He was my mom's baby brother, Albert. He shot himself in the head at the age of twenty-one, playing Russian Roulette. I remember seeing the bullet hole on his temple, and his head was still intact.

I put the gun up to my temple and I cried uncontrollably. I didn't want to live anymore. I cried out to God and begged Him to just take me home. I told Him this life was just too hard and that I couldn't do this anymore. I just wanted the pain to end. I didn't want to be a burden to anyone anymore. I just wanted to be in heaven with Him. I yelled at God for putting me in such a messed-up family to begin with. I told Him that my own mother didn't even love me. How was anyone else supposed to love me if my own mother didn't? I really poured my heart out to God and was crying hysterically with this gun held to my head and my finger on the trigger.

I thought about how the Joneses would feel coming home and finding me dead by Ronald's gun and if Ronald would somehow feel responsible because it was his gun. I thought about how they would feel every time they came into their living room and saw that image of me, dead with a gunshot wound to the head. I'm sure it would have traumatized them. But I was always thinking of the well-being of others. I had to put myself first. I couldn't bear to go another day feeling this way. It was way too much pain to continue on. It would be better for myself and everyone else in the long run if I was just gone. I wouldn't be a burden anymore, and my pain and suffering would finally be over. I would be in heaven with Jesus.

There isn't any pain and suffering in heaven. There would be no more pain, and I wouldn't remember this life once I got there. I wanted to forget everything. My entire life was too painful to remember. I had very little good memories, and even the good memories were tainted with a painful one. The Joneses did a lot for me and took me places, and I got to experience a lot of new things because of them, but I was with the Joneses because my natural family and my mother drove me away and to them. My painful past tainted everything, and there was no way that I could ever run from that fact.

Just as I was about to pull the trigger, the house phone rang and it was right beside the chair I was sitting in. I didn't answer it the first time. I just let it ring, but then it rang again. I picked it up this time, still holding the gun to my head. I had the phone in my left ear and the gun pointed at my right temple.

"Hello!" I said, trying to sound normal like nothing was wrong.

"Andrea, this is Cassie. What is wrong?"

She must have heard the desperation in my voice.

I didn't want to tell her what I was doing.

"Andrea, what are you doing? What's wrong?"

"Nothing," I said, my voice cracking.

"What are you doing? Have you been crying?" she asked.

There was a long silence. I didn't want to tell her because I knew that she would stop me.

"Where is everyone?" she asked.

"Everyone is gone," I said. "I'm home alone."

"And where are you?"

"In the living room."

"And what are you doing, Andrea?"

I couldn't form the words to say it.

"Andrea, what are you doing? Are you hurting yourself? Are you cutting again?"

I started bawling, "I have a gun!"

"What are you doing with a gun, Andrea?"

I didn't respond.

"Andrea, what are you doing with the gun?"

"I don't want to do this anymore! I don't want to be depressed anymore. I just want to go home to Jesus!" I cried.

"Andrea, where is the gun right now?"

"I'm holding it," I said.

"Where?"

"I'm holding it to my head," I said, crying hysterically.

"Andrea, where did you get the gun?"

"From Ronald's and Betsy's closet," I sobbed almost incoherently.

"I want you to go put it back where you found it," Cassie pleaded.

"I can't. I just want to go home. I want to die. I'm tired of living like this. Please, don't talk me out of it."

"Of course I'm going to talk you out of it! I care about you and don't want you to do this! Do you think God wants you to kill yourself?"

"No."

"No, He doesn't. He has a plan and a purpose for your life."

"What plan is that? I can never be happy!"

"God wants you to be happy, and He has a plan for you. We may not know what it is right now, but His plan is not for you to take your life into your own hands. I want you to do something for me. I want you to go put that gun back in the closet where you found it. Can you do that for me?"

I didn't say anything. There was just a moment of silence.

"Andrea, are you still holding the gun?"

"Yes."

"Lower the gun from your head, Andrea."

I slowly put the gun in my lap, still gripping it with my right hand and holding the phone to my ear with my left hand.

"Did you lower it, Andrea?"

"Yes."

"Okay, now I want you to get up, keep me on the phone, and take the phone with you into the closet to put that gun back where you found it, and I want you to tell me what you are doing with each step. Can you do that for me?"

"I'm on a cord. I can't take the phone with me."

"Okay. Can you put me on speaker? Is their room right next to the living room?"

"Yes."

"Okay, put me on speaker and go put that gun back where you found it."

I put her on speaker and slowly got up, still gripping the gun in my hand, and walked into their bedroom and put the gun back in their closet where I found it. Then I walked back out to the living room and sat in the recliner and picked the phone back up.

"Okay," I said, "I put it back."

"Oh, thank God! Thank you!"

Cassie prayed over me, and then the Joneses came home, so I had to let her go. The Joneses never knew about the gun. I tried to hide things from them. I didn't want them to know how unhappy I was. I didn't want to be more of a burden to them. They were doing so much for me already by just letting me be there and getting me out of my mom's house.

My depression turned into pure desperation and utter hopelessness. Not only did I feel like a burden to the Joneses, but I felt like a loser, a failure at life, like a worthless piece of meat—ugly, hated, abandoned, and thrown aside. I felt like a nobody and was better off dead. My own family wouldn't miss me. The Joneses would be sad, but they would get over it.

I felt so alone in the world. I didn't feel like I had a family. The Joneses were a wonderful family, and they tried to make me feel like a part of them, but I couldn't help but feel like the redheaded stepchild. It was my natural family and the estranged—almost non-existent—relationship that I had with them that made it hard and brought up all of these feelings. I wanted more than anything to have a normal family. I saw what Betsy had with Bella and Raegan, and I wanted that too. I knew Betsy thought of me as a daughter, but it just wasn't the same.

My mom didn't know what happened to me with Craig. She didn't even know that I dated Craig. She wasn't a part of my life and didn't make too much of an effort to be a part of my life. She didn't know me. I felt like she was happy now that I was gone because she got her son back. She picked Jordan over me after what he did. I must be a horrible person if she could pick him after what he did over me. I just felt worthless.

I was still trying to process what had happened to me as a child, and then Craig came along and made it ten times worse. My mind and my emotions were overloaded, and I was unable to work through it. My whole life up to this point had been nothing but pain and trauma. I saw my whole life being this way. I could barely get through each day. I couldn't bear the thought of my entire life being this way.

I was so good at pretending. I joked around and put on a smile when I needed to. It was just easier that way. If everyone thought I was okay, then they wouldn't ask me any questions, and I didn't want to talk about it. I just internalized everything and let it fester dangerously within me until I reached a breaking point. I was in a very desperate, fragile state.

One night, I got a hold of some pills. I don't remember what they were, but I crushed a bunch of them up and went downstairs to grab a glass of apple cider. I took it up to my room and sat on the floor next to my bed.

My bed was not up against my wall anymore. I rearranged my room, and it was now in the middle of the room in front of the window. So I was on the other side of my bed away from the door on the floor. I leaned up against my bed and poured all of the crushed pills into the apple cider, hoping that it would disguise the taste. I was horrible about swallowing pills, so I thought that crushing a bunch of them and then drinking them would be easier, and I could get more in my system faster that way.

The pills made a foamy texture in the apple cider and gave it a really foul odor. I had to plug my nose to drink it, and it tasted absolutely disgusting. I forced myself to drink it because ending my pain and suffering was more important than the horrible taste. I also had some pills left over that I didn't crush, and I swallowed a few of them and drank the poisoned apple cider concoction with it.

After drinking the poisoned apple cider, I crawled into bed. I don't know how much time had passed, but Bella came to my room, letting me know that dinner was ready. She tried shaking me and called my name. I was barely conscious with little response. She ran downstairs to get her mom. I vaguely remember the two of them helping me down the stairs and Bella's boyfriend helping me into the passenger seat of the car. Bella got in the back seat behind me while Betsy drove. I was going in and out of consciousness, and Betsy and Bella both had to keep nudging me awake and saying my name. Betsy told Bella not to let me fall asleep.

I couldn't keep my eyes open. My head kept nodding off, and they just continued shaking me until I woke up just to nod off again a minute later. It was a twenty-minute ride to the hospital with them shaking me and calling my name.

I had to get my stomach pumped. They made me wake up enough to drink this nasty tasting black charcoal. I could barely keep my eyes open. I just wanted to sleep and drift off into nothingness. When I wouldn't drink, they threatened to shove a tube down my throat and told me that it wouldn't be pleasant because they would have to hold me down to do it and that I would get a sore throat from it. They were not very nice to me at all.

They had little compassion for people that ended up in the ER due to an overdose. I was a waste of time because there were other people in the ER that wanted to live, and I was taking time away from them. They didn't know anything about me or my history and what I had to go through that led me to this point. They just thought I was just some stupid girl trying to get some attention. I intended on dying. Just how much attention would that give me?

They had to bring in a psychiatrist to come and talk to me and do an assessment. They forced me to go to a psychiatric hospital in Midland. Since I was an adult, I had to go to the adult psychiatric unit. I had to be taken by ambulance to ensure that I would get there. They wouldn't allow Betsy to take me. Betsy went home and packed me some clothes and things in a bag and dropped them off at the hospital before they transferred me.

When we arrived, the two paramedics escorted me inside and took me down a long hallway. Every pair of doors we came to, we had to be buzzed in, and they would immediately lock behind us with a resounding click, letting me know that I was now a prisoner in the loony bin, and there was no escape. I was now at the mercy of the doctors and was there for however long they told me I had to be.

This time, I knew what to expect and knew what I had to do to get out of there faster. I had to be on my best behavior, smile, and do and say whatever I had to get out of there fast. I had to become the best darn actress that even Hollywood would be proud of.

They took me to a small office to get interviewed, the usual "What brings you here?" and all of your medical and mental health information and "Know your rights" garbage when I knew that when you ended up in a place like this, you had very little rights. Then I was taken to another room for the old uncomfortable strip search and bag search before taking me to my new sterile-looking hospital room with the world-class most uncomfortable bed you could ever get with fancy thin hospital bedding that would drive Martha Stewart insane and make her put a gun to her head for ever laying eyes on such a hideous scene, let alone be caught dead lying on. I had my own room at the moment, so I picked the bed by the window which overlooked the parking lot.

It was a totally different experience than the children's psychiatric unit I was in before. In the children's wing, everyone was still normal, other than depression and trying to kill themselves. In the adult unit, there were literally insane people there, and they were scary, grown insane men. This place meant business. This wasn't child's play this time. I was thrown in with the big dogs.

I had two different grown insane men approaching my table during meal times, hitting on me, asking me to take a walk with them out in the courtyard, hinting at sex. I just ignored them and told them I wasn't interested.

I made sure that I ate every meal and took all my meds. I participated in all of the group activities. I tried not to isolate myself in my room. They gave us a journal, and I came out to the common area and sat in a chair instead of the couch so that nobody could sit by me, and I watched TV and wrote in my journal. The nurses came around once a day to do vitals and ask us how we were doing. I was always polite and tried to sound positive. I made it sound like what I did was stupid and that I learned my lesson. I admitted that I really needed help and needed to talk with someone to help me get through some things. I said all of the right things and knew exactly what they wanted to hear. I minded my own business and didn't talk to anyone if I didn't have to.

I was determined to get out in three days which was the legal minimum hold. I was angry when three days came and went and they wouldn't release me. When I asked about going home, they said they were keeping me a little while longer since this wasn't my first time in a psychiatric facility. I became upset, and they told me that I could petition the court, but it would take three days to get in front of a judge, and that was no guarantee. I had to bottle my anger and suck it up. I couldn't give them yet another reason to keep me here longer. I had to do what they said and keep on pretending that I was making progress, all while planning my next attempt, but only this time, I would be dead. I wasn't coming back here.

Cassie called me a few times a day, every day, but we couldn't talk for very long. She offered me to come and move in with her and her family in Clare, Michigan, and I said yes.

After six days of being in the hospital, I was finally released, and Cassie and her husband, Jerry, came to pick me up. I went to my room and sat by the window and watched the squirrels scouring around while waiting for them to pull into the parking lot. I was excited when I saw them and waved at them through the window. They took me home with them.

A few days later, they took me with a van and a trailer to get my stuff. Bella and Ronnie were at school, and Betsy was at work. Ronald wasn't home either. I quietly packed up most of my stuff and loaded it. I also packed up my long haired, Maine coon cat, Sweetie, my two rabbits, Montob and Montel and their outside cage, and loaded them up as well. Betsy came home just before I left, and I told her that I had to get away. She tried to talk me into staying and not going with the Shuecrafts, but I already packed everything up, so there was no turning back.

Betsy gave me a phone card just in case I needed to call her to come home. She told me that I would always be her daughter, that she loved me, and I was always welcome to come back home. We hugged, and I left. I tried really hard not to cry. I knew that I was hurting her. She tried everything she could to help me and took me in as one of her own and did so much for me. She opened up her home, her heart, and her family to me, and I knew she loved me and cared about me. I just wanted to be further away. I was trying to run from my problems. I didn't want to be anywhere where I could run into Craig or the Monteis. I just needed to be out of the area.

The Shuecrafts were a pastor family. I thought I needed that discipline to help get my life back on track, to become closer with God so that I didn't have to go through something like this again. Them being a pastor family appealed to me the most.

Cassie had me write an apology letter to Maddie for punching her in the face. I wasn't sorry and felt that she deserved it because she started the rumors about me and Craig, but she had me write it, anyway, in order to get out of trouble. She didn't want it to follow me to Clare. So I wrote a letter saying how wrong and sorry I was for my actions and left it on her front porch at her house on my way to Clare with all of my stuff. The case against me was dropped, and everything did go away except for the attorney fees I still had to make payments on.

I knew that things were going to be strict. Cassie already warned me that if I moved in with them, then I had to give up wearing pants and had to wear long dresses and skirts. I thought that I could handle that, no problem. It was a small price to pay. I could get used to wearing dresses all the time. Little did I know just how strict and controlled my life would become.

Cassie was allergic to cats, so I had to keep my cat at her mom's house. She lived on a farm with a barn. Sweetie was strictly an indoor cat, so making her being an outside cat on a farm was hard, but I didn't have a choice. I didn't feel like it was right to leave her with Joneses and make them responsible for her. It was a tough decision that I had to make.

I kept my rabbits in the outside cage in the backyard at the Shuecrafts'. During the summer, I kept the rabbits in an outdoor cage, but in the winter time, I kept them in a cage in my room and let them out to play for a couple of hours during the day. I knew that living with the Shuecrafts, they wouldn't be able to come in the house at all.

I had to convince myself that everything was going to be okay. This was for the best. I had to make certain sacrifices to get my life back on track, and the Shuecrafts were going to help me do that. Maybe they would help me find a good Christian guy to court me, and I would get married, have kids, and live happily ever after. I wanted him to be a strong Christian head that prayed and did Bible studies as a family. I wanted a man that was close to God. This would make me happy. This family would give me the discipline I needed to achieve that.

Before I could move any of my stuff in the house, it had to go into the garage for inspection. Cassie sat in the garage with me, and I had to hold up every piece of clothing I had to make sure met her approval. If I was going to live in her house with her husband and three boys, she had to make sure that I dressed modestly so that I wouldn't cause them to stumble. I had to throw away all of my pants. They were not allowed in her house. I had to throw away most of my clothes because they didn't meet her approval. After moving in with the Joneses and receiving that child support money, I built up my wardrobe with nicer clothes. I had to throw them all away, which left me with hardly anything. I had a couple of long skirts I wore for church, but that was it.

Not only did I have to throw most of my clothes away, but I also had to throw away all of my contemporary Christian CDs. They only approved of old hymns. I had little naked angel knickknacks that she made me throw away. I was an artist and spent a lot of time in my room drawing. She made me throw most of it away. I loved to draw people, females mainly, and if they were drawn with pants, I had to throw it away. Anything new that I drew had to be girls with dresses or landscapes, and she had me put a Bible verse on every one. Very little met her expectations.

On trash day, I watched the two garbage men throw all of my clothes, drawings, CDs, and other things into the garbage truck. They were gone forever. Cassie wouldn't even let me donate them because if they were inappropriate for me, they were inappropriate for anyone else too. I was sad watching all of my stuff get hauled away like trash.

I was mainly upset about my clothes. I grew up not having many nice clothes and worked hard on trying to build up my wardrobe just for it to all be thrown away.

I had to convince myself that this was all for my own good. Change was hard, but it was going to get better. I could buy new clothes. I could draw more pictures. It was just stuff. Cassie wasn't trying to be mean to me. She was helping me get rid of everything that wasn't pleasing to God. Although this process hadn't been very pleasant, I would soon reap the benefits from this new life. My life had to change somehow because my life before was leading me down a dark road of depression that was trying to drive me into an early grave. I wanted to be happy. I wanted to live. I wanted my happily ever after with a strong Christian husband with kids. I wanted a man who was a spiritual leader. I wanted to be pleasing to God. I wanted to be strong in my faith.

I convinced myself that this was going to help me achieve all of that. This family was going to help me get to that point, and all I had to do was learn from them, follow their rules, and make some small sacrifices. I had to adapt to their way of living. Change was hard, but it was going to get better. This was all going to be worth it in the end and become second nature.

My bedroom upstairs was right next to theirs. It had a full-size bed and was set up nicely. I've only ever had a twin size bed, so sleeping in a bigger bed was a nice change. It was hard to sleep the first few nights because of being in a new place.

I did manage to talk Cassie into letting me keep my pajama pants as long as I only wore them for bed and not walk around the house in them. I didn't have any nightgowns. I always thought they were for old ladies. I had to take a shower and change right away when I woke up and had to make sure that I wouldn't run into her boys or her husband on my way to the bathroom down the hall. They couldn't see me in my pajamas because it was inappropriate.

Cassie and I were about the same size, so she gave me a couple of skirts and some shirts. She also took me to some thrift stores to find more modest clothing.

If Cassie left the house, I had to go with her because it was inappropriate to be left home alone with her husband and three boys. Cassie did all of the grocery shopping and all of the womanly stuff such as keeping the house and doing all of the cooking, so I had to help with all of that stuff. She was teaching me how to be a good Godly woman and wife.

When we got into the car, she always had to point out when a guy was staring at me in the store and tell me, "That is why it is important for us to dress modestly as woman so that we don't cause men to stumble because God would hold us accountable for it, especially you being a young and pretty girl."

Men were driven by sex, so they stumbled by what they saw with their eyes. I was dressed modestly with a long flowing skirt and a loose-fitted sweater when she said there was a guy staring at me, so I didn't see how that would prevent men from staring. In fact, that made us stand out even more because we looked different. It made us look religious and vulnerable and weak, like an easy target.

Cassie knew about what happened with Craig. She liked to use what happened to me as an example of why it was important to dress modestly in long dresses and why it was important to have supervised courting to assure that nothing like that would happen. I already felt guilty about what happened. She made me feel more guilty about the decisions I had made that led up to that because of what I wore and going alone with him. She drilled it into my head why women had to wear dresses and justified it scripturally. She also blamed the Joneses for not protecting me and allowing that to happen under their roof. She also didn't like the fact that they let their teenage daughter's boyfriend live with them and share the same room and that Bella was pregnant while still in high school and not married.

Cassie really expressed to me everything that was wrong with the Joneses and why they were bad for me. When I talked with her on the phone when I still lived with the Joneses, she would ask me a bunch of questions about them, and she put thoughts and ideas into my head about how they were bad for me and not a good influence. She had me convinced that I was not in a good situation and that they weren't good enough Christians. She was brainwashing me from the start. Cassie had all of the answers to everything. She was a pastor's wife and knew better. She was close to God. So when she asked me to move in with them, I said yes because she already had me convinced that I was not in a good situation.

Cassie didn't let me have any contact with the Joneses at all. I was only allowed to have contact with my mother. I told Cassie about my childhood and my history with my mother. She felt that it was still important to have contact with her because she was my mother. That was my natural family, so that was different. I was tied to them by blood no matter what. The Joneses were not my natural family, so I was not obligated to have any continued relationship with them.

I loved the Joneses more than my own family and tried sticking up for them, but Cassie was very good at planting seeds of doubt and guilt and got me to see things her way. I understood what she was saying, but I couldn't turn off my feelings for them. They helped me so much and took me in as their own and accepted me for who I was. They were my family. I kept my thoughts to myself and just did what they said. She was a pastor's wife. She knew better and was just trying to look out for me. I had to look at it like it was for my own good and protection to help me work through the grieving process. I really did miss them and often wondered if I did the right thing. Was this really what God wanted?

I suppressed my own thoughts and feelings as much as I could and became brainwashed into the thinking and ways of the Shuecraft family. This was my situation, and I had to make the best of it. I just thought it was hard for me because I wasn't raised up this way. I thought that I just had to give myself time to adjust to this new way of life and things would get better.

Her oldest son was dating at the time and already graduated. His prospective fiancé didn't live nearby, and they had a long-distance relationship, so they were on the phone a lot. He was not allowed to talk to her over the phone in private. He had to be on the phone with a cord within earshot of either one of his parents. They called it "supervised courting."

Cassie had a dietician that she consulted and ordered drugs from. She took a lot of vitamins and followed a strict, healthy diet.

She even made her own homemade yogurt. Cassie knew about my eating disorder and put me on the same diet she was on and had me take much of the same vitamins and stuff she was on as well. I weighed one hundred and ten pounds at five feet, five inches tall when I moved in with her. After putting me on this diet, I went down to ninety-eight pounds. When I did eat, I went for sugary junk food. When I lived with the Shuecrafts, I didn't have access to any of that. It was all organic, healthy food.

Clare, Michigan, has a decent-sized Amish population, and Cassie liked to do a lot of her shopping at Amish stores and even got unpasteurized cow milk from an Amish farm. She taught me how to make homemade butter by putting the cream from the milk into a jar with salt and shaking it up until it turned into butter.

When I moved in with them, it was in the middle of my senior year. Cassie homeschooled all of her kids, so she homeschooled me as well. She ordered all of my books, and I got right to work. Cassie was very good at math, which was my weakest subject, and she was very good at helping me with my algebra. Cassie didn't like the public-school system and felt that homeschooling was a safer option for me and her boys because of the worldly influences so prevalent in the public-school system. Cassie worked hard at trying to change my thinking, so she kept me out of the public-school system to isolate me from that.

We also went door knocking once a week. The whole family went door-to-door, inviting people to their church and telling them about Jesus. Jerry and the boys went one way, and I went with Cassie. They were a church plant, so they were trying to grow their church by door knocking. They held Wednesday night services and Sunday morning services in the Clare Elementary School cafeteria where they also had a theatre stage. Jerry set up his pulpit in front of the stage, and we set up chairs in front of that.

Every Sunday morning, we all loaded up in their church bus and went around, picking up the kids for church. Cassie taught Sunday school and had me help her with the kids. We made little snacks for them, and she had me help with all of the crafts.

Door knocking with Cassie, I got to see a lot of poverty and how these poor kids had to live. We went to a trailer park and apartment buildings. Most of the kids that got picked up only came because their parents wanted a free babysitter for a couple of hours. It was sad. Cassie had this box of puppets on the bus, and I helped tell stories with the puppets on the bus and gave them all names to help keep the kids occupied, and we also sang songs.

Door knocking was a brand-new experience for me. I saw how annoyed some people got with us and slammed the door in our faces. It wasn't always pleasant, but I did enjoy it. I felt like I was doing good for God, trying to grow his kingdom. I enjoyed helping out with Sunday school and spending time with all of the kids. The Shuecrafts were teaching me how to be a good Christian and how to grow God's kingdom.

We did Bible studies as a family every night before bed and prayed as a family. Jerry was the spiritual leader of the house. He was the pastor. One of his boys played the piano, so he played the piano for us as we sang and worshipped God every night before bed. He also played the piano for church. We held hands and prayed before every meal. They always sat down and ate as a family. There was a lot about their family and what they did as a family that I loved, but it was still hard getting used to the other stuff.

The Shuecrafts lived on the outskirts of town within the city limits. There was a cemetery right across the street from them. I went for walks through the cemetery and through parts of town, just to familiarize myself with my new surroundings and for a bit of exercise away from Cassie's overbearing watchful eye. Walking through the cemetery got me thinking a lot about death as I strolled through there, reading all of the headstones. I saw quite a few infant grave sites and thought how sad to have died before their lives even began; but how lucky they were to grow up in heaven and not know the pain and suffering this world offered. I wished that were me. I wished I would have died as a baby so I could have been spared this life.

The cemetery was a nice quiet place. I liked walking through there. I even sat up against a tree, reading a book. Cassie took me to the library a lot with her, so I was able to check out some books to read and got into the Beverly Lewis books about the Amish. Since I didn't go to school, I had a lot of time on my hands. I spent a few hours in the morning on my schoolwork and was free the rest of the day.

Spending a lot of time in the cemetery, reading all of the headstones, made me think a lot about death. I tried dying so many times. If I would have succeeded in taking my own life, I would have been lying in the ground, just like all of these people. I often wondered what kind of lives they lived and how they died, especially if they didn't die from old age. Were they Christians? Were they now up in heaven? Did any of these people commit suicide? Walking among the dead was very peaceful, and I wished I was among them for real.

I struggled immensely within my own head. I was a very tortured soul. I put so much blame on myself for what happened with Craig and even used that to blame myself for what happened to me as a small child with Jordan. I wore a mini skirt and a bikini around Craig. That caused him to lust after me. I caused him to stumble, and that's what I deserved. What did I wear as an eight-year-old girl that caused my brother to stumble and lust after me? Did I deserve that too? Was God punishing me? Was I not good enough? Was that why my life had been so hard? I put so much blame and guilt on myself that I couldn't get past it.

Now that I was living with the Shuecrafts, I couldn't go to Cassie and tell her how I was feeling. I internalized everything and tried to deal with things myself. When I was released from the hospital, they had me on antidepressants, and I was mandated to take them along with seeing a psychiatrist in Midland once a month in order to keep getting my script filled.

One night, while everyone was asleep, I snuck downstairs and got my bottle of antidepressants and some water and took them back up to my room. I sat on the floor in between my bed and the wall, away from the door, and took the whole bottle of an almost full-month supply. Then I crawled into bed and went to sleep and hoped that I would never wake up. I would end up in that cemetery across the street and would have no more pain, no more depression, no more sorrow, guilt, or worry. I would be in heaven with Jesus.

I didn't understand why I couldn't run away from my problems. It didn't matter where I lived or who I lived with; my problems were sure to follow. Moving in with a pastor family didn't make my problems go away like I thought it would. I wished I would have stayed with the Joneses. I missed them. They accepted me for who I was. Cassie meant well, but she was molding me into a mini her. I wasn't good enough the way I was. It was so hard living up to her expectations and immediately accepting their way of life when I wasn't raised that way on top of dealing with all of the other stuff.

It was overwhelming. I wasn't used to wearing dresses every day. I wasn't used to wearing my hair a certain way every day. Cassie thought it was disrespectful to have hair hanging down over my face because when people were talking to me, they had to be able to see my eyes.

I woke up in the middle of the night, running to the bathroom and throwing up. I felt so sick, like my insides were going to explode from all of the poison, and I felt so dizzy and lightheaded like I was going to pass out. The pain in my stomach was excruciating. I thought I was going to die. My vision was very blurry when I got up to run to the bathroom. It looked like everything was spinning around me.

After I was done throwing up, I went back to bed. Cassie came knocking on my door a minute later to check on me. She heard me getting sick. I told her that I was fine, and she left. I heard her go downstairs. I thought maybe she was getting something to drink. She came barging back into my room a minute later, asking me where the pills were. I didn't answer her. I knew that I was busted.

"How many of them did you take, Andrea?" she demanded.

I shrugged my shoulders. I didn't count them. I just took them all, hoping that that would do the trick. No, it just made me get sick, and I got busted.

"Where is the bottle?" she barked.

I leaned over the bed and retrieved the bottle from the floor underneath the other side of the bed and handed it to her.

"*You took them all?*" she shrieked.

I stared off in space. I couldn't look at her. I knew she was angry with me, but how could she possibly understand what I was going through? She reacted a whole lot differently now that I was living under her roof. She wasn't as compassionate or understanding this time because I did it under her watch. I somehow betrayed her trust and hurt her feelings. How dare I be depressed and still dwell on the past living with her. I was supposed to be better, and she was going to take the credit for turning my life around for the better.

"Get dressed! You are going to the hospital!" she said.

"I'm not going to the hospital," I said. If I went to the hospital, they would just send me back to that hell, and I wasn't going back there.

"Yes, you are!" she yelled.

"I'll be fine. I don't need to go to the hospital," I begged.

"Andrea Wilber, you took a whole bottle of pills, and it made you sick. You are not fine. You are going to the hospital, whether you like it or not. Jerry will come in here and wrap you up in a sheet and carry you kicking and screaming if he has to. There is nothing immodest about that, but you are going to the hospital, so you might as well just get dressed," she said matter-of-factly.

Cassie left to go get her husband up out of bed. I slowly got out of bed and realized just how dizzy and sick I was. I slipped on a skirt and a shirt. Shortly after that, Cassie was back in my room to check on me. She saw how weak and sick I was and had her husband help me down the stairs and into the car. Cassie woke up her oldest boy and told him what was going on so that he could keep an eye on his younger brothers.

Jerry and Cassie drove me to the hospital and sat with me the entire time while I drank the nasty charcoal to pump my stomach. I was hospitalized again in the psychiatric hospital for another six days. Cassie came to visit me a couple of times. One time, they both came to visit me to tell me that I couldn't live with them anymore. They didn't want to be responsible if anything happened to me, and they couldn't put their boys at risk. I was a bad influence on them, and they couldn't handle it as a family with trying to grow a church. They said that they would help me get a job and my own apartment and that I could still come over for dinner every day and go to church with them, but I just couldn't live under the same roof as them anymore.

I called Betsy while I was there without Cassie knowing. I told Betsy that I was in the hospital again and what I did, but I didn't give her any details on anything else. I didn't want to hear any "I told you sos" when she tried to warn me about how controlling the Shuecrafts were. She was happy to hear from me and begged me to come home and offered to pick me up from the hospital, but I told her I needed to stay in Clare. I had to stay far away from Kingston.

As much as it killed me, I couldn't give into the temptation of going back to Kingston. I couldn't face going back to that school. I had to stay where I was and see it through. Things were going to get better. They had to.

When I got out of the hospital, I went back to the Shuecrafts. They treated me differently after that. Cassie put up a barrier between me and her family. I was no longer welcomed there and could feel that from them, but they had an obligation to help me since they moved me up here to Clare, and I didn't know anyone else there, and they didn't want me going back to the Joneses. That was off the table and not an option. They would rather me have gone back to live with my mother. I know because this discussion came up. They offered to take me back to live with my mother, but I told them that was not an option for me, and taking me back to the Joneses was not an option for them. They wanted to keep me in Clare so that they could still have control over me.

I walked all over town by myself, filling out application after application. I went to just about every business there was, looking for a job, any job to support myself. I still received my child support check, but that wasn't enough to support an apartment, and that was going to stop after I graduated. Cassie even helped me by driving me around different places to fill out applications for a job.

I got called for an interview at a nursing home in Clare. Cassie went to the interview with me. They were going to put me through CNA classes so I could be certified, but I had to work for them for a certain amount of time before I could take my certification elsewhere. They were going to hire me despite the fact that Cassie sat in the interview with me. That was until Cassie asked about the dress code. She asked if I could wear dresses due to religious purposes. Scrubs was the dress code, and that was it. Cassie took right over, and I didn't end up getting that job.

Since the Shuecrafts had connections at the school where they held church services, they were able to help me get a job as a substitute janitor at the Clare Elementary School that would work into full-time. At the same time I got that job, the Shuecrafts helped me find an apartment and paid for the first and last month's rent. It was a very small one-bedroom apartment in an old Victorian style, an orange brick house with a round pillar. There were three apartments in this house altogether. There was an old man that lived in the front downstairs apartment with the round pillar, I lived behind him, and there was a single man that lived in the upstairs apartment who was an art teacher. I never met either of them, but the landlord gave me a brief description of my neighbors for Cassie's peace of mind.

The old Victorian-style house had a large deck on the front that connected my apartment with the old man downstairs. His front door was on the front, and the deck wrapped around the side to my apartment. When you first walked in the door, the small two-person green dining room table with a white table cloth was right there, and to the right was a very tiny living room which was open to a very tiny kitchen with five upper and five lower cabinets, a small gas range, and an apartment-sized refrigerator. If you took a small rectangle and cut it down the middle, the living room and dining room were on one half, and the kitchen was on the other half.

I called that my "Litchen" because the kitchen and living room were together in a small area. There was only room for two small chairs in the living room with an end table in between. The main common area had white beadboard on the bottom half of the walls with a pinkish color wallpaper on the top half with tiny white flowers all over it. The curtains were also pink, the same shade as the wallpaper. Underneath the oak cabinets was white wallpaper with tiny pink flowers all over it, matching the pink wallpaper perfectly. The back door was next to the small single line of cupboards. To the right of that door was a bedroom with more pink wallpaper, and next to that was the bathroom with the same pink wallpaper as well and then the access to the basement. The bedroom and living room had brown carpet, and the kitchen and bathroom had white vinyl lino-leum flooring. The bedroom was bigger than my "litchen" and had a decent-sized walk-in closet.

Cassie helped me get furniture from the lady at the school who helped me get a job as a janitor. She had some old furniture in her basement that she gifted me for free. She gave me a twin size bed, a tan chaise lounge chair that I put in my bedroom, a small green table with two chairs, a brown recliner, and a maroon color rocking chair with a matching ottoman and an end table. She also hooked me up with some old dishes she had in boxes in her basement. She was very generous and didn't charge us anything for it.

Outside my back door, I had a small porch underneath the stairs that went to the upstairs apartment. The back is where every-one parked, and that was the main door that I used.

This was my first apartment and my first real job, and things were starting to look up. I didn't have a license or a car, but I could walk to work. I worked the night shift after school hours and got home around midnight.

I felt lonely most of the time. I was hidden away in this tiny apartment with nothing but my thoughts. I went for walks every day and got lost a few times, trying to find my way around, but I was ultimately alone. I found another cemetery to walk through. I didn't know anyone besides the Shuecrafts. I had minimal groceries such as milk, eggs, bread, cereal, and luncheon meat. Cassie came over every day to bring me over for dinner and to feed my rabbits but then took me home. I was fully dependent on them, and that is exactly where they wanted me.

Cassie also came over before bed and did a walkthrough of my apartment to make sure that I was alone and didn't sneak in any boys. She even looked under the bed, in the closet, and behind the shower curtain and peeked down into the basement. She did that every night as if I couldn't be trusted, given my track record. I worked on my schoolwork, and she helped me with anything I needed help with after dinner before taking me back home or when she came to check on me before bed.

I still had to help her with Sunday school and door knocking, and they picked me up on the church bus on the way to get kids on their route for church.

The Joneses were weighing heavy on my mind, and I missed them. I missed being with them. They were not strict like the Shuecrafts were. They were more easygoing and laid back. I started to feel like a ward of the Shuecrafts with little say over my own life. I was nineteen and an adult and was told what to wear, how to have my hair, what music to listen to, what to eat, when it was time for bed, and who I could associate with. Every aspect of my life was controlled and held under a microscope of Cassie.

One time, she came over to get me to run errands with her. She pulled into the back, and I got in the passenger seat of her car. I was growing out my bangs and had them swept over and pinned on the side. Some of them fell out of my bobby pin and covered my right eye. Cassie ordered me out of her car to fix it before I could get back in and go with her to run errands. It was disrespectful to have hair over my face where people couldn't make full eye contact with me. That is how controlling she was.

I was getting sick of it. I had to break free. When Cassie was making me throw all of my clothes away that didn't meet her approval, she went into the house for something and left me alone out in the garage, and I hurried up and snuck the tightest pair of jeans I owned into the keep pile. I couldn't let go of pants completely, so I saved them and kept them hidden. I put them on out of rebellion and walked up town. It felt so good wearing pants again. I remembered the phone card that Betsy gave to me that I kept hidden away. I walked up to a pay phone a few blocks away, and I called Betsy, crying.

"Hello," said Betsy's voice on the other end.

"Hi, Betsy," I said quietly, my voice cracking.

"Hey, Deedee! How have you been? I haven't heard from you and have been thinking about you!"

"Can you come and get me?" I cried. "I'm ready to come home!"

"Where are you?"

"I walked up to a pay phone. I got my own apartment, but I just want to come back home."

"Of course you can come back home, honey. You know our door is always open. Go back home and start packing, and we will be there in two hours to come and get you. Okay? You are coming home with us today, Deedee! We will be right there as fast as we can, so start packing. I love you!"

I gave her my address and hurried and walked back home and began packing right away. I only lived there a month and never threw away any of the boxes. I brought them all up from the basement and started throwing everything in boxes as fast as I could. I didn't have that much stuff because Cassie made me throw more than half of it away. My adrenaline was pumping, and all I could do was hurry up and disappear before Cassie ever came over to check up on me. I had everything just about packed in an hour and a half.

All of a sudden, there was a knock on the back door. I peeked out my kitchen window, expecting to see the Joneses, but it was Cassie. I got really scared. I panicked. I had boxes everywhere, and I was still wearing my jeans! *Oh no! I'm still wearing jeans!*

She knocked some more, and then I heard her messing with the lock. She had a spare key and was coming in whether I let her in or not. I didn't have time to change back into a skirt really quick. I didn't even know where one was. I opened the door just a crack and poked my head out, trying to hide behind the door so that she didn't see that I was wearing pants—the tightest ones I had at that—that looked like they were painted on.

"What's going on?" she asked.

"Nothing," I said, hoping that she would just go away.

"I came over to take you to do some errands around town. Can I come in?" she asked, pushing the door open, exposing all of the boxes and me wearing jeans!

"What's going on, Andrea?"

"I'm moving," I said meekly.

"Where did you get those jeans?" she scolded.

There was a short pause as she looked me over.

"I'm so done with you?" she shrieked. "I'm so done with you? Really?"

"What?" I said as I looked down at my shirt and realized what she was talking about. I was wearing a brown t-shirt that had Tinkerbell on it that said, "I'm so done with you" on it. *Oh crap!* I did not intentionally wear this shirt for this occasion. I was hoping that I didn't even have to see her before I left. Mix that shirt with the tightest pair of jeans, and that spelled rebellion and was a recipe for extreme offense, and she was furious!

"After all I have done for you, this is how you repay me?" she yelled. "I'm so done with you!" she said angrily as she stormed off and got in her car and left.

I felt terrible for offending her. I didn't mean to wear this shirt specifically for her. It was just a shirt that I threw on. There was no thought behind it. I was grateful for what she did for me and still intended on keeping in touch with her. I just couldn't conform to her world. I wasn't cut out for this way of life. I had so many other things left on my plate. I couldn't deal with the past trauma in my life and try to conform to a totally different lifestyle at the same time. I was going through so much and felt secluded in Clare, away from everyone that actually cared about me.

I wasn't allowed to contact the Joneses after all they had done for me. I loved them. They were my family and they had always looked out for what was best for me without expecting anything in return for them. I was a daughter to them. They were my real family. I was lonely. I felt like the Shuecrafts didn't want me around anymore, but they were stuck with me since they moved me up to Clare. I felt like an obligation to them, like something that needed to be put away and controlled. I was a problem for them, and they had to protect their innocent boys from me. I was more of a project for Cassie, one that she had to change into a meek, weak little girl and brainwashed into submission who couldn't think for herself because she was repro-grammed to think and act like they wanted her to.

Cassie underestimated one thing about me. I was stubborn, and because of the hell I was put through, it gave me the drive and the strength to fight and persevere through any situation. When I wrapped my head around something, there was no talking me out of it, and I was going to see it through. You may suppress my personhood, strip me from my independence, use me, abuse me, control me, and do all manner of things to me—but ultimately, the fighter inside of me will come out and do what is necessary to flee the situation and take back control. You may control me and keep me down for a while, but there will always come a time where I would break the chains that bind me and come out on top, for God is my witness and the restorer of what is good. Enough would eventually be enough, and that is all that it would take.

About thirty minutes after Cassie stormed off angry, the Joneses arrived. Ronald, Betsy, Bella, and Ronnie were in the van, and Raegan and Scott were in another vehicle with their little boy, Tate. They all piled into my tiny apartment and started grabbing boxes and loading them up. I left all of the furniture and dishes behind. I didn't feel like it was right to take them because they didn't belong to me. They belonged with the apartment that Cassie helped me get. I even left the clothes behind that Cassie gave to me. I didn't want to be greedy and tried to leave things on the right terms as best as I could. I didn't mean to disappoint or upset the Shuecrafts, but there was no way of getting around it. I was leaving their controlled environment and going back to the ones they despised the most—the Joneses.

Before coming to get me, Ronald and Betsy got Ronnie and Bella out of school. They were coming to get me as a family, to bring me home where I always belonged and should never have left.

After everything was packed up and ready to go, Betsy had me call Cassie to meet me in town with my rabbits and my cat from her mother's. She told me that she couldn't catch the rabbits or my cat. I would have to come back for them another time and make arrangements to do so. She also told me that I had to meet her in town before I left. She wanted all of the homeschool books back. I was not to receive any credit for it since she bought them. She also wanted the key to my apartment and $400 for next month's rent or she was going to press charges against me. She was basically holding me ransom, and I wasn't allowed to leave unless I met her demands or she was going to call the police.

Betsy had an uncashed check from her second job at the doctor's office with her. We went to the bank for her to cash it to give to Cassie so that she could leave with me.

We met at a strip mall in town. Cassie got out of her car and tried talking me into staying. Ronald got out of the car and stepped in between me and Cassie with his arms up, blocking me from her. She did enough brainwashing. Ronald wasn't going to let her talk me into staying. Ronald was a big guy over six feet with a big belly. Cassie was a small woman, the same size as me. She accused Ronald of pushing her and called the police. She actually ran into him, trying to get to me. Her husband, Jerry, also showed up. He was already at the strip mall, looking at a building to rent for their church to get out of the Clare school. After all this, Cassie was still fighting for me to stay with her. She wasn't ready to give up control over me and especially didn't want me to go back to the Joneses.

Ronald ordered me to get back in the van. He had quite enough of this lady. I was tempted to stay. Cassie was quite persuasive and had a lot of power over me.

The cops showed up, and Cassie gave them this sob story that Ronald pushed her and that the Joneses were kidnapping me and taking me against my will. The cops ordered me out of the van to talk to me. They separated me away from both the Joneses and the Shuecrafts and wouldn't let me look at any of them while they questioned me. They asked me how old I was. I was nineteen. They also asked me who I wanted to leave with. A part of me wanted to stay and try and make things work with the Shuecrafts and try and build a life in Clare, but that was Cassie talking. She had a way with words and made me feel guilty for leaving after all they had done for me. I owed them to stay.

I also wanted to go back home. I wanted to leave with the Joneses. I told the officer that I wanted to go with the Joneses. They asked me about my relationship with the Joneses and how I knew them. They also asked me about my relationship with the Shuecrafts. They were trying to get a feel for the situation to make sure that I wasn't getting coerced to go with the Joneses and being taken against my will.

They ran everyone's names and found out that there was a Ronald Jones in Ionia county who had a warrant out for his arrest, but that Ronald Jones didn't match the description of this Ronald Jones. It was a different person.

The police also viewed the security footage of the strip mall and saw that Ronald did not push Cassie. All he did was step in between us with his arms up, and she ran into his belly.

The cops told me that the Shuecrafts seemed like very nice people. They were a pastor family that took me in and tried to help me and paid for me to get an apartment. They also knew about me getting hospitalized and trying to commit suicide. They knew that I had issues and they spoke highly of the Shuecrafts for taking me in and trying to help me. I knew they wanted me to stay in Clare with them, but I was nineteen. I was an adult, and ultimately, it was my decision. I wanted to go back with the Joneses.

They let me go as soon as we paid the Shuecrafts four hundred dollars for the next month's rent, even though I wasn't going to live there. She also wanted the school books, but they were packed away and buried.

We made arrangements the following month to meet in town in Clare. She got her school books back, and I got my cat, Sweetie, and my two rabbits, Montob and Montel, back. We had a police officer there for the trade-off to make sure everything went okay and that she didn't try to pull something like she did last time, trying to get Ronald in trouble, saying that he pushed her.

When I got home, back to the Joneses, I got a better look at Montob and Montel. They were skin and bones. They were practically starved to death. They didn't bother to feed them. It was not like they had to buy food for them. There was a big tote left full of their pellets, and with the way the Shuecrafts ate, there was plenty of veggie scraps that they could have fed them. No, they left the poor rabbits to starve to death, and they eventually both died, even after getting them back and trying to feed them to fatten them back up. One died a week later, and the other one eventually died soon after that. I felt so bad that they had to suffer like that.

Being a pastor family, I thought that they would have had some compassion for God's creatures and at least feed and water them every day until I was able to retrieve them. I wanted to get them last time before I moved out of Clare, but they wouldn't give them to me then, and I had to leave them and come back for them. Had I known that this would be their demise, I would have demanded that they give me my rabbits back then and have a cop go with me to get them.

Sweetie was healthy for the most part, other than being a long-haired cat that was strictly an indoor cat becoming an outdoor cat, and her hair was severely matted. She wasn't the same after that. I couldn't keep her in the house because she kept wanting to go outside, and I had to shave her down on one side of her body because of the matting, and her personality changed. She was no longer a sweet cat. She became mean to the point where I couldn't even pick her up anymore. She eventually got hit by a car and died because the Joneses lived on a busy road, and we couldn't keep her in the house anymore because she was used to being outside all the time. I found her dead on the side of the road.

Betsy went with me as I scooped her up and I bawled. It was wintertime, so we couldn't bury her. I'm an animal lover, and losing a pet was always so hard on me. Growing up, I lost a few cats, and each time they died, I bawled my eyes out. Betsy helped me double bag her in garbage bags and let me stick her in her upright freezer. I was going to take her to a taxidermist and have her stuffed because she was a very pretty cat, but it was way too expensive, so she stayed in the freezer.

I had another cat named Artheaus. She was a really pretty grey and white tuxedo cat with striking yellow eyes. Having Artheaus made it a little less painful losing Sweetie.

Because I moved to Clare in the middle of my senior year and became homeschooled but was not allowed to receive any credit for it, I couldn't graduate with my class on time. I would have had to repeat my senior year. I didn't want to be a senior at twenty years old. I had to go to an alternative school in Caro for adults and busted my butt and did a full year's work of school in just three months so that I could graduate on time. The school was called Goal. There was a classroom full of adults at different levels of education, and we all had our own work to do, and there was a teacher there to help us with anything we needed help with. We had to be there all day, just like any other school, but we all had to bring our own lunches.

I didn't bother making friends. I went there and worked as hard and as fast as I could to complete my work so that I could graduate in the year that I was supposed to: the year 2007. I did not receive my GED. I received an actual high school diploma but under the Caro school district, not Kingston. I didn't care. I was not going to be a high school dropout like my older sister, like my mother, and like my younger brother. If I wanted to get anywhere in life, I had to have a high school diploma.

There was a small graduation ceremony for the six Goal kids who graduated that year, and my mom, older sister, two younger brothers, my sister's two girls and, of course, all of the Joneses were there to celebrate with me.

That year, I was in the delivery room with Bella when she gave birth to her baby girl Kiara. Watching a child come into the world was the most beautiful thing. Raegan had her baby girl, Alannah, around the same time, so there was a lot of cute baby girl loving to go around. When the girls were just a couple of months old, I did a photo shoot for them. I dressed them in different cute dresses and used different blankets and stuffed animals to pose with them and got a lot of cute pictures.

It was a pretty busy summer of 2007. I stood up for Bella in her wedding that summer and wore a big puffy green dress, and we had our graduation open house with a Luau theme on July 7, 2007, complete with coconut bras, grass skirts, and a mural that I painted with palm trees on a beach for people to get their pictures taken in front of it with different photo props.

Things went back to the way things were before I moved to Clare. I was back to being a part of the family as if I never left. I was only in Clare for three months altogether and never had any more contact with the Shuecrafts. I tried calling Cassie a couple different times after that to let her know how I was doing. I still wanted to be her friend, but she wanted no further contact with me, which was probably for the best.

That was my brush with a cult. I didn't even know that I was in a cult until I got out of it. There are certain signs that identify a cult, and they met a lot of that criteria. The big one was isolating me from people that loved and cared about me. That was how they controlled me. They knew that if I kept in contact with the Joneses, the Joneses would question their authority and get me to think for myself, and then they would no longer have control over me. They opposed critical thinking.

Another sign of a cult is strict rules, such as a dress code. Cassie made me throw most of my clothes away and made me wear long flowing dresses to conform to their way of life. I had to look like them. They stripped me of my own identity. They were extremely controlling and controlled what I ate, what time I went to bed, how I wore my hair, what I wore, what I could or could not draw, what possessions I could or could not have, what music I could listen to, who I could or could not talk to, no freedom of association, or anything. They controlled every aspect of my life and manipulated me in every way possible to conform to their lifestyle. They isolated me so that I was completely dependent upon them. I was at their mercy.

They helped me get a job and an apartment and paid for it to manipulate me into feeling obligated and grateful to them, to bind me to them. They were doing me a favor, so I owed them. They wouldn't let me go to a public school and homeschooled me instead so that they could better control who I had contact with and so that they could isolate me in such a way to where I only had them to turn to. I couldn't make any friends, and I would be left completely helpless with no resources and at their mercy.

There were so many signs that I was in a cult, and Betsy tried to warn me and tell me that they were a cult, but I didn't believe her. I wouldn't listen. I had to find out for myself. Cassie was a very nice person. She was a pastor's wife. She was just looking out for me. She used her status as a pastor's wife to justify her authority and demand respect. When I lived with the Joneses, and Cassie was coming over to do Bible studies with me, she gained my trust and got me to tell her things. She used my trauma with Craig to justify her morals and beliefs to me, such as why women had to be protected, why they had to wear long dresses, and why there had to be supervised courting. She had a biblical reason for everything, and she twisted Scripture in such a way to justify her moral code.

She was very manipulative with her words and spoke in such a way that I thought she knew what was best. She was just looking out for me and trying to protect me, and she was helping me become more godly so that I wouldn't have to go through trauma again. She twisted everything to get me to listen to her and to trap me into her way of thinking. That is how she had control.

I didn't know that I was in a cult until I was freed from it and looked back at all the signs and red flags. It started out subtle and grew in intensity. Once I moved in with them, they knew they had me, and that is when they laid down the law. They alienated me from the Joneses, and I often thought that I couldn't go back to them because I thought they would be mad at me for leaving and not listening to them. I didn't think I had any options and thought I was stuck in Clare. I didn't have a car or a license, and I depended on Cassie for everything.

They were a true definition of a cult, and I am forever grateful to the Joneses for not giving up on me and for opening up their home to me again and providing me a way out of yet another bad situation.

15

More Bad Decisions

After I graduated, I had to start thinking about becoming an adult and finding a job to support myself and move out on my own. Raegan's husband, Scott, was a manager at the Hungry Howies in Caro. I got a job and worked there for a while. I didn't like working there at all and found out that the fast-food industry was not for me. I still didn't have a license, so I always had to have a ride there. I either rode with Scott or I had Bella's husband, Christian, take me. Depending on a ride all the time did not make me feel very good, and I felt like a mooching loser.

I thought about going to college to become a mortician and live on campus, but the only school that offered a mortuary science degree in the state of Michigan was Wayne State. I did not feel comfortable living in Detroit away from everything and everyone that I knew. I remembered how I felt living in Clare, isolated from everyone that cared about me, and I didn't want to go through that again. I couldn't think of anything else that I wanted to do or go to school for. College would just be another place that I had to be driven to, and I already had a hard-enough time trying to find a ride back and forth to work.

Tom was the Joneses oldest son that they "adopted" as their own. His wife, Emily, and her sister, Stephanie, both worked at an AFC home in Cass City. They got me an interview there, and I got the job. I quit Hungry Howies and started working there right away. I loved working there. It was more my style. I took care of people with developmental and physical handicaps. It was a small environment in a house with eight residents, and there were always two people on staff. I had to go through a bunch of training through Community Mental Health to get certified in things like CPR, first aid, HIPPA, and things like that. I also had to get certified in passing meds.

I really enjoyed working there. I loved taking care of the people, I loved the staff there, and I loved my boss and the owner of the company. They treated us good, and everyone was nice. There was also another house a block away owned by the same company that was also an AFC home, and the two houses got together for special events. There was also a house in Caro and an apartment building with four apartments in it that were AFC homes that were owned by the same company.

Eventually, I got to work at all four different places. I didn't work too many shifts at the house in Caro. I only filled in for them a few times, and it wasn't my favorite house. The original house I started working at was my favorite house. The residents were amazing, and they all had fun personalities. One lady loved to sing nursery rhymes, but when she was mad, she would get an angry look on her face and call you a snake in the grass. I loved her. Another lady who wore a helmet and was prone to seizures loved to work on puzzles, and she had the sweetest demeanor. She worked on hard puzzles that were over five hundred to a thousand pieces. She loved having staff sit with her and help her work on them.

There was this one guy there. He was my favorite. He couldn't talk and was confined to a wheelchair, but he could say *baby* and *yeah*. He was the sweetest guy ever and was happy-go-lucky. He loved to blow kisses and was a big ladies' man and a flirt. I loved my job and couldn't be happier working there. I made friends with all of the staff. I couldn't have asked for a more perfect place to work for.

Emily and Stephanie made sure that I got to work, and if neither of them could take me, then Raegan or Bella's husband, Christian, was happy to take me, and I paid them gas money. They were all so willing to help me get on my feet and give me the boost I needed to become more independent and self-sufficient.

There was this guy that worked there that really caught my attention. His name was David. He was a year older than me, and he was about my height and really skinny. He was half-Mexican. His dad was born in Mexico and was brought to the States illegally by his mother, but they eventually got their citizenship. David's dad married a white woman, and they had three boys together.

David had a small Chinese symbol tattoo on each wrist. He also had a snakebite piercing on his lips. He kept his jet-black hair pretty short and always wore his clothes just a little bit baggy. You could tell that he had bad acne as a kid because of the scarring all over his face, and his big brown eyes looked too big for his head. His eyes looked like they were always bugging out of his head, and he had a small head with a big nose. He was a bit nerdy-looking with a very distinct lisp when he talked.

He wasn't the most attractive looking guy, but that is not what attracted me to him. It was his nice guy personality that caught my attention. He was amazing at his job and so good with the residents. I caught myself staring at him and watching his interactions with the residents, and I fell in love with how he was with them. He was so kind, so patient, so gentle, and attentive. He was better with them than I was, and I loved my people. If he was so good with the residents, then imagine how good he would be with kids? He would be very good dad material.

I started working a lot of afternoon shifts with him, and we began to get to know each other. He still lived with his parents and older brother in Caro next to the elementary school in town. He didn't have his driver's license either and had his dad take him to and from work.

The wheels started spinning in my head. I couldn't afford an apartment on just my income, but maybe if the two of us got an apartment together, then we could both stop living with people, grow up, and get a place of our own. He seemed like a nice enough guy. We could become roommates—nothing sexual and not dating—just roommates helping each other out with bills.

I was hanging out at Stephanie's house. She also lived in Caro in town. I was alone, and David came over. The power was out for some reason, and we were just sitting on the living room floor with a candle, just talking, and he leaned toward me and kissed me on the lips. My face turned red. I was really shy and really liked him. He asked me out, and I said yes. So we began dating.

I moved out of the Joneses and moved into Stephanie's basement. Her basement was a typical unfinished basement with cinder-block walls and a concrete floor.

Our friend, Tami, who also worked with us, broke up with her boyfriend and needed a place to stay, so she also moved into the basement. She set up in the main part of the basement, and I set up in the boiler room. I swept and cleaned the basement as best as I could and had a mattress on the floor that I slept on. Tami had an air mattress on the floor. She had her little Pomeranian named Roxy with her, and I had my cat, Artheus, that I kept in the basement.

Neither one of us stayed there for very long, and I got an apartment with David in town right across from the police station. They were all single-story apartments that connected together, and they were pretty decent. We lived in the very front one. It was a brown building with green shutters and some shrubs around the front. We shared a one-bedroom.

When you first walked in, you walked into the living room which was open to the dining room straight back, and the kitchen was directly in front of the door, which had two entrances, one being to the dining room. To the left was a hallway that led to the bedroom on the left, the bathroom on the right, and a furnace and pantry room at the end. It was a small apartment, but it was in really good shape and very clean. The landlord was a really nice guy and hung up all of our pictures for us. He didn't want a bunch of holes in the wall, so we told him what pictures we wanted hung up, and he measured them and made sure they were level and hung every one of them up for us and even supplied the nails.

I got my poor dead cat out of Betsy's freezer and buried her underneath a bush in the front yard of my new apartment.

I transferred homes and started working at the apartments in Caro so that I could walk to and from work and not have to depend on a ride. I walked everywhere. Since we lived in town, everything was easily accessible. The apartments were a lot more challenging to work in because it was more behavioral, and the residents weren't as cute and sweet.

As time went on, I began to see a different side of David, one that I despised. He was a pothead and a partier and started bringing his friends over to our apartment, getting high and drunk off their butts and being loud late into the night when I had to be to work by seven in the morning. I blew up on everyone one time and demanded everyone to leave and kicked everyone out of my apartment and got into an argument with David. I was not into the party scene at all. I had to work the next morning and was sick of it. I didn't like any of his friends. They were all losers. None of them had jobs, and they were all on welfare, smoked pot, drank, played cards and video games all the time.

One time, I got into a big fight with David because he spent all of his money on pot and alcohol instead of helping me with bills. I kicked him out of the apartment and locked him out. He came back hours later, drunk, pounding on the door, demanding me to let him in. I was on the phone with the Sandefurs, telling them what he was doing. They begged me to call the police on him, but I didn't. I had to let them go when David managed to crawl through a window. He tackled me and pinned me down, sitting on top of me, holding my arms above my head. He acted like he was going to hit me, but he didn't. He let me go, and I ordered him to leave and go sleep at his parents' house for the night. They were only three blocks away.

He did leave, but not before he tried to smooth things over and make up with me. I wasn't having it. You don't make a redhead that mad and expect to butter up right away. It doesn't work that way.

David soon just up and quit his job. He was scheduled to work a midnight shift, but instead, he sat in the bedroom on the floor, Indian style, meditating, and ignored work when they called and asked where he was. I had to call work and tell them he wasn't coming in. He was a no call, no show. When I tried to reason with him, he ignored me and just kept meditating. He was into Buddha and yoga and meditation. He was a very weird and strange individual.

To make more money to help pay for bills, I got a side job with Stephanie. Stephanie also worked as a stripper, and she was talking to me about how much money she was making. I wasn't too sure about it. I wouldn't feel comfortable making a living that way. I didn't feel confident in myself to be able to take my clothes off for money.

After I graduated, I started gaining weight. I got tired of starving myself, so I didn't feel like I had the body to be a stripper and never thought I was very pretty, so I didn't have that going for me either. I wasn't a dancer. I didn't know how to dance.

She told me about what the other girls looked like. Some were a little chunky and had butter faces, and they still made money. She tried to convince me that I would do well. Men just cared about seeing boobs. It was no déjà vu. It was just a small hole in the wall with one stage and one pole, and since they served alcohol there, it wasn't full nude. It was just topless. I told her no the first time she asked me, but then I talked to David about it, and he talked me into it because we needed the extra money. He wanted me to do it. He was okay with his girlfriend being a stripper.

So I bought some sexy underwear and lingerie and these really high-heeled white boots that screamed stripper, and I went to work one night with Stephanie. It was about a forty-five-minute drive away. I was extremely nervous and didn't quite know what to expect or what exactly I had to do.

My first impression of the place was that it looked like a dump. It was very dark and dingy on the inside. The dressing room wasn't that big. It was off to the side by the bar, and the bathrooms were on the other side of the bar. They were disgusting, and there were dirty needles in the trash can and all over the floor. The girls there were also high on coke. I guess they would have to numb themselves somehow to be able to do this kind of work. The roof leaked in some spots as well.

The main way the bar made money was by the customers buying the girls drinks. We had to accept drinks if a customer offered to buy one for us. When it wasn't our turn to dance, we either had to be at the bar with the male customers or out on the floor doing lap dances.

I was very nervous my first time up on stage. The dancing part wasn't as hard as I thought it was going to be. I watched what the other girls did and just followed suit. I had a very innocent look to me. I didn't look like any of the other girls that had been doing this for a while. I was literally fresh meat.

I felt very dirty as a stripper. I felt like a piece of garbage. I felt like I was victimizing myself. I had to do what I always did to get through something. I made my mind go blank, blocked it out, and just went through the motions and tried not to think.

I was not a drinker. I didn't like the taste of alcohol, but I did drink if guys bought them for me. I mainly just drank shots because they were smaller, and I could slam them down easier than a big glass of something. The alcohol did work as far as numbing me to get me through the night.

Lap dances were the hardest part. It was more physical, and the guys that came in were mainly dirty old men. I got fingered a couple of times during a lap dance. I knew what I was doing was wrong and hated every minute of it. The voice inside of me told me to get far away from that place and never come back.

I did make money doing it, but no amount of money was ever worth what I had to put myself through to get it. I felt like I was victimizing myself by subjecting myself to it. I had stooped to an all-new low.

I went with Stephanie a few more times on the weekend, but then I quit. I couldn't do it anymore. I felt embarrassed and terrible for ever even considering it as an option. I felt unbelievably dirty, like the vilest of sinners. I'd rather be homeless and starving than to ever have to do that for a living.

My sister, Jennifer, popped in unannounced one time to visit. She had the kids with her. The girls had to use the bathroom, so I took them down the hall to show them where the bathroom was. My purse was sitting next to the couch on the floor. A few minutes later, she asked me if I would go to Rite Aid with her. I had to print off some pictures anyway, so I went. When I went to pay for my pictures, I had no money. I just got paid, and my four hundred dollar rent payment was due, and my money was gone. Jennifer said she had the money to cover my pictures, so she paid for them for me. I knew it was Jennifer that took the money. She was a known thief and a liar and couldn't be trusted.

I asked her about it, and she denied it. She blamed it on David and asked me if he would have taken it out of my purse.

I knew she must have taken it when I showed the girls where the bathroom was. They were just a diversion.

I never got that money back, and I had to call my landlord and explain to him what had happened. He was a very nice guy and very understanding and wasn't mad. He just asked that I would pay it back when I could by just adding extra onto the rent until it was caught up. It wasn't easy, and I was already living paycheck to paycheck, as it was, and David wasn't helping at all. He would borrow my money to buy drugs so that he could sell the drugs to make a profit, but he just smoked it instead. He was the worst drug dealer ever.

David tried to get me to smoke on multiple occasions, but I wouldn't touch it. Not only did he smoke marijuana and drink alcohol, but he also took mushrooms and other drugs. I don't know what all he did because I never hung out with him and his friends. I worked my butt off and picked up extra shifts while he went out and partied all the time. I was no fun because I would never touch drugs or drink with him.

I was getting to the point where I couldn't do it anymore. I had to give up the apartment. I couldn't afford it on my income alone.

David talked me into moving in with his parents. His parents' house was very run-down and not the cleanest. It was in such bad shape that there was a hole in the bathroom floor from being rotted, and the kitchen floor was very wavy. The whole house was very cluttered, especially the living room, and they didn't own a vacuum.

David's dad sat around watching TV most of the time. He was a nice enough guy and was always nice to me, but his mom annoyed me. She was a little slow and very clingy and always wanted to talk to me, but I just couldn't handle her most of the time. She was always asking me for money and wanting me to go to the dollar store with her. She also kept bugging me for grandkids and kept telling me to put on slow music and how to be romantic with her son. She tried to talk about sex with me, but I always cut her off. It wasn't any of her business and not very appropriate.

There was no sex with her son, and there never was. He was impotent, and that's all I'm going to say about that. We were never intimate and lived more like roommates, even though we shared the same bed. David never even tried to have sex with me because he knew that he couldn't perform. There was something medically wrong with him, but he was too embarrassed to go and get it checked out. I was perfectly fine with that arrangement and never pressed the issue.

I stayed with him and put up with his family because I didn't have anywhere else to go. I started visiting an older lady that used to go to the Kingston Wesleyan church. Her name was Kathy. She was a heavy-set lady and the sweetest soul. She was so willing to help anyone in need. She worked as a social worker for DHS. She also sponsored me to go to church camp as a teen one time. I started walking to her house after work every once in a while. She didn't live too far from where I worked.

I started to tell her my situation with David, and she insisted that I move in with her. She only had a two-bedroom house, and her brother lived with her, but I could stay in her basement.

I broke up with David and took her up on her offer. I was with David for about two years. I didn't tell him where I was going. I waited until he was gone with friends, packed up all of my stuff into Kathy's car, leaving so much behind, and I left.

Her basement was very dark and cluttered. It smelled like a basement. She had a couch down there with a pullout bed, and that's what I slept on. I knew this wasn't a permanent arrangement. This was just temporary until I figured something else out. She was just trying to help me get out of a bad relationship.

David only found out where I was staying because he went to my work and waited for me to get out and then followed me to her house. He kept stalking me, showing up at my work and following me home, begging me to come back to him.

Stupid me, I gave in and went back to him for a short time.

I eventually got sick of him and called Raegan up to ask if I could move in with her. Raegan lived far enough out of town where David couldn't easily get to me. He didn't have a license, so he wouldn't be able to bother me anymore. I had to break free from him. He was only holding me back. He was a loser that was never going to amount to anything. There was no future with him. I had to get away from him. I had to get out of town.

Raegan lived in a very small house. She had two kids, so each of them had a room, and their rooms were really tiny. Every room in the house was small. She didn't even have a full-sized couch in the living room. She just had a loveseat and one of those round papasan chairs. There wasn't any room for me in the house, but she had a pop-up camper that I could stay in.

16

The Pop-Up

When I moved into the pop-up camper, David had his mom and dad drive him out to Raegan's to talk to me. His parents stayed in the car while he barged into the pop-up like he owned the place. He begged me to come back with him. He literally begged. He got on his hands and knees and begged me to stay with him. He didn't want to lose me. He promised to change. He told me that I was good for him. He wouldn't be able to find anyone else to put up with him like I did.

I heard the same speech from him a few times before. It was so pathetic, and I was embarrassed for him. It got even more pathetic when he got out this ring and proposed to me. I will never forget what this ring looked like. It had the biggest rock that I have ever seen, and it was green. At least he got my favorite color right. He took it out of its package and put it on my finger and asked me to marry him. I was really shocked. No one had ever proposed to me before, and he was a bit unconventional.

"No," I said, "I will not marry you" as I put the ring up to my mouth and tasted it. *Hmm. Green apple. It tastes good at least*, I thought to myself.

"You are a loser, David! A candy ring? Really? Who proposes with a candy ring? You are so pathetic. Get out of here and leave me alone! You can't even keep a job. All you want to do is hang out with your friends and play video games and live with your mommy and daddy. Just get out of here! Grow up! You are embarrassing yourself!"

He stood up with a bewildered look on his face like he lost his best friend.

"Please?" he begged.

"Pease, what? I said no. Leave!"

"This ring is only temporary. It's all I can afford right now. I'll buy you a new ring, any one you want. You can pick it out! Marry me!" he begged.

"I don't want anything from you, David. Just get out of here. You're making this harder than it has to be."

David turned and walked out of the pop-up. I stood in the doorway, watching him. He went over to the passenger side window to his mom and told her that I said no. She handed him something, and he walked back toward me and got back down on his knees and held out a different ring, this time nonedible. I recognized that ring. His mom showed me that ring a few times. It was her own wedding ring.

I just rolled my eyes at him. He was so pathetic and desperate to hold on to me. No girl would date him because of his problems, and all his friends had girlfriends, and he would have no one. They already thought for the longest time that he was gay.

Raegan came walking up to see if everything was okay. I told her that he refused to leave and that he was trying to propose to me.

David got up and took my hand that he put the lollipop ring on and bit my big green rock off, and then he turned around and left.

"Hey!" I hollered. "You ate my ring!"

David never bothered me after that, and I never did get to enjoy the lollipop ring that he gave me. I liked green apples.

Raegan couldn't understand why I ever dated him. He was a loser, pathetic, and not even good-looking. I guess I didn't understand it either. I was desperate to have an adequate place to live and knew that I couldn't afford an apartment on my own. He didn't have his own place either. He seemed like a nice enough guy, and I thought it would help us both out. I wasted about two years of my life with that loser and basically supported him the entire time.

The pop-up camper was not in the greatest of shape. I moved in there in the summer, so it wasn't so bad at first. I cleaned it out thoroughly to make it somewhat livable. I chose to sleep in a bed next to the table. It was easier to climb into bed on this side because of the bench seats. The outside canvas that wrapped under the bed was ripped, but I always just made sure it was tucked underneath the bed good. The mosquitos were bad, and there was always a ton of them that came in, especially through that hole, and Raegan's house was surrounded by woods.

Mosquitos were the least of my worries when it started to get cold out, and I was still living in the pop-up. I had to do something. I couldn't keep living like this. Nobody at work knew how I lived aside from Emily and Stephanie because they picked me up most of the time. I was basically homeless without a plan. I had to do something. I needed to find someone to help take care of me. That was the only way I saw to survive in this world. It took two incomes to make it in this world. I couldn't do it by myself. It was at that moment that I realized why my mom thought she had to have a man to help support her, especially with five kids. Going it alone was frightening, and your odds of making it were that much better with someone there to help you through.

I started going on dating sites and creating a dating profile. I didn't get out much because I had no license, so I couldn't go out to meet new people. This was the only way that I knew of to meet prospective dates. This was also a way of getting around my social awkwardness and getting to know someone online without doing it face-to-face. I could hide behind a screen and behind texts. I was so desperate to get out of my situation. I was willing to do anything to get out of it, even jumping headfirst into another bad situation which seemed like a pretty typical move for me anymore. I always jumped into another bad situation just to get out of another bad situation.

This guy from the Bronx in New York City started messaging me, and we exchanged phone numbers and started talking to each other over the phone. He wanted me to move to New York with him. He offered to fly me out for a weekend to meet first. He worked as a construction worker and had his own place. He was Italian and had that mafia sounding accent. He wasn't some pitiful loser like David was. He was a real man and had a lot going for himself.

Because of where I was at and not having the greatest cell phone service, especially being a prepaid cell phone, I had to walk up and down the road to get reception in order to talk to him. We talked to each other for weeks. We both really wanted kids, and he told me that he would have me preggers within a month.

I knew deep down inside that this was all wrong and a very bad idea, but I didn't care. I was desperate. I had to get out of this pop-up. It was about to be full-blown winter in Michigan, and I had to do something. I couldn't stay here. I was already getting really cold at night and had nowhere to go. There was no way that I was going back to my mother. If this guy turned into an ax-murdering pimp, I was still better off. I always wanted to live in the big city anyway.

I didn't have to have a driver's license living in the big city. I could take the subway, a taxi, or a bus. There were many different modes of transportation. I could basically be independent and not have to rely on anyone for a ride to work. There were many things that appealed to me about moving to New York. The main thing was getting the heck out of here and starting over away from my family. New York was far enough away to run from all my problems.

The conversations sort of died off, and he wasn't serious about sending me plane tickets to come out to meet him. So I had to move on to the next guy. Talking to the guy in New York actually got me to seek out other guys that lived in a different state. I needed a change of scenery and needed far away from here. None of them really panned out, and I kept finding myself back to square one.

Everyone that I talked to was all about sex. I always had this fantasy of saving myself for marriage and finding a great Christian man, but it didn't seem like a very realistic reality anymore. If I wanted to get out of this pop-up, I had to let go of that. That was some fairy-tale dream that you only saw in movies. I had to let go of that and do what I had to do to survive. This was about actual survival now, and when you get to that point of being in survival mode, you have to do things that you don't want to do in order to survive.

Men were all about sex and they wouldn't be with a girl who wouldn't give them that, not in today's society. Waiting until marriage was old-fashioned and didn't happen anymore.

I was shocked to get a message from a guy that was just a mile down the road. He came over that very same night that he messaged me. I didn't want to have sex with him, but I was desperate and wanted out of that pop-up and wanted him to like me so that he could help me get out of the situation that I was in. I felt super uncomfortable and hated doing this. I knew that it was wrong and that it was a sin, and I was terrified of getting pregnant by him. I didn't know anything about this guy, and he was very scruffy-looking with a beard and was fourteen years older than me. What did I get myself into? I instantly regretted my decision but forced myself to go through with it because I didn't see any other way out. I was backed into a corner and a victim of circumstance.

This guy's name was Devlin. I soon found out just how wicked this man was and how closely he resembled the devil himself. He was a predator, and I was his wounded prey, an easy target, desperate and deeply broken.

*****

This was the beginning of a very long relationship with Devlin. He was much older than me by fourteen years. I was twenty-two when I first met him that fateful night. Everything that I had ever been through thus far in my life with Jordan, Clayton, Craig, the Shuecrafts, my mother, being hospitalized multiple times, all of the depression and anxiety which lead to an eating disorder, self-harmful behavior, suicide attempts, the alienation and rejection I felt by my own family—all of the hell that I have laid out for you in my story thus far was a cakewalk. It was nothing compared to the hell that this guy, Devlin Lane Edwards, put me through. Nothing! I shouldn't have even made it out alive. He should have killed me. He almost did. God must have had *big* plans for me, though, because it was only by the grace of God that I'm alive to tell my story today.

That first night after meeting Devlin, and he was getting ready to leave, he staked his claim on me right off the bat.

"You're mine now, right?" he said.

"Do you want me to be?" I asked, not knowing where this was actually headed. I was a smart girl and picked up on things, but I was also naive and dumb. I knew what I was doing, and there were so many red flags, and I had such an uneasy feeling about this guy. He smelled of danger and warning labels. He was a bad boy, and I knew it. He made every hair on my body stand up. I knew there was something off about him, but I didn't understand it at the time.

Since I was desperate, I turned off the fire alarm and ignored the smoke signals. Nobody knows exactly to what lengths they would go when they reach the point of desperation where you are willing to do just about anything.

Imagine being on the *Titanic* when it was sinking. You either drowned with the ship or you jumped into shark-infested waters, hoping that someone somewhere would hear your faint whistle blowing and pull you to safety. Getting eaten by a shark was a grave possibility, but it was a risk worth taking because doing nothing was not an option. Doing nothing was a sure way of drowning. I couldn't just do nothing.

After that night, I saw more of Devlin. He took my phone and deleted all of my dating profiles eventually. At first, he just made sure that I was inactive and didn't respond to anyone else, and if he did think I was online, he made sure to ask me about it. He kept his dating profiles just to keep an eye on me to make sure I didn't talk to anyone else. That was the first sign of him being controlling. I belonged to him and him alone. He took possession of me.

I tried to remain willfully ignorant when it came to Devlin. I had this idea of what I wanted in a relationship and put the blinders on to any red flags. I didn't want to see that he was bad for me. I didn't want to see the signs that told me to run away from the very beginning. I wanted out of this pop-up, so I had to make this work.

You see? There is something you have to understand about me, something I didn't recognize myself for the longest time. I didn't love myself nor respect myself. I never have. Other people in my life hurt me, yes, but I put myself through hell. I hurt myself. It was me that told myself that I was ugly. It was me that hated everything about my looks, my hair, my complexion, my glasses, my body. I always told myself that I was fat, so I starved myself down to nothing. I always told myself that I was never good enough. I wasn't worthy of my mother's love.

Jordan had more worth than I did, even after what he did, so I must be pretty bad. I put so much blame upon my own shoulders. It was my fault that my family was messed up. It was my fault that Jordan did what he did. It was my fault that Clayton went to prison. It was my fault that my mother had to choose between two of her kids. I hated myself so much that I put myself through hell. I cut myself and caused myself so much pain and misery. I was hateful and bitter. I never stood up for myself. I blamed myself for Craig. Everything was always my fault. I was my own worst enemy. I didn't love myself enough to want to live. I didn't deserve the very breath in my lungs. I was my own worst critic. I never had my best interest at heart, which was why I made some of the decisions I did.

I wasn't interested in boys because I never thought I was good enough for anyone. I never thought any boy would be interested in me because of my looks, and I was damaged goods.

So the first boy that paid any interest in me I went for because I never thought that I could do any better. I didn't expect any better because I didn't feel worthy enough to demand any better because I never thought that I could do any better. This was the best it was going to get for me. I had low expectations in men because I had low expectations for myself. I had low expectations for my living arrangements because I never thought I deserved better. This is why I put myself through so much and why I went through so much hell. I never valued myself enough to be valued and respected and loved by anyone. I didn't expect any better, so I didn't get any better.

I put up walls and barriers around myself and didn't truly let anyone in. I thought I did that for my own protection so that I wouldn't get hurt, but it was because I didn't deserve that close human connection. I was poisoned. I poisoned my own family. Every relationship I had was poison because it was me that was the poison.

So when you as the reader ask why I didn't do this or why I didn't do that, why I stayed and put up with so much, that is why! Because I didn't love myself enough and because I never thought that I could do any better. That's why. I settled for what I thought I deserved. That's why I fell for Craig and David, and this is why I fell for Mr. Devlin Lane Edwards, the spawn of Satan himself, and that is no exaggeration. Devlin was the very definition of evil and was wicked right down to the very core of his being. It took years to realize the full capacity of what he was capable of. It started out okay at first until his horns started poking through. By that time, it was too late, and I was eyeball-deep, staring at the Devil right in the face.

Devlin lived with his mom and dad and little brother. We will call his mom Rita and his dad Bob. His little brother's name was Josiah. Rita and Bob had an older daughter named Libby. She was the oldest. They adopted three sisters from foster care. That is where little brother Josiah came from. One of the sisters who had him couldn't take care of him, so Bob and Rita took him in and adopted him and raised him up. He was about eight at the time when I met him.

They lived in a really nice two-story home on a Christmas tree farm with about forty acres of woods behind their Christmas trees. They were only about two miles down the same road as the Joneses. Rita was a township treasurer. I don't remember where Bob was retired from, but they made a pretty decent living and lived comfortably.

Ironically enough, Rita was actually a member of the Kingston Wesleyan Church. Once I found out that I actually knew of his mom, it kind of settled all of the uneasy feelings I had for Devlin and made me relax a little. It gave me a false sense of security about this guy. He can't be too bad if his mom was Rita. She belonged to the church I grew to love.

Devlin was just a little rough around the edges. He smoked cigarettes and pot and occasionally drank alcohol. He even smoked pot driving down the road with me in a truck. I always hated it when he smoked. He had a sleeve of tattoos up both arms and some on his back and chest. One of his tattoos was that of a scorpion, and some were lizards. His nickname was Lizard, given to him by his friends.

We'll get into his friends and the kind of people he associated with later.

He had a pretty scruffy-looking beard and dark brown hair with the bluest eyes. He was about five foot seven and a hundred and forty pounds and wore glasses. He wasn't terrible looking for a scruffy guy. He was a little charming in a bad boy sort of way.

Devlin loved to listen to rock and roll such as Kid Rock, Janis Joplin, AC/DC among others. He always kept a big CD case full of rock and roll in his small green S10 pickup truck. He loved his music, and he was always jamming to it. The way he played the air drums on his steering wheel and sang along with his not so great singing voice as he was driving was actually pretty sexy. He knew how to make me laugh. He dedicated a song to me called "Blue Jeans and a Rosary" by Kid Rock. I was his "good" church girl, and he was my "bad boy." As time went on, I actually grew quite fond of him and fell in love with him. He was the very first man that I actually fell in love with.

My future looked bright. I was going to marry this man. I was finally going to have the family I always wanted. He came from a very good family, and I got to know his mom pretty well. She would have made a great mother-in-law.

Although I was with Devlin, he didn't whisk me out of the pop-up right away. I spent the entire winter in that pop-up, and it was brutal. It was amazing that I didn't freeze to death. I had this tiny little space heater that I sat on the table facing the bed. I was literally two feet away from it, and it barely put off any heat. I couldn't sleep most nights because of how cold I was.

The hole in the canvas was right by my head, and the cold wind always managed to rip through there. That was also the way my cat Artheaus came in and out of the pop-up.

I wore long johns, pants, four shirts, a hooded sweatshirt, four pairs of socks with thermal socks, my winter jacket with my hood from my sweatshirt tied tightly on my head, and my hood from my coat on as well. I even wore gloves and had like ten heavy thick blankets. I slept like that every night and was still freezing so cold that the chattering of my teeth and constant shivering of my entire body kept me awake. January and February are the coldest months and the most brutal. I basically slept in a glorified tent all through a cold snowy Michigan winter. My life couldn't get much worse than this… or so I thought.

This was what it was like for the homeless in the wintertime. This was torture and brutal and frigid cold. I remember that winter perfectly. We received a lot of snow that year. Some winters in Michigan can be mild with not as much snow and not many nights of subzero temperatures. That winter was especially cold that year.

I don't really think that Raegan and Scott really knew just how bad it was for me because I didn't complain too much. I knew that was the best that they could offer me since there was no room in the house. They did me a favor by allowing me to stay in their pop-up when I had no place else to go.

Sometimes, when I couldn't stand it any longer because I was so cold, I went in the house and slept on their loveseat. I didn't like to do that because I didn't want to be a bother. I didn't want to be in the way. I couldn't stoop much lower than this. This was as bad as it could possibly get. I felt like such a loser. How did I get to this point? As if I didn't beat myself up enough already, this made me feel even worse about myself, and the only way I knew how to fix it was to get into bed with the Devil.

17

The Big Secret

I'm going to be transparent here because I have told a lot of lies about this particular revelation that I am about to reveal next. I haven't told the truth about how this all came out, and I want to clear it all up here. I was talking to a friend recently about this subject, and she made me realize all of the lies surrounding this big secret which had a serious negative effect on this whole situation. Well, the truth shall set you free, so here it goes.

After a few weeks, things started to get more serious with Devlin. Devlin had a big secret to tell me about himself before we wasted too much of each other's time. He knew that it would be better for him if he told me up front than if I found out about it later on my own, and I respected him for that. It was pretty brave of him to come out with such a big secret like this, knowing that there was a possibility that I would turn and walk away from this relationship after he told me. It could have been a big deal breaker for me, and it should have been. But let me tell you again that I was naive, dumb, and desperate to be with someone because of the circumstances in which I found myself. I ignored the smoke signals and threw every form of reasoning out the window and had a death grip on getting out of the pop-up and having a boyfriend that would take care of me, no matter who he was or what he did.

There was that initial moment of shock after he told me this big kept secret, and at first, my head was telling me to run far away from this guy. He was dangerous. He was bad news. He had a criminal record. He wasn't worth it. I would sacrifice so many of the things I wanted out of life if I stayed with him. I wouldn't be able to adopt or do foster care or anything like that. Not with him; not with his secret. If we ever had kids together, would they be allowed to have friends over because of what he was?

At the time, I was living in the moment, day to day. I couldn't let myself think that far ahead. You can have dreams all you want, but that doesn't mean that it will be a reality. Remember when I said I was *willfully* ignorant?

Here was this guy that liked me. If I stayed with him, then he would help me rise above this situation. You have to remember, I was living in a pop-up that was in poor condition, no heat, in the winter in Michigan, no driver's license, and I was at the lowest point in my life that I could possibly get. Also, I thought very little of myself and didn't think I could do much better. He liked me, so I guess at the time that was the main qualifier of staying in a relationship with him in spite of this "secret" because who else would want me? I didn't give myself very many options at the time. I saw this as my one and only choice, so I had to make the best of it. I had to believe him. I had to make a pact with the Devil.

Devlin picked me up one day in his truck. He told me that he had something to tell me. So many things ran through my mind on what he possibly had to tell me. Was he unable to have kids? He was fourteen years older than me which made him thirty-six at the time, and he didn't have any kids himself. Was that it? That would be a disappointment because I really wanted kids. Did he have some kind of terminal illness? Okay, I could deal with that.

Was he actually adopted? His mom was so prim and proper, and he was, well, not. Bob was not his real dad. He seemed like he was the odd one in his family, so that would have made sense. Devlin wore Rock band t-shirts and stained jeans. He had tattoos all over and he smoked. He was the only one in his family like that. He didn't fit in. His little brother was adopted, and he had three adopted sisters. So maybe that was his secret. No, that wasn't it. He was Rita's real son.

So was he some kind of criminal? Did he do time for something? Was it drugs? DUI? Robbery? People do stupid things when they are young. I'm not that unforgiving. I could handle that as long as that is who he was in the past and he was a changed man now.

I had so many things running through my mind as to what his secret could possibly be. I never imagined it to be what it actually was. It was worse than I thought. I could have handled all of the other things I mentioned. This one was a little too close to home. I only wished it was any other secret but this. I knew that this would make things a little more difficult, not only for me but for him. Would the Joneses accept him? Would my family? This is why there were so many lies around this issue. I had to lie to protect him and had to lie to protect myself.

Mainly, I lied *to* myself. I had to suppress any reasonable thought process and believe the lie he fed me because I had to believe that he was as innocent as he claimed he was. I had to believe that he was innocent because if he wasn't, then what did that say about me? How could me, of all people, after all that I have been through, fall for someone like him of all people? If he really wasn't innocent, then that put me in the same category as my mother with the choices she made. I could *not* admit to that. I was deeply offended. I'm not my mother. I'm nothing like her.

So I lied. I lied to myself, mainly, and allowed myself to believe the lie he fed me so that I didn't have to admit that I was somehow just like my mother. I hated my mother and judged her for what she did and what kind of person she was and for the choices she made. There was no way that I could be like her. I'm not a hypocrite. That is the main reason why I lied. I lied about him telling me this secret because I chose to stay with him even after he told me. I made myself believe a lie because I wanted him to be innocent. He had to be innocent in order to ease my own conscience.

I also lied because I was afraid of what others would think. They would try and talk me out of this relationship because of what he was, and then I would have to start all over again finding someone else. I already invested a few weeks into this relationship. Not only that, but I was already sleeping with him, which had me even more invested because I basically sold myself out, knowing that he wouldn't have anything to do with me unless I had sex with him and needed him to like me because I wanted out of this pop-up. So if I broke up with him over this, regardless of if I believed he was innocent or not, then who knows how much longer I would have to live like this?

There were so many reasons why I lied, even though none of them was a good enough excuse. I should have been honest with myself and with the Joneses and with Reagan. I should have told them as soon as I found out because if I had then, he would have been out of my life for sure, and I would have been much better off, even if I had to live in that pop-up for another winter. Anything was better than the hell this man put me through.

Devlin texted me and told me that he was on his way to get me. When he pulled into the driveway a few minutes later, I walked out of the pop-up and got into his truck.

He sat back in his seat for a minute and just stared down at his lap. There was something on his mind that he needed to get off his chest. I just didn't know what. Was he breaking up with me? If only I had been so lucky.

"We need to talk," he said.

Uh-oh! This doesn't sound good. "About what?" I asked.

He sat forward, looked out the windshield, took a deep breath, shifted his truck in reverse, and backed out of the driveway.

I knew how I was when there was something difficult that I had to say and couldn't form the words, so I didn't press him. I sat there, patiently waiting for him to speak.

He drove all the way to Caro and pulled into Walmart without saying anything. It was a twenty-minute drive of silence. That's why my mind was going a mile a minute, driving me crazy, trying to figure out exactly what it was that he wanted to talk about.

He parked way out, more by the gas station at Walmart, and turned the truck off and sat back slowly.

"What's the matter?" I asked.

"I really like you and I'm falling for you…hard. I've never met anyone like you before. You are way too good for me, and I don't deserve you," he said.

There was a long pause of silence, and I just sat back and stared down, not looking at him, waiting for him to finish what he had to say.

"There is something you need to know about me," he continued, "and it's been really bothering me because I don't know how you will take it, and I'd rather you hear it from me."

"Okay."

"If you don't want anything to do with me after this, I completely understand and will take you back home, and we can go our separate ways, and I won't bother you ever again."

This is starting to sound really bad, and I was nervous.

"I spent ten months in the Georgia state prison."

Oh yeah, this was bad. This guy was a criminal. Just my luck. I just couldn't catch a break.

"What did you do?" I asked.

"I met this girl online from Georgia. We talked back and forth for months. We even talked over the phone. She told me that she was eighteen years old. We sent nude pictures back and forth. I sent her a cell phone and paid for the minutes on it because she didn't have the money, and I wanted to be able to talk to her. As soon as she graduated, I was going to pay for her to take a bus up to Michigan, and we were going to get married. We got really serious. She wanted to come up here and go to school to be a nurse. I had a really good job, making good money as a crane operator, and it came with a house. Everything was all set for her to come to Michigan.

"I loved this girl. It turned out that she wasn't eighteen. She was actually fifteen and lied to me. Her mom got a hold of the phone I sent her and saw all of the nude pictures we sent back and forth and called the police. I got arrested and was extradited down to Georgia. I had the book thrown at me and had a piece of shit attorney. That little witch ruined my life with her lies.

"When I was released on good behavior, I came back to Michigan but wasn't allowed to get out unless I had some place to stay. I lost my house and my job when all of this happened. So my mom had to come down to Georgia to sign a bunch of paperwork and vouch for me. I had to move in with my mom because I had to register as a sex offender and needed a permanent address. So now I'm on probation and I have to take these group sex offender classes once a week. It's hard for me to find a real job because I have a felony, so I'm working under the table for my friend, remodeling his house down in Warren, but I'm tied up here in Caro once a week because of these classes and going to see my PO.

"I'm innocent. That girl told me that she was eighteen. She was very developed in her pictures. She looked like she was twenty-five. My mom can vouch for me. She will tell you that I'm innocent. She went to court with me and heard all of the evidence. I would never hurt a child. That girl lied to her mom to get herself out of trouble when she got caught and she lied to me.

"So now because of all of her lies, I'm in all of this trouble. I can't be around little kids unsupervised. I can't live by a school or a playground. I have all of these rules that I have to go by. I never met that girl in person. It was all over the phone, but because we were sexting back and forth and she was a minor, I got slammed. I just wanted to be honest and up front and let you know what was going on because I wanted you to hear it from me and not find out about it on your own. I will completely understand if you don't want to see me again. I really like you. You are beautiful. I've never been with a redhead before, and I would like to see where this goes."

Whoa! That was a lot to take in. *So he is a sex offender? Oh man! What did I get myself into?* My mind was racing, and I couldn't say anything. We just sat there in silence for a few minutes after he revealed all of this to me. I didn't know what to think. I was just taking it all in and trying to process it. If I walked away from this, then where did that leave me? I really needed this. His story sounded pretty convincing to me. That did happen. I'd heard of a lot of cases like this where the girl lied to get out of trouble or lies just to get the guy in trouble.

"Say something," he said, breaking the silence.

"My uncle is going through the same thing right now. He's my mom's younger brother. He was dating this woman with a teenage daughter and teenage son. They even had a little girl together. He caught the teenage girl smoking pot in her room, and he tried to take

222

it away from her and threatened to tell her mom. She claimed that he raped her. So now he is currently in prison, doing six years for it. He had his own auto mechanic business and everything, and he lost everything. So I know that does happen," I said.

"So do you believe me?" he asked.

"Yes," I said, nodding my head.

Devlin let out a deep sigh, and he looked at me and smiled. "Do you still want to see where this goes between us?" he asked.

I nodded my head yes before I could even give myself time to think this through and think about what this actually meant, what I would be giving up, what it would do to my reputation when people found out that I was dating a sex offender. People would think that I was sick for being with him. But if he was innocent, then why shouldn't he deserve to be happy with someone? Why should that girl's lies cost him a happy relationship. He was already paying for it by having to be on the registry and being a felon, which comes with all sorts of challenges. It was not fair for him to not have a girlfriend because of this.

I threw all proper reasoning out the window. I didn't even consider the possibility that he was lying. I didn't allow myself to think too much into it. I grabbed onto his story that he was innocent and ran with it. I needed a boyfriend. I needed this to work. I needed help rising out of my situation. I wanted out of this stupid pop-up. He would have to take care of me because who else would put up with him and his criminal history? I, at least, needed help getting back on my feet and out of this pop-up. Then, if things didn't work out, we could go our separate ways. I was going to use him to get what I needed.

Devlin grabbed my hand and squeezed. "You make me so happy," he said, bringing my hand up to his mouth and kissing my hand. "I don't deserve you! How did I get so lucky? And you were only a mile down the road!"

Devlin took me right to his parents' house. He sat me at the table with his mom, and his mom went over everything with me and reiterated everything that Devlin told me but in much greater detail. She was even more convinced of her son's innocence. I really thought that he was a nice guy that just got a bad rap. I believed he was innocent. His own mother, who was a member of the church I loved, had me convinced that he was innocent, but now I think that Devlin had us both fooled. What mother would want to believe that her son could be capable of such heinous crimes?

Right after that, Devlin was as sweet as can be to me. He treated me like a queen and worshipped the ground I walked on. He spent so much time with me. He swept me off my feet. He made me feel special. He kept telling me how beautiful I was. He made me feel good about myself, and in return, I gave him what he needed as a man. I gave him my trust and overlooked his criminal history. I believed his story and stuck by him in spite of everything. Just like the snake in the garden of Eden, he charmed me into his lies. He roped me in and had me right where he wanted me, an innocent girl who had been through so much already, a wounded bird trapped in a net of crafty deception. I was easy, vulnerable, gullible prey so desperate to get out of her current situation I leapt onto the back of a dangerous crocodile to get away from the seaweed that threatened to pull me down.

18

Vagabond

I believe Devlin's mom, Rita, told Devlin once he started to bring me around that he better tell me about him being on the registry before I found out on my own. I think that is why she really jumped into the whole story of innocence when he brought me over and sat me at the table. His mom was very convincing.

I told Raegan that Devlin was in trouble with the law one time because he was on probation but never told her for what. She asked me if it had anything to do with murder or rape or any sexual crime, and I told her no. We had been dating awhile when they found him on the sex offender registry, and they were mad because I lied. They had two small children at the time, one being a little girl. I never thought those kids were in danger because I was convinced that he was innocent, and I saw him around his little brother and his nieces and nephews. He was good with kids. Also, I never left him alone with the kids. I was not going to justify having him around. I was blind and willfully ignorant and desperate. I knew that they wouldn't approve, which was why I never told them. I completely understand why it was wrong, regardless of the state of mind I was in, and I don't blame them for being angry.

Raegan and Scott were pretty upset, and they had to protect their kids. When they sat me down to tell me that he was on the registry, they were pretty upset that I already knew. They just thought he lied to me about why he was in trouble. They didn't know that I knew, and when they found out that I knew about it, they were very angry. I tried to tell them his story that he told me and what his mom said and how convincing they were, but I don't think they believed it. They had a bad vibe from him from the start.

A couple of months later, Stephanie came and got me to hang out with her at her house, and I got a text from Raegan, telling me that all of my stuff was outside in the snow and that I needed to come and get it. They were sick of the lies surrounding Devlin and didn't want him around, so they kicked me out of the popup.

Devlin was very upset that they found out and about their reaction to it. That is when his horns started poking through, and I saw the evil side of him.

Scott was the one that was packing up a lot of my stuff. He was getting my stuff out of the bathroom, and he mistakenly put Raegan's hair straightener in my stuff. Both of our hair straighteners looked a lot alike. A couple of weeks later, Raegan was texting me and asking me about it. She accused me of stealing her straightener. They had all of my stuff packed up and outside. I never went inside to retrieve anything, so how could I have taken it? I had my own. Everything was already packed up and waiting for me outside. She threatened to get a hold of Devlin's PO and get him in trouble if I didn't return it. It was not a very pretty situation, and a lot of ugly things were said on both sides. We did return the straightener and put it in her mailbox.

Devlin was angry. That is when I found out about his gang friends. He told me that his Scorpion friends were nobody to mess with and that he would have them up here and they would kill their whole family, including all of the Joneses and all of the kids. They would wipe out their whole family and leave no witnesses if anything ever happened to him. Whoever was responsible for putting him back in jail would pay with their life, and the Scorpions would take care of him. He was fuming.

That was the first time I ever saw him really angry. His face turned beet red, his eyes and lips were pierced tightly together, his knuckles turned white, and he was breathing out of his nose like a bull ready to charge. That was the first time I became pretty terrified of him, but I just thought that he was angry because of Raegan threatening to call his PO. He was afraid of getting into more trouble and was already in enough trouble, and Raegan was making threats against him to get me to return her dumb straightener that she thought I stole. Little did she know just how dangerous making such threats were. Her whole family could have been wiped out. I had to convince Devlin to let this go. He was ready to retaliate and make promises out of his threats.

When I got kicked out of the pop-up, Devlin helped me get all of my stuff out of the front yard and the snow. It was dark outside when I went to get it. I had nowhere to go. I had to quit my job. I thought living in the pop-up was as low as it got. Now I was officially homeless.

This part of my life is a little hazy because I bounced around so much. I became a vagabond, bouncing around from one couch to the next. I had no choice but to return to my family. I stayed with my youngest brother, Theo, down in McComb for a few months. That is when I got my CNA license, but I had to be driven back and forth to class which put a heavy strain on my brother and his girlfriend at the time because my classes were all the way in Sandusky, Michigan.

Devlin paid them rent for me to stay there for a few months since I didn't have any income. When things no longer worked out there, I stayed with my other brother, Joshua, and his girlfriend and two kids at the time in Marlette. He was living in an income-based apartment, but shortly after that, they rented a house two blocks away.

Joshua's girlfriend, Ashley, was a royal piece of work. She tried to act like my mother and tell me what to do. I had to be home at a certain time. I had to tell her where I was going and spent less and less time there, even though I kept all of my stuff there. I had the whole upstairs, and they liked to use my room as their marijuana smoking room because it was away from the kids. Devlin still paid her rent for me to be there, even though I hardly stayed there. I was with Devlin most of the time. Ashley and I almost got into a fistfight in her front yard one time, and I had to restrain myself and walk away because I was trying to get my life together, and she was a cop caller. I didn't want to get an assault charge and ruin my chances of ever getting a job in the medical field.

I went back to my mother. She was my last resort, and I had nowhere else to go. She and Dwayne were renting a tiny one-bedroom house on an old dirt road in Deford, Michigan. It was heated with a woodstove that was in the one and only bedroom. The living room was open to the kitchen. There was no dining room, so they had a small table in the middle of the kitchen. It was a very tiny house. I had no job and was sleeping on the couch at my mother's. Of course, Jordan came over often, and so did all of their friends who came over to smoke pot. They even smoked it in front of me sometimes.

That house ended up getting condemned because the sewer was leaking into the creek out back and was an environmental hazard. The health department had to come out to give them a notice to vacate the property.

They found a little one-bedroom house in Cass City on the outskirts of town that they rented. It was a cute little house with a cute fenced-in backyard. I stayed there for a little while and slept on the couch. I walked all over Cass City, putting in application after application, trying to find a job. My stepsister, Molly, worked at the nursing home in Cass City. I had my CNA license, so I tried to apply there. In the application, it asked if I had any family members that worked there and wanted to be truthful, so I listed her.

Molly got really angry about it and yelled at me for putting her down. She had a good thing going there and she knew nothing about my work ethic, but I was not going to make her look bad. Her place of work was off-limits to me. I really needed a job so that I could get on my feet, and she ruined a potentially good thing for me. I kept calling on my application in spite of her blowing up at me, but I could never get the job there. I never listed her as one of my references. I didn't expect her to help me get that job. I didn't want anything from her. I was being truthful on a job application so that it didn't come up later that she was my stepsister and I didn't divulge that information. I was trying to better myself so that I could get out of this hole that I was in, and I didn't want anything to mess that up.

Neither one of my stepsisters really cared for me. I didn't fit into the family. They thought I was a Goody Two-shoes because I didn't smoke or drink and party with them. They thought I was too good for them. Plus, I believe not having anything to do with Jordan had a lot to do with it as well.

Every day I walked all over town, putting in applications or checking on applications. I was determined to find a job—any job. I didn't care what it was. I needed something to help me get out of this hole. It got discouraging at times, but I didn't have a choice but to keep pressing on. Giving up meant I wouldn't get out of my mother's house. I would forever be a loser sleeping on my mother's couch. That wasn't an option for me. Giving up was not an option.

I went to my old employer at the AFC home that I used to work at in Cass City and practically begged for my job back. My boss hired me back, but I had to work at the other home in Cass City which was right next to the nursing home that my stepsister, Molly, worked in. There were only part-time hours available, and I had to work the night shift, but it was better than nothing.

I was finally starting to generate some money and was one step closer to getting back on my feet. I only saw Devlin on the weekends. He came up Friday to see his PO and then went back down state Sunday night. He worked for a friend, remodeling his house in a ritzy community.

When Devlin came up, we always had a hard time finding a place to be alone. Neither one of us had our own place, so he had to get creative. Sometimes he would make me have sex behind the shed outside at night. Sometimes he would take me to a dirt road and pull over.

His family owned a small rock cabin not too far from his parents' house on a dirt road. It used to be his Uncle Garth's house, but when he passed away, it was willed to his mother.

I actually remember going to this house as a kid. My mom and Dwayne were friends with Garth. Garth had a bunch of cats, and his yard wasn't kept up very well. I got a pure white kitten with the bluest eyes from him. I named her Yemen. I only had her for three years, and she passed away. I found her stiff and dead on the floor in front of the bathroom when I got home from school. I believe that she was poisoned because Dwayne never liked her. She was always attacking his feet while he was sitting at the kitchen table. When he was bouncing his leg up and down under the table, she would sneak up behind him and wrap herself around his ankle and bite and then take off running when he hollered at her. It was funny, but he hated her. She would even attack anyone's feet that came into my room. She was strictly my cat.

I loved that cat. She was so beautiful, white as snow with gorgeous sky-blue eyes. She was healthy and only three years old. I have always believed that Dwayne did something to her. I was devastated when I found her dead. I scooped her up and took her to my bed and curled up in bed with her, holding her tight and bawling my eyes out until my mother came in to take her away so that they could bury her.

I've lost so many cats growing up, and each time was heartbreaking. One got hit by a school bus. One broke his back because he got outside and went across the field and a cow kicked him. When I was coming home from school, he was dragging himself up the porch, and I saw him. He was missing the night before, and I was sad that I couldn't find him. His name was Precious. That poor cat dragged himself home. He couldn't walk on his back legs. He was purring and snuggled me as I held him, crying. Dwayne had to shoot him. It was the day my mom took us to Teen Ranch to visit Jordan because he waited until we all left to shoot him so that he could bury him before we got back home.

So not only did I have to deal with the tragedy of seeing my beloved cat like that, but I had to go to Teen Ranch to visit Jordan, which was traumatic enough, knowing that Dwayne was home, shooting my cat, and he wouldn't be there when I got back.

Devlin's family cabin was a small two-story rock cabin with an outhouse. The only running water there was at the kitchen sink. When you first walked in, there was the dining room and the kitchen. The stairs were right to the left next to the door. The end of the stairs butted right up to the wall, so you had to step over the side of them to go up or down. There was one big bedroom upstairs with four different beds of different sizes. When you walk through the dining room and kitchen, the small living room was on the left.

Rita and Bob cleaned up the cabin and got rid of all of the junk in the yard. Bob and Devlin shot all of the cats. There was also an old barn in the back and a nice-sized pond. Devlin liked to take me on the paddle boat on the pond. They also had a fenced-in garden. They planted a bunch of veggies in the summer between Rita and his sister, Libby, and they did a lot of canning. I helped work that garden with them. They also had family get-togethers there at the cabin during the summer, and Bob used it as a hunting cabin during hunting season because behind the pond, there was woods.

It was a nice little cabin that got utilized a lot throughout the year. It was very secluded. The only house around there was an abandoned house just a little way down the road within sight of the little rock cabin. Devlin made me go to that abandoned house with him to tear scrap out of there for money. The yard was full of junk that we took in for scrap.

Devlin took me to the cabin a lot to spend the night with him. A lot of things happened at that cabin that I will get into a little bit later.

19

Devlin and Devil Are One in the Same

Devlin helped me get an apartment in Cass City. He paid for my first and last month's rent. The apartment building was on the other side of the nursing home, so I didn't have far to walk. When there wasn't a bunch of snow, I just cut through the nursing home parking lot and walked up the hill to work. That job eventually did move into full-time. It didn't pay that much above minimum wage, so it was really hard trying to pay bills, but Devlin did help me with that. He stayed there with me most of the time, even though he wasn't supposed to because he was registered at his mom's.

I worked there for maybe six months until I found another job that paid just a little bit more money. I started working at an assisted living facility just a half mile down the road from my apartment, so I was able to walk to and from work. That was my all-time favorite place to work. I loved working there. I became really good friends with a Christian lady in her fifties named Colleen. We worked well together, and I confided in her about things. We talked a lot about my relationship with Devlin, which was unhealthy and abusive.

My apartment was upstairs, and it was a two-bedroom, one bath. My living room was pretty spacious, and I had a balcony. I was so thrilled to finally have my own place and a job that I loved.

I was looking through a newspaper one day and found an ad for some free kittens. Devlin took me to this horse barn, and inside a cage in the middle of the barn floor was a tiny longhaired orange kitten. It was love at first sight. Devlin took me to get everything we needed for him and a few toys to spoil him with. We ended up naming him Clyde.

Just like any kitten, Clyde was very playful and full of entertainment. What made him unique was that he liked to play fetch like a dog. Having Clyde around really helped me get through the times where I was lonely and depressed and hurting. He was a comfort to me and put a smile on my face when I needed it. He slept with me and was right there beside me when I needed him.

My relationship slowly progressed with Devlin into something I couldn't climb out of. He became extremely controlling. He controlled my bank account, my social media, and who I could associate with. When I first opened up a Facebook account, I wasn't allowed to post any pictures of myself or post anything personal because he used my Facebook account. He wasn't allowed to have any social media accounts of his own due to the terms of his probation.

He called me constantly, especially if he knew that I was with friends. If I went to the store with friends, I had to take a picture of who I was with and where I was at. I tried to go to a church in Cass City one time, and he ordered me to take a picture of myself inside the church to prove that I was there. That was just embarrassing. Who takes a selfie in the middle of church? I never went back to church after that. I didn't want to be subjected to the embarrassment that he caused me while I was there.

I stopped hanging out with my friends. Every time I had friends over, he would call me a million times. At first, I spent my breaks with Colleen at work, and then I had to call him all the time on my breaks, and if I didn't take my break around the same time because I was busy with work, he would flip out on me. He isolated me from everyone. I had to devote my time solely to him.

Devlin had tried to teach me how to drive, if you call screaming at me the entire time a good teaching method. He tried to make me drive with only one hand on the steering wheel and screamed at me every time I did something wrong, which led to more mistakes. It always ended up in a huge argument. He made me extremely nervous and on edge so that it was hard to relax and learn how to do something that was already nerve-racking enough. When he had enough, he made me get out so that he could take over and tell me that I would never get my driver's license.

Every time I made an appointment to do my driver's test, he would make the night before a living hell so that I couldn't concentrate, and I would either fail the test or just cancel. I even paid for private driving lessons because I couldn't take Devlin trying to teach me screaming at me the entire time. The guy came right to my apartment, supplied the car and everything. I was trying so hard to get my life together and knew that I needed a driver's license in order to be more independent. I loved my job, but what if something happened and I had to get another job or move? I couldn't always depend on being able to walk to work.

Cass City was just a small town. I couldn't depend on rides to take me grocery shopping or anything like that. I had to have a driver's license. It was essential to live in a rural community. Devlin made it so hard and frustrating, and I became scared of driving, so I gave up on trying to get my driver's license. I hated driving and still do because he had always made it a stressful experience full of yelling, belittling, and arguing. I think he did that on purpose so that I would never get a driver's license. That would make me more dependent on him so that he could control me better.

One time, Devlin got this German Shepherd puppy, and he made me babysit it overnight at my apartment. I wasn't allowed to have dogs there, and the puppy was not potty-trained. I kept it in the bathroom so that it was easier to clean up any messes. That dog cried and howled all night long, keeping me awake, and I had a driver's test the very next morning and failed. I was so exhausted from hearing that dog cry all night. I couldn't concentrate. Devlin slept peacefully at his mom's, of course. When I complained to him about the dog crying all night, he was very unapologetic.

When I first met Devlin, he worked off the books for a friend of his who went by the name of Kid. He did odd jobs such as remodeling a house or house-sitting and even some mechanical work on semis. His rich friend, Kid, who was remodeling his house, bought another house on the dirt side of Eight Mile. Devlin told me that Kid planned on flipping this house for a profit. It was an estate sale and needed a lot of work. He took me there one time to see this house. It was a beautiful older house with so much potential. There was a large greenhouse and tree nursery business behind it not associated with this house. It wasn't long after he bought that house that he turned it into a place where he started growing a massive amount of marijuana complete with hydroponics and grow lights.

It was Devlin's job to babysit that house and take care of the plants. He showed me pictures of the operation and the stages of growth. It was a massive operation, and the whole downstairs of this house was a pot nursery with different hybrids and breeds. Every time Devlin came home, he reeked of marijuana. He even supplied my mom and stepdad with marijuana and smoked with them.

My mom and Dwayne both really liked Devlin, in spite of him being on the registry. They knew about his criminal record but didn't care. Devlin seemed like a nice enough guy to them, and he had good weed. The three of them would all smoke in front of me, knowing that it bothered me. I would have to get up and walk away.

My mom kept asking me when I was going to give her grand-children. Every time I saw her or talked to her over the phone, she would ask me that. She didn't care who I had them with as long as I gave her some, which was odd because all of my teen years, I remember her telling me over and over again that she hoped I would never have children. She told me that because of how strict I was with my nieces and made them mind and because I made comments about how I wouldn't let my kids believe in Santa Claus due to religious purposes and because of the unique names I picked out for them. I had Christian values and morals and discipline that I would make my kids abide by, and she didn't like that.

She was never joking when she told me that. She was quite serious. Apparently, her parenting method was better; you know, the kind where you turn a blind eye to your daughters getting molested and then telling her that back in the old days, incest was normal, so get over it. Yeah, her parenting skills were great.

Devlin treated me a lot differently when other people were around, especially around his mother. He was the perfect son and perfect boyfriend around his mother. He had everyone fooled about who he really was. Behind closed doors, he was controlling and verbally, physically, and sexually abusive especially.

Devlin made my life a living hell. He was addicted to porn. Not just normal porn, but sadistic, snuff, BDSM, torture porn that he made me act out with him. He even watched porn in front of me and watched it while having sex. He has choked me on a number of occasions, almost to the point of passing out, slapped me around, pulled my hair, and used electric shock toys on me. It was always about him and fulfilling his own sick fantasies. He had me terrified of him. He was a very dangerous man that took pleasure in making me suffer. He would find any reason at all to punish me just so that he could justify performing these abusive sexual acts on me. The things he did would make Christian Grey from *Fifty Shades of Grey* blush.

The things he did to me are so unimaginable that I can't bring myself to repeat them. He could have very well destroyed my chances of ever bearing my own children because of the horrific things he put me through.

Devlin was affiliated with the Scorpion Biker Gang out of Detroit. He loved to threaten me with them to force me into submission. He told me about how he used to have a drug-running operation with them across state lines and about how they have killed people. The Scorpions were a brotherhood, and they took care of their own. Nobody messed with them.

Before I got my apartment, he became an over the road truck driver for his friend. He had to get permission from his PO since he was crossing state lines. He took me on the road with him, delivering hay down to Arkansas and Texas. I had to help him tarp the loads, and he screamed at me if I wasn't doing something right. I thought it would be somewhat enjoyable going over the road with him, just because I wanted to see new places because I never traveled anywhere except to Erie, Pennsylvania. No. He made me help him tarp his loads, which was not an easy task, and screamed at me the entire time to the point where I told him to do it himself and sat in the cab of his truck. When he became frustrated because something wasn't going his way, he became a raging tyrant, and if I was there, I was his verbal punching bag. I learned to stay away from him if he was working on a vehicle in his mom's garage.

When we got down to Arkansas, we had lunch with his ex-wife, Melanie, and her husband. We even stayed the night at his ex-wife's house which was very odd to me. Melanie took me out to get my nails done with her to have some girl bonding time. She told me that she was happy that Devlin found himself a new girl and was glad that I made him happy. She also said that she and Devlin were better off as friends. They never got along when they were married. She confirmed Devlin's innocence and said that he got screwed over royally by that girl. She was married to Devlin for a number of years, and he wouldn't hurt a fly. Devlin told me that they got divorced because Melanie would never have sex with him, and all she did was lie around all day.

We delivered a load of hay to a farm in Texarkana. They had cows, goats, pigs, chickens, and a lot of lizards running around. Some of their pigs were pregnant and due any day. They were a very hospitable family and served us dinner while we were there.

At a truck stop in Louisiana, I stayed in the truck while Devlin ran inside. I saw a few women walking around to all of the semis, soliciting the men. One woman was actually invited into the cab. A woman who looked to be in her thirties, dressed very provocatively with smeared makeup on her face, approached our truck, but Devlin wasn't around. She wanted to know if me and my man wanted to have a good time.

"No, thank you," I said.

Later, I found out that those types of prostitutes that hung around truck stops are called Lot Lizards, and that particular truck stop was always heavily worked. I wondered if Devlin ever had a Lot Lizard and if that was the reason why his friends called him Lizard.

On our way back to Michigan, we stopped in Anderson, Indiana, to stay with the Sandefurs for a night. The Sandefurs moved to Indiana shortly after I graduated to pastor at a different church. Devlin sure did put on a show for them and was as nice as can be. I was thrilled to be able to see them. I missed the days where I spent every Wednesday before church at their house and Sunday mornings, sitting next to Regina in the pew. While I was there, I was thinking how nice it would be if Devlin just left me there with the Sandefurs. I hated him, and he made the entire trip miserable.

Even though Devlin was on the road a lot, he still had control over me. He had to come home on the weekends due to probation.

A police officer showed up at my door, looking for Devlin. They were checking up on him and trying to see if I would say that he was staying there because he wasn't allowed to stay the night at my apartment since he was registered at his mom's; therefore, he had to sleep at his mom's. I had to lie and say he never stayed there. I was so afraid of what Devlin would do if I got him into trouble. He had always made it very clear that whoever was responsible for him getting into trouble would answer to his Scorpion buddies. The police knew where I lived, where I worked, and what shift because they were there not even ten minutes after I got home from work. They knew everything about me and that I was dating Devlin.

Devlin did stay at my apartment on multiple occasions, and his mom would get after him for it because he could get into a lot of trouble if he ever was caught. His probation officer also did surprise visits at his mom's and searched his bedroom to see if he had anything he wasn't supposed to. He kept all of his marijuana paraphernalia at my apartment.

I tried to leave Devlin. I wanted to leave him shortly after his horns started poking through. He would not let me leave. I belonged to him and was his property. I never thought that I was strong enough to leave him. I had no family support. I had to distance myself from the Joneses to protect them from him. I had no further contact with them. They were mad at me for choosing to be with Devlin and for some of the choices that I made, but I wanted it that way. They needed to stay away from me and out of my life. I had to convince Devlin to not send the Scorpions after them. They were safe as long as they stayed out of my life.

I was scared to ask the few friends I did have for help because of how dangerous Devlin was. I didn't want Devlin to go after them for helping me leave him. He did a good job of isolating me. I was all alone. He was the only one that I could depend on for anything. I *needed* him. My mom and Dwayne lived just a few minutes away on the other side of town, but they never came to visit me. I could never depend on them for anything, and they liked Devlin.

I didn't know what to do or how to get out of this. I was all alone. How do you escape the grips of a man so dangerous with nowhere to go and no one to turn to? He wasn't even a man. He was far too evil to be a man. He was the Devil, and he had me right where he wanted me, firmly in his grasp, crushing my spirits and will to live, forcing me into submission to accept the living hell that I was in. There wasn't much of a difference between Devlin and the devil. That is how sadistically monstrous that man was.

20

The Devil Rages On

How was I going to free myself from the grips of the Devil who held onto me so tightly that he literally was squeezing the life out of me and my willpower to live? What would make him leave me? He wouldn't let me leave him. What did I have to do to make him want to leave me? What if I cheated on him? That would be enough to break up any relationship.

I created a dating profile on the Plenty of Fish dating site. I caught the interest of an older married man in his fifties and met up with him. I'm not proud of this and hate myself for this, but I had to do what I had to do to escape the abusive controlling relationship that I was in.

One day, Devlin took me up to Michigan Works in Sandusky, and I left my phone in the truck. I was only going to drop something off really quick. When I came back out, Devlin was looking through my phone, and he was angry. He threw my phone on the floor, and the back of the phone and battery came out. I was so terrified of what he would do next.

This is when the controlling behavior and the abuse went from bad to worse. I tried telling him that I wasn't happy and that I wanted to leave. The only way that I was leaving was in a body bag, and now that I was acting like a whore, he was going to treat me like one.

He threatened to tell the Sandefurs how much of a whore I was. He knew how important they were to me, and he wanted to ruin

240

their perception of me. They were not going to think of me as an innocent little Andrea church mouse anymore. He wanted to ruin my reputation and isolate me even more.

I begged him to leave them out of it. What the Sandefurs thought of me meant so much to me. The Sandefurs were my biggest support system, and I loved them more than my own family. If I lost them, I would literally have no one.

Shortly after this all came out, Devlin picked me up one summer night. He didn't say a word to me. I didn't know where we were going at first. I could tell Devlin was lost in thought and that he was very angry. When he pierced his lips tightly together and flared out his nose and squinted his eyes, I knew that the rage was boiling inside of him and to look out, especially if he refused to talk to me.

I knew that we were going to the cabin when we went past his mom's and turned down a dirt road. I started to get scared. Why was he taking me to the cabin late at night? Did he get the key from his mom? Before, when we stayed at the cabin, he had to get permission from his mom and get the key from her.

I didn't like being alone with him when he was mad. When he pulled in the driveway, he pulled alongside a row of sheds. This angry man who refused to talk to me got out and started rummaging through the sheds, looking for something. I had a really bad feeling about this.

I got out of the truck and went over to the shed and peeked in to see what he was doing.

"What are you looking for?" I asked.

Devlin continued looking around, ignoring me. What was he doing here this late, rummaging through the sheds? And why wouldn't he answer me? I had never seen him like this before. I had seen him pretty angry before, but this was different. This was pure rage, and the look on his face was pure evil.

I became very scared once I realized that he brought me to this cabin late at night for a reason. What was he looking for in the shed? Something to use on me? To kill me? Was he looking for a shovel to dig my grave?

The night had a putrid smell of danger, and every alarm bell was going off in my head. I could feel the knot swelling up in my gut as I looked around, assessing my situation. This man was going to kill me. I had never seen him this angry before. I was wearing flip-flops. I couldn't run too far in those. There were no houses around. We were on an old dirt road. There was no place to run or to hide. I could scream, but nobody would hear me. This was it. This was my fate. I couldn't outrun him in the truck.

He was going to kill me for cheating on him. In the past, he had said the only way I could leave him was in a body bag. Was he making good on his promise?

My head started racing. I thought I was going to die that night. I started confessing all of my sins to God. I wanted to make sure that I was right with God before this man killed me. I should never have cheated, but I wanted out of this relationship, and he wouldn't let me leave him.

"Get in!" Devlin barked, distracting me from pleading with God as he came out of the shed with what he was looking for in his hands. It was a long wooden dowel with fresh holes drilled into each end, but that was not what he was looking for. He planned this. He drilled those holes recently. What he was looking for was rope. This was it! My fate was sealed! Was he going to tie me up and bludgeon me to death with that stick? No! He had something far more sinister planned.

I got in the truck, and he threw the rope and wooden dowel in the back and drove us out back by the pond. I wish he had killed me that night. It would have been far more merciful than the hell he continued to put me through.

"Get out and get undressed," Devlin ordered.

I slowly got out of the truck but just stood there. I didn't want to have sex with him. He was angry and looked like he was about to kill me.

"Take your freaking clothes off!" Devlin yelled.

"I don't want to. I don't want to have sex with you when you're mad."

"Oh, so you can give it to every other Tom, Dick, and Harry, you whore? You belong to me, and if I want it, I'm going to take it whether you like it or not! If you're going to act like a freaking whore, I'm gonna treat you like the freaking whore you are! Now take your freaking clothes off, you freaking whore!"

I slowly got undressed and stood there with my arms wrapped around myself, concealing my nakedness. Devlin got the wooden dowel out of the back of his truck and fed the rope through the holes. Then he walked over to me, put the wooden dowel behind my head, and snatched my arms up and tied my hands to the ends, putting me into a cross position. He tied the rope so tight around my wrist that it was cutting into my skin.

Devlin shoved me to my knees, which was difficult when you don't have hands to brace yourself. He unzipped his pants and made me perform oral sex on him. He was pulling my hair and was being very rough while shouting profanities at me and calling me his whore.

Devlin grabbed my hair and yanked me forward. I couldn't brace myself with my hands tied to this wooden dowel in a cross position, so my face fell into the dirt. Devlin got behind me and raped me repeatedly, both vaginally and anally with my face in the dirt. I could not brace myself with my hands tied to this wooden dowel in a cross position, so all of the weight and force was put on to my face. He was very rough like a crazed animal, and he kept hitting me while he was raping me. He kept shouting profanities at me and calling me his whore. He kept telling me that I belonged to him and if I ever cheated on him again that he was going to kill me. If I ever tried to leave him, he was going to kill me. If I wanted to leave, it would have to be over my dead body. He also told me that he was going to start treating me like the whore that I was. Devlin also threatened to take me down to his buddies and let them toss me around like a whore. He told me that they have already seen my pictures and liked what they saw.

When he was done, he smacked me on the behind really hard. He got in front of me and he pulled up on the wooden dowel, help-ing me to my feet so that he could untie me. I got dressed, and he took me home and dropped me off. I took a shower and cried hysterically. The only way that I was going to leave this man was if I was dead. He was the very personification of the Devil, the most wicked evil man you could ever imagine, and I was stuck with him. Death would be the only way to separate myself from him.

21

Leaving in a Body Bag

The controlling and abusive behavior intensified. When he came home from trucking on Fridays to go to probation, he made it a point to make my life hell and called me a whore every chance he got. He would spend all week over the road, watching porn while he was driving to get more ideas of what he wanted to do to me on the weekends. He even sent me videos of the things he wanted to do. The things he did are far too graphic and horrific to repeat and are exceptionally painful. Some of the things he did makes me wonder if that is the cause of my infertility. Could he have done permanent damage to my reproductive organs?

When Devlin took me to Walmart in Caro to go grocery shopping, he would make us sit out in the parking lot for a while, watching other young women come and go. He was a sexual predator hunting for another victim to join in on his games. He wanted another girl to do a threesome with.

"What about that one?" he would say, pointing out different girls. He tried to pick some out with the same body type as me because he knew I was self-conscious.

I would always tell him no. I was not into girls. He also looked on craigslist under the personal ads and even created ads, looking for another girl who wanted to do a threesome.

Nothing ever came of it, but he did try to set something up on a number of occasions. He even tried to set something up with his cousin, but schedules were always conflicting. Devlin also talked about swingers' clubs and tried looking into joining one.

One time, Devlin took me to the Deja Vu strip joint where he paid a skinny black girl with a big gap in her two front teeth to give me a lap dance. She even pulled my breast out and bit my nipple in front of everyone. I learned to just go with the flow when it came to Devlin. If I protested very much or told him no, then I would just pay for it later. He did everything he could to punish me. My life was a living hell.

His family really liked me, and his mom even drove me to a tiny white chapel on a dirt road in Snover, Michigan. She wanted us to get married and really pressed the issue. If we were going to be together, she wanted us to be married to make things right in the eyes of God. His mother didn't have a clue that her son was the spawn of Satan himself.

Devlin was a very good pretender, and I learned how to pretend just as well. On the outside, we looked like a normal couple. I smiled and waited on him in front of his family. He was a doting gentleman. Things seemed nearly perfect to any onlooker who didn't know any better, but I knew better, and Devlin knew better. He was my master, and I was his slave, his prisoner left to his mercy to which he had none.

Rita not only had her own house and the rock cabin that was willed to her by her Uncle Garth, but she also had a double-wide willed to her from her dad that was sitting empty, just the way her dad left it. It sat that way for a few years. Rita and Devlin talked about Devlin taking over that house and paying her for it. Devlin and I went to look at it.

It was very old and dated but had a lot of potential. It also had a full-sized basement with a bathroom and full-sized kitchen, living room, and a couple of bedrooms down there. Everything in the basement was covered in black mold and would have to be gutted and redone. This house was located on M-46, just a few miles outside of town. Behind the house was a decent-sized pole barn and a shed. Behind that were woods that contained a short trail to Devlin's uncle's house. His uncle's property butted up to the back of that property.

Rita was talking to Devlin about marriage and letting him have that house. She thought she was doing us a pretty good favor. Devlin would have to clean it up first to make it livable, and then his probation officer would have to do an inspection to change his address on the registry. This house was Devlin's dream. The house sat back from the road, secluded by trees with a long driveway. You couldn't see the house from the road. I would have to quit my job and not work at all due to not having a license. I would basically be a prisoner in that house with nowhere to go and his uncle right behind me to keep an eye on me. I wouldn't be able to see Colleen anymore, the only real friend I had at the time. I would be completely isolated and cut off from the rest of the world. It was the perfect set up for Devlin.

I wanted to leave him a long time ago, but his dad passed away from lung cancer, and I didn't want to try and break it off from him after his dad just died.

I dreaded the weekends and always looked forward to going to work. Even during the week, when he was hundreds of miles away, he still managed to make my life a living, breathing hell.

I had to leave him. I couldn't live like this any longer. My life was a living hell, and I had no one to turn to. I could talk to Colleen from work, but all she could do was pray for me and try to encourage me to leave him or go to a women's shelter. She didn't understand just how dangerous this man was. He had made it very clear that the only way I was leaving him was in a body bag.

Death was better than the hell this wicked man put me through. I had to die, but first, I wanted to explain to everyone why I had to commit suicide. I wanted to write an expose, a tell-all called *Andrea's Pandora's Box*, much like what you are reading now. Anyone who read my story would understand why I had to commit suicide. Some people would have killed themselves a long time ago if they had to go through half of what I went through. My story would be a Pandora's box releasing all of the family secrets that my mom tried so hard to keep hidden. It would also expose Devlin for the Devil he really was. My story was essentially going to be my suicide note. It was written in such a way that portrayed such hatred and anger toward all those who hurt me, especially my mother.

I got right to work writing my book. I walked up to the Dollar Store and bought four different leather journals. Devlin never allowed me to go anywhere or do anything with friends, so I was able to spend every waking moment after work and before work writing this book. It took me a couple of months to complete, but it was something I had to do. It was something that I had to leave behind before I died. It was my revenge and final kick in the gut to all those I would be leaving behind.

I walked up town to the Dollar Store after work one day to purchase over-the-counter sleeping pills and Aspirin. I chose Aspirin because it was a blood thinner, and if I took a bunch of them, I would bleed to death internally, and the sleeping pills would put me to sleep and I wouldn't feel a thing. I would just go to sleep and never wake up. It was going to be peaceful, and I was finally going to be free of the Devil who had his claws sunk deep into my flesh.

Devlin was up for the weekend, and this was the weekend I wanted to free myself from him and life in general. The cops showed up at my apartment just a few days before, looking for Devlin again. They were checking up on him to make sure that he wasn't there.

It was late at night, and we were in my living room on the couch, watching TV with all of the lights off. I knew that it would be a matter of time before Devlin wanted to have sex before he went back home to his mom's, and I didn't want to have sex with him. I had to get rid of him somehow. As soon as he got up to go to the bathroom, I texted Colleen and asked her to call the cops on Devlin for me because I didn't want to have sex with him and I wanted him to leave. Colleen knew everything about Devlin and how he treated me.

A little while later, three officers were knocking on my door. I played dumb like I was surprised that they were there. Devlin knew that the cops kept coming to my apartment to check up on him because I told him every time they did. So he just thought that this was the time that they finally busted him. He never thought that I was responsible for them being there because he was with me the whole time. I had Colleen call them for me and deleted our messages right away because Devlin did go through my phone all the time. It worked out perfectly.

I let the officers in, and they talked to Devlin about the terms of his probation and the curfew. He wasn't supposed to be out this late at night. He had to be at his mom's by a certain time.

I could tell that Devlin was sweating bullets and thought that he was in big trouble. He hated cops. I was thanking Colleen over and over again in my head for getting rid of him for me. He was none the wiser.

The cops gave him a warning and asked him to leave. After he left, they questioned me for a few minutes. Colleen kind of filled them in on the situation. They knew that he was abusive and that I didn't want him there. They didn't let Devlin know why they were there. They just acted like it was a routine checkup. They asked if I wanted to press charges or file a PPO against him, and I told them no. I didn't find it necessary.

As soon as they left, I was going to take a bunch of pills and go to sleep forever. I wasn't going to have to worry about Devlin any longer. I was finally going to be free of him. My plan worked, and I had Colleen to thank for that.

Devlin called me as soon as he got home and wanted to know what the cops said after he left and what I told them. I just told him that they were there to check up on him like they always did. He was satisfied with my answer, and we hung up.

I texted Colleen to let her know how things turned out and to thank her for helping me get rid of him. Then I deleted my messages. I had to work the next morning. When I didn't show up, Colleen would know that something happened to me and come looking for me, but I would already be dead. It would be unusual for me to not show up or call. I was at work every chance I got.

Colleen knew my situation with Devlin. She even got worried about me and reported me to HR after I started telling her that the only way that I could ever leave Devlin was if I took my own life. HR tried to help me at the time and gave me information about battered women and how to leave an abusive relationship. They tried to set me up with an appointment to talk to someone about it. But they didn't understand how dangerous Devlin was. He was affiliated with the Scorpion biker gang. He was a pedophile and a sexual deviant. He was abusive, controlling, and wicked right down to the core. I appreciated the help, but the only way that I was leaving him was in a body bag. He had made that perfectly clear.

The cops showed up earlier that day to do a wellness check on me because HR reported that I was suicidal. They came into my apartment to do a suicide assessment on me, but of course, I lied and told them what they needed to hear to get them to leave me alone. If only they knew that later that night, I would be saying goodbye to this cold cruel world for good.

Life had not been very nice to me. It had been extremely hard my entire life. My whole life, I had been fighting. My fight would finally be over. I would finally be at peace. I was going to take a bunch of pills, beg God for forgiveness, and then run into His arms, leaving the pain and torture of this world far behind me. God would wipe all the tears from my eyes, and I would remember this life no more. I was looking forward to that. I didn't want to be in pain anymore. I didn't want to be Devlin's play toy that he could abuse whenever he wanted anymore.

My life had always been hard. I was only in my twenties. I had my whole life ahead of me. I couldn't stand the thought of living to be eighty years old and having my life be this hard and painful the entire time. I could barely get through each day, let alone another fifty to sixty years. I didn't see how things could ever get better.

When I was a kid, I had dreams of becoming a mother. That was the one thing I always wanted more than anything. I couldn't have that with Devlin. I didn't want that with Devlin. He was too dangerous. Who knows what he would have done to his own daughters? There was no way I could foster or adopt with him either, not with his record. He was the place where my dreams came to die. Life was not worth living. I didn't have anything to look forward to or to live for. All hope was lost. I didn't have a future with him and didn't want to spend the rest of my miserable life with him. I didn't see any other way out. My only option was to leave him in a body bag.

After the cops left, I went to my bedroom and got in bed under the covers and sat up for a while, petting my cat, Clyde, and crying. I was crying to Clyde and telling him sorry for leaving him like this, but I couldn't go on like this anymore. I told Clyde that I didn't have a choice. This was my only way to get away from him. Devlin had made that very clear. He wouldn't let me leave, and I couldn't stand to be with him any longer.

Clyde was purring very loudly and walking all over me, kneading me with his paws, wanting me to scratch his head as he softly meowed at me in-between purrs. He even put his face up to mine and rubbed his head on me. He was a good cat and he was trying to make me feel better. Clyde sniffed my nose and rubbed his head across my face. He was a hairy cat, so I pushed him away and wiped the hair off my face.

I got my phone out and texted Colleen, thanking her for everything she had ever done for me and for being a great friend. I told her that I was sorry but that I didn't see any other way out. I had to do this to get away from him. Then I turned on Christian music from a playlist that I created. I had it on repeat so that the music would be playing when someone found my body. I took out the bottles of pills and a bottle of water and started swallowing pills one by one. I took a bunch of Aspirins and a bunch of sleeping pills and I lay there, waiting for death to find me and release me from the chains of this life.

I could feel myself getting really sleepy but at the same time, I felt really sick. My stomach was starting to hurt, and I could feel the pills starting to take their toll. I could feel the poison working through my body. I became very queasy and light-headed. My head felt like it was spinning. My body felt extremely weak. My arms and legs felt like they weighed a ton, and I could barely lift them to move. I sunk down in bed and laid on my back with my hands folded on my stomach like how you see a body positioned in a casket. I wanted to be found, peacefully in bed, no longer in pain or torment from this life with my cat, Clyde, curled up beside me.

I woke up, running to the bathroom to throw up. I called Colleen and left her a voicemail, telling her how sorry I was. As I was stumbling out to the living room, I collapsed on the floor and passed out. I was going in and out of consciousness.

I was aware of what was happening to me. I could literally feel my soul separating from my body. I felt myself dying. It was not a peaceful experience. I felt total darkness, and everything was void of God. I had never felt so far away from God in my life. Out of all of the pain and hell that I'd been through, I had never felt such a distinct separation from God before. It was the most empty feeling you could ever imagine. I knew without a doubt that I was headed straight for hell. I thought my life was hell now; just wait until I was actually in hell.

Every human being on this earth, regardless of the status of their salvation has a direct link to God. Anybody can come to God at any time as long as they still have breath in their lungs. The moment a lost person takes their last breath is the moment that direct link to God is severed for all of eternity. Once that link is severed, it is a done deal, and you will forever spend all of eternity void of God. It is a feeling of total despair and hopelessness. When you are void of God, you are void of everything God is. God is the God of hope, and without Him, you are hopeless. God is love, and without Him, there is hate. God is peace, and without Him, there is no peace. God is holy, and without Him, there is wickedness and everything unholy. God is happiness, and without Him, there is total despair. God is the light of this world, and without Him, there is total darkness.

If you are void of God, you are void of everything God stands for. That in itself is hell. There is more to hell than just the lake of fire. Being void of God is the scariest part of spending all of eternity in hell. It is worse than the fire itself. If you have ever felt hopeless in your life, you have a tiny inkling of what that feels like.

God allowed me to experience what that void felt like. Regardless of that prayer I said in the fifth grade, asking God into my heart, regardless of all the times I went to church and sang in the choir and in the praise band, I was lost and on my way to hell when I took all of those pills and felt my soul start to separate from my body. I walked away from God a long time ago, and every decision that I made was my own decision on my own path without seeking guidance from God. I put myself through hell with all of the choices that I made.

Instead of trusting in God, I created a dating profile which landed me in the hands of the Devil. I was impatient and tried to do things my own way, so God allowed it all to play out and culminate for this very moment. If I was going to be rebellious and do things my own way without God, then God was going to allow me to feel what it was like to be separated from him for all of eternity. He was going to allow me to feel the heat of those consequences.

I can't accurately describe the total disparity of what it felt like to be severed from God to experience that total void of everything God stands for. Trust me when I say that nothing in this life is worth that experience. It was the most horrific feeling you could ever imagine. Any hell this life puts you through is worth going through over and over again if it means the end result is not spending an eternity in hell. Any trial and tribulation this life offers is nothing compared to what is waiting for us after this life, whether it be heaven or hell.

All I could do at that very moment when I felt my soul start to separate from my body, and I knew that I was dying and headed for a far worse hell than the one I was trying to run from, was to cry out to God and beg him to save me. I couldn't speak because I was going in and out of consciousness, but my mind and my soul were crying out to the only one that could save me.

My Jesus! My Savior! My God! Don't let me slip from one hell into a more permanent one! Don't let me die and go to hell! Please, save me! I don't want to die! I don't want to go to hell! Save me, Jesus, because you are the only one that can!

At that moment, there was a knock on the door, and I heard a familiar voice. It was Colleen begging me to open the door. I couldn't move. I was still passed out on the floor, even though I was still aware of my surroundings.

She ended up calling 911, and the paramedics came. Colleen came running up to me and tried shaking me awake. She was crying. The paramedics turned me onto my back and started rubbing my sternum very hard. That didn't work, so they shoved a salt stick up my nose, and that made me sit straight up. They searched my apartment for the pills and asked me how much I took, but I couldn't answer them because I didn't know and was too weak to speak.

Colleen called Mandy from HR over to my apartment to support her because she was really upset about me. They loaded me up on the gurney and hauled me off to the Cass City Hospital just two blocks away. Colleen and Mandy followed me up there and sat with me as I was made to drink the nasty charcoal.

According to Colleen, Devlin did show up at the ER and asked to talk to me, so she left him with me and waited in the waiting room with Mandy. I remember him being there, but I don't remember the conversation that I had with him. Colleen said that he came out to the waiting room to talk to her, and she fed him a line about how much I cared about him, and then he left. Devlin was a very dangerous man, and she knew it, which was why she had to be careful what she said to him. He couldn't know that I was leaving him.

I was really worried about Devlin finding out what I did and what he would do to me when he found out. I wasn't dead, so he was still a problem. How come I couldn't get away from him no matter how hard I tried? I asked God for help. I asked him to save me and help me get away from Devlin. I didn't see it at the time, but this was him helping me finally break free of Devlin.

I had to be hospitalized for six days at Bay Med in the psychiatric hospital, but it was a blessing in disguise. This was my breakaway from the Devil. I was safe there. They helped me come up with a plan to break free from Devlin once and for all.

Still, to this day, I'm not sure exactly how Devlin found out where I was, but he kept calling the hospital where I was at. The workers came up to me and asked me if I wanted to talk to him, and I said no. They just kept telling him that they could not confirm nor deny that I was there due to HIPPA. Still, he called every day at least twice a day. I was scared of him. How did he find out where I was? And what was going to happen when I went home? I was as good as dead. Why did God save me from killing myself when I was just going to be released back into the hands of the Devil when I got out? Things were going to be even worse for me. He would probably kill me for real this time for trying to leave him again. I couldn't do anything without his say so. I couldn't even die without his say so. I had little faith. God had this, yet I refused to see it at the time.

Colleen kept in touch with me every day and let me know what was going on. She took Clyde to her house to look after him for me because she didn't want to go to my apartment with Devlin lurking around. It was far too dangerous. Devlin had my apartment watched. He was friends with an older couple in their fifties who lived downstairs. He sold them pot and smoked with them on occasion, so he had them watching my apartment. He got a hold of my contact list from my cell phone provider and started calling everyone on my contacts, asking them where I was at. He kept calling my job every day, asking them if I was there. They had to tell him that I no longer worked there. He even showed up at my job, asking for me, and then had one of his Scorpion buddies go to my place of work and asking about me.

My employer had to take desperate measures to ensure the safety of everyone that worked there as well as the residents who lived there. Colleen told HR just how dangerous Devlin was and that he did have guns and that he was violent and abusive. They held a staff meeting about him and put a plan in place in case he did show up looking for trouble. They had a picture of him and the description of his truck by every exit and every phone in the building. They, as a company, had to file a restraining order against him because he kept harassing my work, asking about me. The Cass City sheriff had to drive through the parking lot frequently throughout the day. It was an assisted living home full of vulnerable people, and Devlin was a crazed madman who was unpredictable. My work even had to hire a security guard, and I was required to file a PPO against him in order to return to work. It was a very dire and sensitive situation.

When I was released from the hospital, I could not go home right away. It was too dangerous, and my apartment was still being watched. I had to stay with a friend who lived behind me in the backside of my apartment building, and I had to make sure that I was wearing a disguise if I left her apartment. If I had to go to my apartment for any clothes or anything, I had to go there at night, escorted by my friend, and wear a disguise. I also had to get a hold of my landlord to get my locks changed.

As soon as I was released, my friend took me to the police station to file a PPO against him. I also called Devlin's PO and made an appointment to go and see her. If I was going to try and break free from this man once and for all, I had to get him in as much trouble as I possibly could to make him go back to jail so that I could be safe, at least until he got out.

When I talked to Devlin's PO, she set the record straight on a lot of things. Devlin's whole story that he roped his mom and ex-wife in about him being innocent was a load of crap. He was a sexual predator, and that little girl was actually thirteen, not fifteen. He bought her a phone so that he could groom her and sexted back and forth with her without her mom knowing. He was also planning on going to get her from Georgia and bring her to Michigan.

She also told me that she knew everything about me. She knew where I lived, where I worked, my schedule, who my parents and siblings were, and where they lived. She knew everything. The cops had been watching me and kept an eye on me. She knew that Devlin was manipulative and that I probably didn't know the truth about him, and she was trying to catch him in the act of violating the terms of his probation.

I told her about the pond incident and how controlling he was. She said that she wasn't the least bit surprised. She dealt with a lot of sex offenders on a daily basis, and Devlin was the most manipulative and conniving. She said Devlin thought he was smart and that she was stupid. She knew that he was a liar. She knew that he had a cellphone under my contract. She knew everything. They were just waiting to catch him in the act.

His PO spent about an hour with me going over everything. I came prepared. I handed her the wooden dowel and rope that Devlin used on me. I gave her his Scorpion t-shirts, all of his marijuana paraphernalia, bongs and papers, and even showed her my Facebook account where he was using my messenger to communicate with his friends. I did everything I could to get him into as much trouble as I possibly could. I knew that I was risking my life talking to his PO, but it was a risk that I was willing to take. I wanted him out of my life, and if he came after me and killed me for it, so be it. He would be doing me a favor.

I became very paranoid after I left Devlin. I had to lock my doors at night and then go back and make sure they were locked like three times. Every time I had to do laundry, I was very quick about it and made sure that I was aware of my surroundings. I was constantly looking around me, scared that I would find Devlin lurking around the corner or a Scorpion. I didn't like leaving my apartment. I never felt safe. Devlin would get me sooner or later.

22

The Scorpions Killed My Cat

It was late at night when I heard a knock on my door. I wasn't thinking straight, and I opened the door instead of looking through the peephole first. Devlin barged into my apartment with a few of his Scorpion buddies. They grabbed me and threw me down on the couch. I was scared. What was he going to do to me now? I had a PPO against him. He wasn't supposed to be here. He was going to punish me for leaving him and talking to his PO.

Clyde, my cat, came walking down the hallway, and one of the Scorpions grabbed him and started petting him roughly, telling me what a pretty cat he was.

"Let him go!" I begged.

Clyde was hissing at him and trying to get away. The guy walks over to the dining room and opened my microwave, threw him in, and shut the door. Clyde was howling, growling, and hissing, trying to get out.

Devlin and another guy grabbed me and dragged me over to the dining room in front of the microwave. They each had an arm and held me there on my knees. Another guy was behind me, holding me by the hair to make sure I watched as they turned the microwave on and cook my cat alive as he screamed and flopped around inside the microwave until he was lifeless.

I was crying hysterically and begging them to stop. They are all laughing. I tried not to watch, but the guy behind me had a hold of my hair and made sure I watched the whole thing.

Devlin knew that I was an animal lover and how much I loved Clyde. He took great pleasure in making me watch them kill Clyde in the most horrific way possible. Devlin was evil right down to the core, and so were his buddies.

I woke up in a sweat and started crying. It was all just a dream, and Clyde was curled up, sleeping beside me, safe and sound. It seemed so real. I picked Clyde up and held him, crying, thanking God that didn't really happen.

I got up and checked my apartment and made sure that my door was locked. I walked over to the sliding glass doors in my living room that looked out onto the parking lot to make sure that I didn't see Devlin's green S10 pickup truck or any other vehicle I didn't recognize. I also made sure that my slider was locked as well.

After leaving Devlin, I lived in a constant state of fear. I was afraid that he would eventually come after me. I could no longer walk to and from work. Colleen picked me up and dropped me off or another coworker did. I could no longer go for walks through town. I was free of Devlin, but he still had me trapped inside my apartment. He still had control over my life.

I had nightmares about him kidnapping me as I walked to work. There was a golf course in between my apartment and where I worked, and I was always so paranoid that he would be parked there, waiting for me.

He was a truck driver. He could literally be anywhere or take me anywhere, and no one would find me. Every time I was out and about, I was so paranoid. Was that guy a Scorpion? Or that one?

I had to get out of Cass City. I had to get far away from here to eliminate any possibility of ever running into him.

I decided to go back onto the dating sites. I needed to find a man to protect me and get me far away from the thumb of Michigan. I couldn't stay here any longer. A PPO was just a piece of paper. That would not be enough to keep that monster away from me. He violated his probation all the time. He was a rule-breaker. There was no way that I was safe here any longer. It was only a matter of time before Devlin came after me, and I was just a sitting duck. He knew where I lived, where I worked, where my family lived, and where the Joneses lived. I had to leave. I was tired of living in a constant state of fear, always looking over my shoulder, constantly double-checking and triple-checking my locks.

23

A New Life

I met a man named Frank on a dating site. He was a pure blood Mexican, born and raised in Mexico. His mom brought him and his two sisters to the US for a better life. He lived in Grand Rapids, Michigan, just outside of downtown Grand Rapids in an upstairs two-bedroom apartment. Frank was an accountant and co-owner of a small accounting firm.

Grand Rapids was two and a half hours away, and I moved in with him almost immediately after meeting him. It felt good getting out of Cass City and made me feel so much safer. I was still a little paranoid when I went for walks and went exploring. Devlin was a truck driver. It would be nothing for him to drive to Grand Rapids. Just down the road from Frank's apartment was a park with a paved walking trail along the Grand River where people went to run or walk and feed the ducks. It was very pretty and serene for being inside a city. I loved to go for walks there and went a few times a week.

On our way to Grand Rapids with all of my stuff and Clyde, we stopped and picked up a cute grey and white kitten and brown tabby kitten. We named the grey one Professor and the brown tabby Nemesis. We kept Professor and Nemesis together for a few weeks and then gave Nemesis to his sister who lived in Grandville with their mother.

Frank loved cats, and he adored Clyde and the two kittens. When we went to visit his sister and mother, we always took Professor with us to play with his brother, Nemesis.

A few months after moving to Grand Rapids, Frank took me on a big trip with him to London, England, for a whole week. Outside of Erie, Pennsylvania, and Michigan and going trucking with Devlin, I had never traveled anywhere, especially out of the country, so it was pretty exciting. We had to fly to Canada to get onto a connected flight to Heathrow Airport in London. I felt so on top of the world. None of my family traveled outside of the country, much less outside of Michigan and Pennsylvania. It felt like a huge accomplishment.

When we landed in Heathrow, we had to find our way to a tube station to get to our hotel. A tube station is a subway. That is the main mode of transportation in London. It was fun trying to master the tube station and figuring out which sites were at which tube station.

London also have so many stairs you had to climb up and down to get down to the tube station. Our favorite tube station sites were Piccadilly Circus, which is comparable to New York's Time Square, and Camden Town. Camden Town was a shopping center where we got most of our souvenirs.

Frank and I had a whole itinerary planned out and purchased tours in advance. We went on a Beatles Tour and got to walk across Abbey Road, see the rooftop where they last played, and ate at the Hard Rock Cafe where so many of the great music legends had their stuff displayed.

We also went on a Jack the Ripper Tour which was fascinating. We went to Buckingham Palace, saw Big Ben, and saw the redcoats march around. We also walked across the London Bridge and went on the London Eye which is the world's largest Ferris wheel. Riding on a double-decker bus was fun but very crowded. So many people were standing in the aisle; it was so full!

I had so much fun on this trip, and it was an experience of a lifetime. Frank really spoiled me and showed me a good time.

London is a very vibrant city, full of life and street performers. We ran into a couple of ladies who were Americans and from California, so we hung out with them and got to know them. We stood around this group of singers from Russia and got to talk with them. I was immersed in so many different cultures. They say

America is a melting pot, but I really think London is a melting pot of so many different cultures and people of all walks of life.

One complaint I had about London was how congested it was. It was very difficult for two people to walk side by side because you had to constantly weave in and out of crowds of people. Other than that, I had the time of my life, and that is when I fell in love with traveling. Frank gave me an experience that I will never forget.

Frank loved to travel and had to take a trip every year. The year before he met me, he traveled to Spain. Frank also took me to Chicago for the first time. We went with his mother and one sister, Maya, and her son, Christopher. We went to a museum with a planetarium. Frank loved the finer things in life. He loved to go to live plays, and we went to see *Bye-bye, Birdie* and *Legally Blonde*, the live plays. We also went to a live concert that looked and sounded like the Beatles and played Beatles music. He took me to a hockey game and also to see Jeff Dunham live. He lived in a cheaper apartment because being able to do fun things was more important to him. It was a completely new lifestyle for me that I wasn't used to.

I also loved living in the city and having the option of doing so many fun things without having to drive far to do them. The city life was a different culture within itself, and I loved it. I fell in love with Grand Rapids. Frank would just take me downtown at night just to go for a walk because that is when the city comes to life. I was born a city girl and was back in my natural habitat.

I didn't have a license, which made it really hard trying to find a job. I really wanted to be independent and contribute. I didn't want to be that girl that stayed home while her man made all the money. It didn't feel right to me. I found a sales job selling gas for a company called Just Energy. I quickly became the number one saleswoman in the state of Michigan and made really good money in commissions. It was a really hard job, though, especially in the wintertime. We were dropped off in a neighborhood and assigned a specific area and had to knock on doors to get people to switch the gas provider for their gas company in order to lower their utility bill. I'm a very shy person and not one to strike up a conversation with strangers, but I managed to stick to my script and do really well.

The hardest part was trying to find a bathroom to use. Sometimes a customer would allow us to use their bathroom, but sometimes I either had to hold it or find a secluded place in a patch of trees or somewhere to go. Most times, we didn't have access to a public restroom since we were dropped off in residential areas.

Grand Rapids is brutal in the winter because of the lake effect, and I had to sell gas door-to-door in a blizzard. Most people were so nice and let me come in to get some hot chocolate and use their bathrooms, even when they weren't interested in switching their gas providers. I found that it was much easier to sell in inclement weather such as rain or snow because people took pity on you. People wouldn't try to scam you in the pouring rain or a blizzard. It wasn't a scam, but a lot of people were leery because most people don't know that you can change the provider of your gas company. You can't change your utility company, but you can tell them where you want them to get your gas from for a cheaper price.

I did this job for a few months but decided I couldn't do it any longer. The biggest problem I had with it was not having access to a bathroom. I couldn't handle that. It wouldn't be a big deal for a guy, but it made it very difficult being a female.

I applied for a job at the Grand Rapids home for veterans, which was right down the road from where we lived. As a matter of fact, the park I loved to go to was in between the nursing home and where we lived. It was perfect. I got the job and loved the convenience of being able to walk to and from work. Sometimes, I went for a walk through the park on my way home from work. Living in the city was nice, but it also enabled me to keep putting off getting my driver's license. I was scared to death of driving but mainly because Devlin made me that way. He screamed at me the entire time and made me terrified of it, like I was never going to be good at it.

I talked Frank into letting me get a puppy. I had always wanted a Yorkie, but I could not find any Yorkie puppies for sale at that time. I came across an ad online for Maltipoo puppies that was downstate by the Ohio border. I had never heard of Maltipoo puppies before, so I looked them up to see what they looked like and fell in love. They had long hair, and I wanted a little girly dog that I could dress up and put her hair in bows and ponytails. Maltipoos are a hybrid dog that are half Maltese and half poodle, and they only get to be around ten pounds. I was super-excited.

Frank drove me down to get her. It was about a three-hour drive, but when we got there, I was very disappointed and almost went home empty-handed. The place was a dump. The house was very disgusting, comparable to hoarders on that TV show. They had just small pathways all throughout their house and they had a bunch of cats and dogs running in and out. They had a room off their living room with wall-to-wall cages of birds. I was very leery of buying a puppy from this lady. What if the puppy was sick from being in such a dirty environment? What if I wasn't paying for a high-quality dog?

This lady had two different female puppies in a small hexagon playpen. One was a purebred toy poodle, and the other one was the Maltipoo. They were from two different litters of puppies. I looked at them both and considered them both but ultimately decided on the Maltipoo. I couldn't leave her there in that environment. I felt like it was more of a rescue, and I was buying her a new life of health, safety, and happiness. I paid $450 for her, and we made the long trip home, trying to come up with a name for this adorable little girl. She was pure white and had a fat round belly. She had the cutest little face, and I was overjoyed. I couldn't be happier. It was instant love at first sight. I always thought that whenever I got a female puppy, I was going to name her Pita, which stands for "pain in the arse," but that name didn't fit this little girl. She was a princess and needed a princess name.

At the time, I really enjoyed the *Twilight* movie series and had a thing for unusual names and fell in love with the name Renesmae. I never heard that name before, and it had a beautiful princess ring to it. I wanted to keep with the *Twilight* theme, so I decided that her middle name would be Rosalie after another character. Her name was now Renesmae Rosalie, and I called her Esmae for short.

Esmae was a true prissy princess right from the start. I dressed her up in cute little pink dresses and put bows in her hair, and she loved every minute of it. She was very good with the cats, and I often found her curled up with Professor, sleeping. She had the sweetest demeanor.

I did fall in love with Frank. He was good to me for the most part. He was nothing like Devlin. He showed me how good things can be. The one thing about Frank that really bothered me was that he was a huge momma's boy, and his family spoke in Spanish in front of me and carried out full conversations that I could never be a part of because I didn't understand Spanish. I always thought that was disrespectful.

Frank and I did get engaged. We were going to get married in Frankenmuth, Michigan, at the old theater and have the reception at the Zender's Restaurant. His mom made the bouquets and did a beautiful job, and I ordered a beautiful puffy wedding dress with roses on it. The colors were going to be blue and silver with a winter wonderland theme. I made all of the centerpieces. They were little trees with crystal garland hanging from them. The aisle was going to be lined with trees painted white with glitter on them. It was going to be like walking through a winter wonderland. It was going to be a beautiful wedding.

Frank and I started fighting, but mainly because his one sister, Rocio, didn't like me. Rocio was a pediatric doctor at the Grand Rapids hospital. She thought that her brother could do better than me. I didn't wear name brands and wasn't trophy wife material. To top it all off, there was a possibility that I could not have kids of my own due to PCOS and a previous abnormal pap which resulted in a cone biopsy. Frank wanted kids of his own, especially a little girl he wanted to name Michelle and call Millie for short. His mother wanted grandbabies from her only son.

Frank would go outside and sit at the top of the stairs and talk in Spanish to his mom and sisters over the phone about me. They talked him into breaking things off with me. Frank was planning another trip to Spain, which I originally was going to go on with him. I told him to go without me. We needed a break from each other, and he needed that time alone to reflect on things and decide what he wanted to do about us. I was willing to make things work, but he needed to stick up for me and not let his mother and sisters bad-mouth me. Rocio hated me the most, and I only met her one time.

Frank dropped me off at my mom's for two weeks while he went on his trip by himself. When he came back, we talked on the phone and both agreed to end the relationship. I couldn't handle his mother and sisters. His mother and one sister, Maya, were nice to my face, but they, too, wanted Frank to end things with me. Their biggest thing was that there was a big possibility that I could not have children of my own.

I had to find a ride to Grand Rapids to pack up all of my stuff and retrieve Clyde. I had Esmae with me at my mom's. Frank's mother and sister, Maya, looked after Clyde and Professor while he was gone on his trip.

Cris and Jim Archer got a hold of me on Facebook and offered to help me. I went to school with their son, Christopher, and they attended the Kingston Wesleyan church. I didn't really know them but knew of them. Cris approached me a few times in church, and she seemed like a very nice lady, and we were friends on Facebook.

They lived about fifteen minutes away from my mom. Cris and Jim picked me up and took me to Grand Rapids. They helped me pack up all of my stuff. Frank showed up at the end and asked me to leave him my fifty-inch flat-screen TV. I worked hard to buy that with my own money before I even met him. He practically begged me to leave it behind. He made good money. He could buy his own. The TV was the last thing that I packed up, but I did take it with me. I left him my entertainment center but only because I had no room to take it with me.

Frank also tried to talk me into leaving him Clyde. Clyde and Professor became very close, and he didn't want to split them up. I told him to get another cat, and I packed Clyde up and left, and that was the end of Frank, the momma's boy, and potential bad in-laws that caused me nothing but grief.

24

Greyhound to Texas and Back

I became very depressed living with my mother and stepdad again. They lived in a three-bedroom single wide trailer in between Dwayne's oldest daughter, Molly, and his brother, Martin, and his wife Cindy. So there was family on both sides of them. Dwayne's mom, who lived in Tennessee, bought that trailer and property and rented it out to them to ensure they always had a steady place to live.

My mom was a pack rat, so their house was very cluttered. She was also very obsessed with her grandkids, so she had a whole area off the living room with a bunk bed and a bunch of toys. They also had a playground in the front yard with two different wooden swing sets, a sand box, four tractor tires half buried in the ground, a teeter-totter, and a bunch of bikes, cars, and toys. It looked like a day care. She was a much better grandma than she was a mother, and I have a theory about that. She was such a horrible mother; her grandkids were her redemption. That was her way of making up for it.

I stayed in the spare bedroom, but I had to deal with all of the pictures she plastered on the wall, and yes, some were of Jordan. I just tried not to look at them. This was temporary until I could figure something else out. Jordan came over a lot, anyway, so I was always seeing his face. I stored most of my stuff out in the pole barn. I gave my TV to my mom for allowing me to stay there.

Devlin finding me was always at the back of my mind. He knew where my mom lived. I tried so hard to get away from here, and here I was, back to square one.

With my last check from my job at the Grand Rapids nursing home, plus a little bit of money I saved up and my tax return, I was able to buy an old '98 Buick LaSabre for $800 and still had money left over to live on for a while. I saved it and tried not to spend any of it because I needed it to get back up on my feet. I didn't have my license yet, but I was determined to get it because I had to have it in order to survive.

I spent every day looking for a job and filling out applications online, but I was very limited. There weren't any jobs around. Even when I did get a job, I would be faced with the dilemma of finding a ride.

I got a job working in a factory making headliners in Marlette. I hated it, but I had to do what I had to do to get back on my feet.

My friend, Tami, drove me back and forth, but what I had to pay her in gas took almost my entire check. My mom's friend, Andrea, lived in Marlette, in town, so I had to stay with her a few nights a week to save on gas and just walked to work from her house. I hated staying with her, though, because she had cockroaches, and her house was dirty. I was so paranoid about the roaches. I made sure I checked my stuff over before leaving her house and only took the bare minimum with me.

Working in the factory, I was exposed to fiberglass. I started breaking out from it. I tried wearing long sleeves to protect myself a little bit from it, but it only made it worse because the bits of fiberglass would get stuck to my shirt and poke through the fabric and irritate my skin even more. I also had issues with the fiberglass going down my shirt and into my bra. I found out I was really allergic to the fiberglass, and it was breaking me out in hives, so I had no choice but to quit after only a month of working there.

I found a sales job online that came with a place to live and food. It paid to relocate people to where they needed them. The job was in Texas. Perfect! I could move to Texas and start all over and just forget everyone in Michigan. I didn't have much of a family anyway.

ANDREA SHERMAN

This was an opportunity to have a brand-new life far away from my old one. I would go down there, make a bunch of money, and then come back for Esmae and Clyde and the rest of my stuff and move down there for good, leaving Michigan and everyone in it behind and never looking back. I planned on starting over in Texas and cutting ties from everyone in my old life.

I bought the largest plastic tote I could find and filled it with all of my clothes and duct-taped the lid on it really well. I also packed two large suitcases.

I said goodbye to Esmae and Clyde and left them in the hands of my mom and Dwayne. My mom and her friend, Andrea, took me to the bus station in Flint and dropped me off. I got on a Greyhound bus, and it took two days going from one Greyhound bus to another to get down to Texas. The dredges of society travel by Greyhound, and it was extremely scary. I'd had to sit next to strange, sketchy men. It was dangerous being a young girl in my twenties, traveling alone by Greyhound. I had to constantly be aware of my surroundings. Human trafficking was on the rise, and I could have very well been served into the hands of human sex traffickers.

The ad I responded to about this job was very promising. I didn't look too much into it. I kind of knew that it sounded too good to be true, but I was desperate and wanted to get as far away from here as I could.

I did not like being back in the thumb of Michigan. That is where Devlin was from and where David, Jordan, and Craig lived. Kingston and Caro were small towns. There was always a chance of running into somebody I knew. Every time I ended back up in the thumb, I always felt such a huge feeling of oppression and anxiety, even when I just went back to visit. I never wanted to stick around long. I never wanted to stop anywhere, like at a store or anything.

One time, I went to Kingston to visit my mom and stopped at the dollar store in town and saw the Monteis in there. I hid from them and avoided them like the plague. I wasn't trying to be rude, but I get major anxiety from seeing people in my past no matter which role they played. When you run into people you know, generally, the conversations start out with, "How have you been? What

270

have you been up to? What are you doing now?" That is the kind of conversation I tried to avoid and run away from because I never wanted to answer those questions. I would have to lie and didn't want to do that. I got really nervous and anxious if I ran into anyone that I knew from that area and that part of my life. It didn't matter if I went to school with them and never talked to them or if they used to be my friend in grade school.

So getting out of Kingston was a major priority for me. Nothing good ever came of Kingston, aside from the Sandefurs, and they no longer lived there. Kingston offered me nothing but pain and memories. I couldn't stand being back there. Every time I found myself back in Kingston, my spirit didn't sit right at all. If this didn't work out in Texas, I would have to figure something else out, but right now, I had to just get out of Kingston and go from there.

The company I was going to work for paid for my Greyhound ticket, and my boss picked me up from the bus station. He drove me to a really nice house in an upscale subdivision not far from Houston. That is where other people like me were housed that came from all over the US, looking for a job and a fresh start with a new change of scenery. I had to share a room with another girl from Wyoming. We had twin mattresses that sat on the floor, and the room was small. Our bedroom was upstairs, off from a large landing where they held meetings before each workday.

I was going to be working in sales, selling two different Satellite TV services, and it was all commission-based. I was really good at selling gas. How hard could this be? The first two weeks were training. Texas was blazing hot in the summertime, and we were dropped off in a residential area to go door-to-door, selling satellite TV. We could have an ice-cold bottle of water to start out with, but in the Texas heat, it would be warm within thirty minutes. We were at the mercy of customers to give us something cold to drink and let us use their bathrooms. We would be out in the Texas heat all day, walking around, going door to door.

Texans are very hospitable people. They gave us bottles of water and allowed us to use their bathrooms, even if they were not interested.

One day, I was taking a break from the Texas heat and sat on a rock wall flower bed that had the name of the subdivision on it, and I was talking on the phone with the Sandefurs and heard the rattle of a rattlesnake. I jumped up and took off running away from there. I wasn't taking any chances and wasn't going to look for it.

I also got chased out of a junkyard with two big pit bulls, and just as one jumped up to lunge at me, I made it out of the yard. It had an invisible fence, and the dogs had shock collars on. They made my heart leap out of my chest. I thought I was going to be dog food!

I came across another yard with a pit bull on a chain, and he was jumping up and swinging from a tree branch by his mouth. I wasn't going anywhere near that house!

I quickly realized that this wasn't going to work out. When they said that food was provided, they meant ramen noodles once a day. I had a few hundred dollars left that I was saving that I went down there with, but that wasn't going to get me very far. I tried not to spend it, but buying drinks and cheap sandwiches from the gas station really ate up what little I had.

This house was a coed house. There were two other girls and about five guys living in this house together. The guys were all downstairs, and the girls got the upstairs. In the middle of the night, the boss would sneak up to the room I was sharing with one other girl, and they would have sex in her bed right beside me, thinking that I was asleep. It was more of a party house where they also drank beer and smoked marijuana. Everyone was in their twenties, including the boss.

No matter how hard I tried, I couldn't make a sale, so the boss had me go door knocking with him to teach me some pointers and see what I was doing wrong. During the alone time with him, he told me he had a daughter in Florida that he paid child support for, and he came to Texas to build a team so that he could go back to Florida to be with his daughter. He was also hitting on me. He hit on the other two girls that lived there and was having sex with my roommate. Shortly after, he started putting the moves on me. I knew I had no choice but to go back to Michigan.

There was no future in Texas. I didn't make a single sale. This house was a party house, and I just didn't fit into this scene. I came here to better my life and was very disappointed when it didn't turn out how I imagined it.

I was there for about six weeks and told the boss that I had to go home due to a family emergency. That was my excuse as to why I had to go home. I really missed Esmae and Clyde. I didn't belong in Texas. As much as I hated Michigan and Kingston, I had to go back. I packed up all of my stuff, and the boss drove me to the nearest Greyhound bus station and paid for my ticket back home.

It took me three days to go back home, and it was three days of hell. The layovers in between buses were long, and I was making the long journey home by myself, which was scary. It was hard to sleep on the bus because I was scared of strange men and couldn't sleep at the bus station either because I was scared of missing my next bus. It was the longest three days of my life. Going down to Texas and back by Greyhound was the first time that I ever traveled by myself.

When I finally made it back to Michigan and my last bus took me from Flint to Saginaw, the Archers were there to pick me up, and that is when I discovered that they lost my big tote full of clothes. I had to leave without it and call customer service to try and locate it. It never got on the right bus, but they did manage to find it, and I had to wait a week before it would be at the Saginaw bus station. They offered a discount off my next Greyhound bus ticket, but I told them I never planned on another Greyhound trip.

The Archers drove me back up to Saginaw to retrieve my lost tote, and that is when I discovered my digital camera missing that I had hidden at the bottom underneath all of my clothes, and my tote was shoveled through.

I moved back in with my mom, and Esmae was super-excited to have her momma back. I started spending a lot more time with the Archers and eventually moved in with them.

The Archers loved animals. They had five dogs, a bunch of cats, a bird, two ferrets, and other animals over the years. At one point, they even had a potbellied pig named Honey Boo Boo. They welcomed Esmae and Clyde into their home, and Esmae took to Jim right away. She loved Jim. He had treats for her every morning, and food was the key to her little heart.

Cris and Jim had a good-size pond in their front yard with a ton of goldfish in it. They swam in their pond a lot and had big floaties to lounge around on. Cris and Jim loved being outside. They had a large deck on the back and sat out there, drinking their coffee in the morning while the dogs played outside and the cats came up to say hello. Jim was a retired shop teacher.

Cris loved to do arts and crafts and was big into sewing. She made Esmae a cute little pink and green princess dress and embroidered "Princess Esmae" on it. Cris tried to teach me to sew, but I could never get into it.

The Archers used to go to the Kingston Wesleyan church, but after the Sandefurs left, they started going to the Marlette Baptist church, and I went with them.

The Archers were wonderful people and treated me very well. They had a big empty house and gave me one of the bedrooms. They never charged me rent. They tried teaching me how to drive so that I could get my driver's license.

There was an upcoming craft show coming up that I was helping Cris prepare for. It was at the Cass City High School gym. I helped Cris and Jim bring all of the stuff in and helped set it up. I had my wedding dress there from when I was going to marry Frank. I wanted to try and get rid of it.

The gym filled up quickly with vendors and customers. There was one customer in particular that kept circling our table. He would come to our table, strike up a conversation, go look at all of the other vendor's tables, and then come back to our table. He would go look at other tables and then come back, and he did that at least four or five times.

Cris and Jim got up and left me to man the tables for them because they knew this guy was hitting on me and wanted to give us some privacy. His name was Matthew, and he asked for my phone number because his little sister was getting married, and she needed a wedding dress. He also asked me out on a date, and I agreed.

25

My Happily Ever After

Matthew picked me up from my mom's later that day after the craft show, and we went to Murdog's, which was a small burger and fry joint in Caro. Matthew got the big Murdog burger the size of a plate. If he was able to eat it all, he would get the meal for free, but he was unable to complete the challenge.

Matthew was not from the thumb area and was there on business. He worked for the government under federal contract with the Michigan State Police, doing fingerprinting for background checks for preemployment checks, concealed carry permits, adoption, foster care, and things like that. He was doing a special in Caro, and it wasn't his normal site that he went to.

As fate would have it, he heard about the craft show going on in Cass City and thought that he might as well check it out while he was in the area. Christmas was next month, and he wanted to get a head start on Christmas shopping. He was from the West Branch area which was almost two hours north.

I never saw the end of Matthew after that. We called and texted each other a lot, and he took me on more dates. He was a really nice guy, and we found out that we had a lot in common. We shared the same political views and were both very passionate about politics. His grandfather was actually a Wesleyan pastor in Caro. I went to a Wesleyan church. I even found out that we went to the same church camp as kids. His mother was also a redhead, and so was mine.

Red hair ran in both of our families. Matthew even had a red beard, even though his hair was jet black. His grandmother's name was Rosalie. My dog's middle name was Rosalie. We couldn't get over how much we both had in common, and it seemed like it was meant to be, like fate brought us together. He came to Caro the same day the craft show was going on. People told him about the craft show going on in Cass City which was only twenty minutes away. He lived two hours north, and we magically came together that day.

Matthew lived with his parents because he was single, and his parents needed him to help with the house. He took me to meet his family shortly after that, and I started spending the weekends with him.

His mom, Donna, was a very sweet woman who was soft-spoken, walked with a walker, and was on oxygen. Donna always wore long skirts and her hair up in a bun. She was a very religious woman and always had a smile on her face. She had the joy of the Lord living inside of her. She had pulmonary lung disease, which did not give her long to live. Donna and I hit it off right away and built a close relationship. His dad, Dick, was a talker, which I learned was a family trait that Matthew inherited.

Matthew has an older sister named Laurie who is married to a pastor named Clinton with five beautiful kids, has a younger brother named Brian who is married to Tonya with four beautiful kids, and a younger sister named Kat who has two beautiful kids and a step-daughter. Matthew has a pretty large family, and they are all close, unlike my family.

It wasn't long at all before I moved in with Matthew at his parents' house. They had a large two-story five-bedroom, three-bathroom house back in the woods on forty acres. They built that house in 2007, and most of it was built by the Amish.

I was moved in before Christmas and was able to bring Esmae with me, but I had to leave Clyde at my mom's. Dick was not a big fan of animals, so bringing Esmae was really pushing my luck enough. Donna absolutely adored Esmae, and Esmae loved her as well. Esmae loved to sit on her lap, and Donna spoiled her. Donna got a kick out of how much Esmae loved to wear dresses and get her hair done. Esmae got so excited to get dressed and went nuts when she saw her hair box. She loved the attention and loved looking like a little princess.

Matthew and I got along great. We couldn't have asked for a more perfect match. By April the following year, we were engaged and were married four months later on August 16, 2014. We met and got married in a nine-month time frame. He was a great guy, and I wanted to snatch him up right away. Also, we were living together and not married, and I really wanted to make things right with God. I strayed away from God for so long, which was why my life was a mess. I wanted this time to be different. I wanted things to be right with God. Matthew was different from all the rest, and I knew right away that he was the one.

We got married so quickly because we both felt like we needed to make things right with God. Matthew wasn't a Christian at the time, but he grew up in a church. His grandfather was a pastor, and his mother was a very devoted Christian woman who always had her Bible open. She loved the Lord, and she was a praying woman. I grew to love her like my own mother and really appreciated the fact that she raised a good son that God brought into my life.

Our wedding, though rushed, couldn't have been more perfect. I ordered a simple white dress with some beading on the bodice online from China. Donna was the one that shared that mother experience with me when I tried my dress on for the first time. She was the one that was there to zip me up in the back and helped me figure out my veil. She was there every step of the way in the wedding planning process. She helped me make the little fans that I made up with the list of the wedding party on them. She helped me get the invites out. She did the job that my mother should have had. Donna was very much involved and was very happy to help.

I couldn't get my mother to help me with anything. I tried to involve her because I thought it was the right thing to do, but she wanted no part in the wedding planning, even though she was there for my youngest brother Theo's wedding and helped them make stuff for their wedding. Having Donna help me kind of relieved those hurt feelings I had about my own mother not being there for her daughter's wedding. Donna was there where my mother couldn't bring herself to be. Donna fulfilled all of those motherly duties and then some.

Someone asked me not too long ago why I even invited my mother to my wedding after all that she had put me through. She was my mom, and I felt like I had an obligation to involve her as much as possible. It was easier to just have her there than it was to explain to people why she wasn't. I wanted to keep the peace and also because she was my mother. I wanted more than anything for her to be there in spite of everything. It also had everything to do with portraying a somewhat normal family.

I wanted her to play and look the part. She lit the unity candle with Donna. Dwayne and my mother posed in pictures with me. Dwayne even walked me down the aisle and gave me away. I never invited Clayton, let alone have him take part in anything.

My sister, Jennifer, never even bothered to come, let alone congratulate me in any way. We were both not on speaking terms and pretty much went our own separate ways. She had only called me a couple of times since then to ask for money but ceased all contact with me when she found out that I wasn't going to give it to her. It really upsets me how her life turned out. She didn't have a good childhood either and probably had it worse than I did, but she chose a path of destruction and refused to climb her way out of it. She lost custody of all four of her children and was not a good mom at all. She lived with people and refused to grow up and take responsibility for her life. She was in the party scene and loved to drink and do drugs. She was a pathological liar, and I just couldn't trust anything that she said. She was also a known thief.

I wish I was close to my sister, and it hurts to see that her life ended up that way, but I couldn't allow her to poison me with her drama and suck me into her mess. I have tried to reach out to her on several occasions, but she has been unwilling to build a relationship with me because we are total opposites, and she feels that I am a Goody Two-shoes.

Jordan was not invited to my wedding, and I had to make it very clear to my mom that he wasn't allowed to be there because I knew how she was. She wanted him to drop her off at my in-laws. Neither my mom or Dwayne had a driver's license because they both got their license suspended for driving without insurance, so they had to depend on a ride. Matthew and I couldn't come and get her because we were busy planning a wedding and getting ready. They had to have Dwayne's cousin drop them off. He promised to come to the wedding, but he never showed. He was getting high with friends in a nearby town instead.

It sort of floored me that she would even consider having Jordan drop her off, but I should not have been surprised. She had tried her hardest to shove Jordan into my life whenever she could. I did not want him to know where I lived, and this was supposed to be the best day of my life where I married the man of my dreams. Why would I want to see the very face that had ruined my life all those years? I was never sure if my mom did these things to intentionally hurt me or if she was just so selfish that she only thought of herself and was incapable of thinking of my feelings at all. Either way, I had to learn to accept that it was who my mother was, and she was never going to change.

Once I learned to accept that, it took the sting away every time she did something that hurt me. She still left a welt, but that initial sting dissipated. It didn't even seem like my mom wanted to be there. She didn't help in any way. She was just there, going through the motions. I even had to buy her outfit and Dwayne's tie because they couldn't afford to buy nice clothes, and if they were going to be in pictures, I wanted them to look presentable.

My mom and Dwayne stayed the night in one of the upstairs spare bedrooms. Theo and his wife, Robin, and Joshua and his girlfriend, Jessica, at the time stayed out in tents in the backyard. Joshua's two little blonde-haired girls, Raylyn and Layla, were the flower girls.

I tried to involve everyone on both sides and didn't want anyone to feel left out. Matthew's brother, Brian, was the best man, and my friend, Tami, was the maid of honor. I wished Bella was my maid of honor or my own sister, but they were not a part of my life anymore. All of Matthew's nieces and nephews were in the wedding. We had a large wedding party.

Betsy, Ronald, Raegan, and Raegan's daughter, Allanah, did show up, though. They were a big part of my life, and I wanted them to be a part of my special day.

All six girls wore simple black dresses, and they each had a different color sash that matched their shoes and simple Gerber daisy bouquet that Matthew's Aunt Karen made. All of the guys wore black dress pants, white button-up shirts, and different color suspenders to match the girls' sashes. The colors were all bright colors of pink, purple, blue, orange, green, and yellow. Everyone had a different color.

I made my own bouquet and had all of the colors in it along with one big white flower in the middle, and on the stem, I attached my Grandmother Phyllis's broach. I tried to make everything as affordable as possible for everyone. It was such short notice I didn't want to make the girls buy a fancy expensive dress they would only wear one time.

The Sandefurs lived in Anderson, Indiana, at the time, and they drove all the way to Michigan for our wedding, and Pastor Ken was the one to marry us. He played a huge role in my life, and it was very important to me that he was the one to perform the ceremony, even though Matthew's brother-in-law, Clinton, was a pastor. I made Clinton an usher and had him do a game at the reception. Matthew's sister-in-law, Tonya, was our photographer.

Matthew made all of the centerpieces out of white birch logs that we put candles in. He also made two wooden benches for everyone to sign on instead of doing a traditional guest book that would only get shoved in the closet.

We got married in a private subdivision tucked away in the woods where Matthew grew up. This subdivision was on a private lake with a campground, a park with a large pavilion, and a clubhouse overlooking the long three-mile lake with a large sandy beach. We had our ceremony under a large pavilion and the reception in the clubhouse. It was very simple and affordable.

It rained that morning, but as soon as it was time for me to walk down that aisle and become Mrs. Matthew Sherman, the rain stopped, and the sun came out, and the weather was beautiful. It was like God was telling me, "Before this day, your life may have been rainy and gloomy and your skies were grey, but now your dreams of happiness, love, safety, and being a part of a real family that loves you will become your new reality, and the Son of God is going to shine down on you and bless you."

Before I met Matthew, my skies had always been grey, and my tears rained down quite frequently throughout my life. I could never find happiness or sunny skies until this very moment when God brought us together. This moment was life-changing, and my life was going to be better from here on out.

One of the many blessings that God has bestowed upon me was watching Matthew grow from a decent man but did not have a personal relationship with Jesus Christ to a man of God on fire for the Lord and very knowledgeable about the Bible. We started going to church together, and he became water-baptized, and I couldn't have been prouder.

Now he is an admin in several Christian social media groups and a founder of a few. He is very involved in teaching others about the Bible and rightly dividing the word of truth.

A few different people approached us over the years and told us that they saw a big change in Matthew after we got together. He used to be an atheist and a totally different person before he met me, and I changed him for the better from what I have been told. They never would have thought that he would start going to church and get baptized and start living for the Lord, and they thanked me for the changes in his life. I deserve none of that glory because all of the glory belongs to Jesus. Without Him, we are nothing. Without Him, nothing is possible. He makes something out of nothing and is the Author and Finisher of our faith. To God be the glory and honor in everything.

One of the first things Matthew did for me when we first got together was teach me how to drive without yelling and screaming every time I did something wrong. I failed the first driving test, but with more practice, especially on the parking and backing up, I was able to pass it the next time around and finally got my driver's license at the age of twenty-six. It was such a huge accomplishment for me. I never thought I would get my driver's license because Devlin always drilled it into my head that I would never get it, and he caused me to have great anxiety over it. I still have anxiety when it comes to driving and don't like to drive, but I'm able to drive myself wherever I need to go.

We waited a year before we went on our honeymoon aboard the *Carnival Glory* cruise ship to the Caribbean. That was the *best* vacation ever, and we had so much fun visiting other countries and trying new things, getting immersed into different cultures. We left Esmae with a friend who was more than happy to spoil her rotten for the two weeks that we were gone.

We had to leave from Miami, Florida, so we decided to make a two-week vacation out of it. I had never seen the mountains before, so we took the scenic route and went through the Kentucky Blue Ridge mountains on our way down to Florida.

My mother's nephew lived in Jacksonville, so we stayed with him for a few days and Matthew and I went to the Jacksonville museum and planetarium and saw all of the dinosaur displays. We also checked out the hurricane simulator.

We went down at the end of August, so the weather was still blistering hot, and it was during hurricane season, but we welcomed the warmer weather, being from the colder climate of Michigan. To be able to look outside and see palm trees was very exciting to me. I also secretly loved the big cities and driving around Jacksonville—the United States' fifth largest city was right up my alley. I was right in my element, taking it all in. I think it is safe to say that we both fell in love with Florida on this trip, and the conversation came up about moving there. Matthew and I both hated the cold Michigan winters and dealing with the snow. It seemed like our summers were not long enough to enjoy them.

My cousin, Mike, took us out to eat gator tail for the very first time, and we both thoroughly enjoyed it. It really did taste like fried chicken, only better. We both loved to try new things, and this trip was all about experiencing many new things together.

When we boarded our ship, we were both very excited. This was it. It was finally here. This was the moment we have been waiting for. We planned for this trip months in advance and saved up for it. It seemed like this day would never come, and we were finally here. We watched video upon video about the *Carnival Glory* and videos about the different excursions we were going to go on at each port. We were super-hyped up about this trip and put in a lot of time planning and working extra hours to pay for it.

We were very impressed with all of the decor and the amenities the ship offered. Everything was beautiful. The grand staircase, the little shops, all of the different restaurants, the indoor pool, the pool deck with the water slide, hot tubs, pool, and big movie screen. Everything you could ever want out of a tropical vacation was on that ship.

We had an exterior room with a balcony, which we took advantage of. We spent our mornings and evenings out on that balcony watching the sunset and the sunrise and got many beautiful pictures. Watching the waves coming in and out and crashing against the boat was very mesmerizing. We thanked God every day for such beauty and sitting out on that balcony watching the sea never got old. There was never a dull moment on that boat.

We spent a lot of time in the hot tubs both on the pool deck and the adult area, meeting and talking to new people. The cruise ship was so massive in size, you could spend an entire day just touring it. They had a theater room where we got to see a live show of singing and dancing with a lot of graphics and lights. They also had an arcade area where we tried our hand at the money claw machine. Yes, that claw machine wasn't stuffed with useless childish toys; it had bundles of money for prizes. Even though it was disappointing to come out empty-handed, it sure was exciting and fun to try.

Matthew and I both loved to try new foods and took advantage of the opportunity to do so. We got to try Calamari, which is baby octopus, and escargot, which are snails. Both were very good. The snails were roasted in butter, garlic, and cheese and tasted just like whole mushrooms. Their lobster tail and chocolate lava cake were to die for. All of the food was very good and presented very well.

Our first port of call was Cozumel, Mexico, where we got to go ziplining through caves and waterfalls. That is where Matthew and I both discovered just how out of shape we were. If you ever want to prepare for a marathon, go ziplining in Cozumel, Mexico. The four-teen different spiral staircases taller than the treetops that you have to climb up to get to each zipline will surely whip you into shape. You can't do just one. Once you start it, you have to complete every one of them in order to get to the end.

Ziplining through waterfalls into caves may sound cool until your zipline stops you underneath a waterfall and you almost drown due to panic and sheer shock that you are unable to paddle yourself backwards out from underneath the waterfall that is trying to pelt you into an early grave. Yeah, that was me. If you ask me if I ever want to go ziplining through waterfalls again, the answer will surely be a definite no. One time was enough for me. Well, fourteen times because that is how many ziplines we had to do.

After the ziplining, we got to go on ATVs through the caves and bumpy trails. Matthew drove while I sat in the passenger side and enjoyed the ride. That part was actually a lot of fun. They provided a meal for us, and we were expecting a traditional Mexican meal which we were excited about, but it was not Mexican food. It was very Americanized but was still excellent. They had a large food buffet set up inside a cave, and we got to eat just inside the cave. There was this cute little friendly orange cat that was hanging around for food handouts. He was the cutest little Mexican.

Matthew and I got a few souvenirs from the shops inside the cave. That was the first time that either one of us got to go inside a cave. We had so much fun at the Xplor Park in Mexico, even though climbing all of those steps were exhausting and I almost drowned under a waterfall.

Our next port of call was in Belize. This shore excursion was very welcomed and at a much more relaxing pace. Belize is a small country south of Mexico that is very tropical and stays in the sev-enties and eighties year-round. Their official language is actually English, but most everyone there speaks both English and Spanish.

When I first got there, a Belizean woman talked me into letting her braid my hair for money. She did a small French braid at the front going down the side. It was a neat experience having her do my hair for me.

Our excursion was about an hour and a half inland, so we had to take a bus which gave us an excellent tour of the country. There was a lot of poverty in Belize, but there were some parts that had really nice modest houses, and all of the houses there are all painted bright colors. Belize is such a beautiful country, and as a native Belizean would say, "Belize is '*unbelizeable*,'" and it truly was.

Matthew and I instantly fell in love with Belize. Before we took this trip, we researched every country that we would be visiting, and Belize is the country that we were most looking forward to. When we were there and got to see what it was like, we were sold on that country, and that was it. When we retired, we were going to buy property and move there. Belize would be our home one day. We were kind of tossing the idea around of moving somewhere in South America, and Belize really caught our attention because their official language was English, and we didn't have to learn how to speak Spanish. So when we found a cruise itinerary that included Belize, we were excited.

The tour guide on the bus did very well at telling us the history of Belize, and she also had a page of laminated currency so that we could see what their money looked like. When we finally got to our destination, it was tucked away in a rural area, and we had to walk about a half mile to our poolside retreat through the rainforest. We walked across a handmade bamboo bridge, and our tour guide pointed out different plants that they used for medicinal purposes. There was some kind of nut they used to put in small piles everywhere to burn, and it kept all of the mosquitos away. Whatever it was, it worked, and we didn't see a single mosquito.

The pool was beautiful. On one side there was a little man-made cave with a waterfall that had a hidden waterslide on the side of it. There was also a bench built into the inside of the cave made out of rock where you could sit. After the waterfall incident the day before in Mexico, I vowed to never go through another waterfall ever again. I've had my fill of waterfalls. Matthew talked me into sitting under the waterfall with him, so I did. It was just a small man-made waterfall. I could handle that.

There were little tables along the pool with grass umbrellas and hammocks to lounge around in. A little walk away from the pool was a large pond with lily pads all over it, and on one side of the pond, there was a large pavilion with a grass roof that overlooked the pond. They had canoes stacked up on one side that you could rent, but nobody did because there was a young alligator that just took up residence in that pond. Not only that, there were also piranhas. I wouldn't want to take a chance of capsizing the canoe in that pond. I wouldn't be sure if the alligator or the piranhas would get to me first.

They did provide a traditional Belizean dish of chicken, rice, beans, and fried bananas in some type of sauce which was very good. After the meal, they took the leftover chicken and threw it in the pond to feed the piranhas and alligator. Watching the swarm of piranhas tear that chicken up was quite entertaining and confirmed to me that renting a canoe to go on that pond would be a really terrible idea.

We just had a very quiet and relaxing time in Belize. There weren't a whole lot of people there, so it was very nice. It really did feel like paradise on earth, and we never wanted to leave. It was so "unbelizeable!"

Our next shore excursion was in Roatan, Honduras. Roatan was a small island off Honduras where pirates hid their treasure. Honduras is beautiful but also very poor. When we boarded the small boat to get to shore, there were a bunch of shops there where you could buy souvenirs. They also had natives there playing the drums and maracas and dancing in traditional native garb with headdresses and everything. We got to pose in a picture with them and took videos of them playing their instruments and dancing. It was very fascinating to see a bit of their culture. There were also a couple of guys playing the xylophone, and it just reminded me of Caribbean music as they played.

We had to board a bus to go to our excursion and had to drive at least an hour inland to get to our destination. Since Matthew really pushed for the ziplining in Mexico, I pushed for seeing the monkeys in Honduras. I loved monkeys and really wanted the opportunity to hold one. So we went to a zoo called Gumbalimba Park. It was a privately owned ecoadventure and history park. There were many activities there that included a museum, a pool, animal interactions where you get to hold large tropical birds and monkeys, several botanical gardens, and a waterfront with a beach and submarine activities.

Our tour guide was very knowledgeable, and she also gave us the history behind Honduras. She took us through a little cave where they had a display of pirates, and we also went to a building where they had a bunch of dead bugs dried in frames on display. It was kind of cool seeing all the different species of bugs, especially butterflies. They come in so many beautiful shapes and sizes and colors. God is truly the Master Artist and Creator. He created everything so intricately with much detail and beauty. It was more like an awe moment and reflecting just how great God really is.

The park only had animals that were native to Honduras, and most of them were not in cages or any type of enclosure. There were a ton of lizards and iguanas running around, sloths, white-faced monkeys, macaws, hummingbirds, peacocks, turtles, *guatusas* or "island rabbits," as well as other animals. I love animals, so it was all fun for me. Matthew is not a big animal person, but he agreed to go because I really wanted to hold a monkey, plus I did the ziplining with him and nearly drowned under a stupid waterfall.

When we finally got to the animal encounter, I could hardly contain my excitement. I was in heaven, and the pure joy plastered onto my face as I could not stop smiling from ear to ear. The monkeys were not in cages, and they were trained to come down from the trees and interact with people. The handlers fed them sunflower seeds, and the monkeys just came down and climbed all over everyone, going from shoulder to shoulder. Matthew took a bunch of pictures and videos of my interactions with the monkeys. The monkeys climbed onto Matthew as well, and even though he claimed that he didn't care for the monkeys and he did it only for me, I knew that he secretly enjoyed it.

He told me when we first got together that he didn't like animals or dogs and cats in particular, but he could have fooled me. Esmae had him wrapped around her little paw. He just liked to portray himself as a tough guy that doesn't like animals. Aside from the monkeys, we also got to hold a macaw on our shoulder and saw toucans up in the trees.

Our last and final port of call was Grand Cayman in the Cayman Islands. The Cayman Islands is a territory of the UK. Everything was very expensive there and looked much like any upscale modern city in the tropics.

We participated in two separate shore excursions. The first one we did was parasailing. We went out on a small boat with a group of about twenty people, including us, and we all took turns parasailing.

It was so beautiful there. The water was so clear and so blue, you could see the bottom of the sea floor.

I wanted to chicken out of going up in the parasail and made Matthew go first. Once I got up there, though, the sights were so amazingly beautiful. Flying high in the sky over crystal blue water, seeing the coral reef below, and getting a bird's-eye view of the city was truly money well spent.

Our next excursion was the underwater sea trek. We got on another boat with a small group of people, and we had to wear these large space helmet-looking things on our shoulders. When you tipped a glass upside down and pushed it into the water, no water went into the glass. That is how these helmets were designed to work.

There was this long ladder that we had to climb down from the boat to the sea floor about seventy feet down. With every step down, you had to plug your nose and pop your ears due to the pressure. Some people have more sensitive ears than others, and people with tubes in their ears could not do this excursion because it does hurt your ears going that far down to the sea floor. I got halfway down the ladder and had to go back up because it hurt my ears so bad, but then I went back down and made it to the sea floor. Once we were all down there, we got to walk around and see all of the coral firsthand, and there was a ship wreckage that we got to see as well. There was a school of fish swimming around in front of our faces, and we also got to hold a sea urchin, which was pretty cool.

Matthew and I purchased an underwater digital camera specifically for this excursion, and we got a few pictures. It was a little difficult because the pressure from the water made it hard to push the buttons on the camera.

We had so much fun on this trip, we never wanted to go back home, but I was missing my baby girl, Esmae.

When we got off the boat, we drove to Weeki Wachee, Florida, to visit the Sandefurs at their condo where they ended up retiring. Everything was so beautiful in Florida, and the more of it we got to see, the more we fell in love. Their condo was on a river that had manatee, and they also had a small sandy beach. It was a beautiful condominium. Their son and daughter in law also had a condo there, and their other son lived with them.

Regina really out did herself and put on a large spread with cake for dessert. Then we had a fun time of fellowship, playing cards and board games.

We stayed the night and went to Sunday church with them. They went to a very large church, and the service was great. I sat next to Regina, and it was like déjà vu, like old times when I was a shy little kid sitting next to her in church in Kingston.

We planned on staying two nights with them, but Matthew got called back to work a day early, so we made the long drive back home.

*****

The next morning after we got back, we went to pick up Miss Esmae, and she was so excited to have her mommy back. She literally climbed up my legs and leaped into my arms, giving me a ton of kisses. When she realized her daddy was standing next to me, she leaped over into his arms and gave him kisses as well. She really missed us during those two weeks.

Our friend that had her was an older guy named Dave Ryan and his wife, Tina. They had two Maltese dogs of their own that Esmae got to play with. Dave was a longtime family friend of the Shermans and knew Matthew's grandparents very well. He spoiled Esmae immensely while she was there and gave her lots of treats and started calling her Goofy. She loved Dave and loved going to his house to visit.

A couple of years later, we bought a house that was a major fixer-upper and in desperate need of repair. It was actually the house that Matthew grew up in as a kid and in the same subdivision where we got married, so getting this house really meant a lot.

Every single room needed to be gutted right down to the studs and redone with all new electrical and plumbing. We couldn't afford to do it all at once, so we have been slowly working on it one room at a time.

The living room was the very first room to be redone, and the first thing we did was rip up the old carpet. There was also a fireplace that had old red brick that made the room look really dark, so I repainted it a light grey, brick by brick, and painted all of the grout white with a tiny paintbrush to give it a fresh look. We ripped out all of the old paneling and replaced it with drywall. The living room didn't have any overhead lights or ceiling fans, so we put in four can lights and two ceiling fans. What I love most about the living room is that two of the walls are pretty much all windows which let in a lot of light. We also widened the doorway between the living room and dining room to open it up more.

Every room has wood paneling that will be replaced with drywall. By the time the house is done, it will be pretty much a brand-new house with all new insulation, wiring, plumbing, duct work, furnace, and drywall. When we bought it, it was a three-bedroom, one-and-three-quarter bath. We are converting it to a two-bedroom, two full bath to make a larger master suite with a larger bathroom and walk-in closet. It still needs a lot of work, but it has been fun tearing down walls, painting, and ripping up flooring. We are trying to appeal to a retired couple when remodeling this house because we do live in a predominantly retired community. As soon as the house is done, we want to sell it and move south to a warmer climate.

There was an old wooden swing set in the backyard that we wanted gone, so I called my mother up and asked her if she wanted it. My brother, Joshua, brought her and Dwayne up and tore it down to take it home with them. We had planned on them staying to visit for a few hours and bought steaks to cook out on the grill for them. My mom only cared about coming to get that swing set. We had to beg them to stay for dinner. As soon as they were done eating, they packed up and left.

I was very upset that my mother only came up because there was something in it for her. She didn't come up to see me or the house. She only came up to get the swing set and was only there long enough for Joshua to tear it down and for them to eat. They were probably only here for an hour, tops. The fact that I had to actually beg them to stay for dinner was a real slap in the face. I felt really used and hurt by that. My mom really hurt my feelings. If I didn't have anything to offer her, she wouldn't have come up at all. She never told me she was proud of me for buying our first house. We gave her a tour, but we didn't get any emotion or feedback from her. She didn't care. She only came for the swing set. She didn't care about seeing the house or me, for that matter. At least, that is how she made me feel.

My mother and Dwayne only came up one other time a couple of years later because I invited them to the annual ox roast for our subdivision and already purchased the tickets ahead of time. They tried to back out of that, but I told her that I had already bought the tickets, so they had to come.

Matthew and I did go visit my mom often, especially in the summertime. I felt an obligation to go down and see them and really did try to have them a part of my life, in spite of everything that I had gone through. Most of the time, when we were there, Jordan showed up. I tried not to let it bother me and never spoke one word to Jordan. I knew that this was the way it was going to be. Jordan was always going to be around, so I had to learn to accept it, but I didn't have to talk to him or have any type of relationship with him. Things were never going to change. My mother was always going to pick Jordan over me.

Some would think that my mom chose both of us equally and didn't pick one of us over the other, but that's not true. My mom didn't have to pick either one of us over the other. She could have been every bit involved in Jordan's life since he lived nearby but asked him not to come over while I was visiting. That would have been respectful. No, my mom made it a point to have Jordan come over while I was there. She tried her hardest to shove him in my face every chance she got. When I called her on the phone, she wanted to talk about Jordan. When she messaged me on social media, she wanted to talk about Jordan and send me pictures of his baby boy. She threw him in my face every chance she could.

When Jennifer came up from Ohio, my mom guilted me and even had Theo guilting me to come down to pose in a picture so that my mom could have a picture of all five of her kids together. I didn't want to do it. I didn't want to be in a picture with him, much less see him, but I did it for my mother and because a part of me wanted to see my sister, even though the reunion with her was a huge disappointment.

I felt very disrespected and couldn't wait to leave. That was the first time I had seen Jennifer in probably eight years or more. She ignored me at first and then decided to give me a hug, but it was just a formality. We barely even talked. It was around Christmas time, and my mother had this huge blow-up Santa out in the yard that she wanted us to stand in front of for a picture, knowing that Matthew and I did not celebrate Christmas and wanted nothing to do with Santa Clause. My mother only thinks of herself and what she wants, so that may have slipped her mind since she is not used to thinking of others. I talked her into doing the picture in front of some pine trees instead. As soon as she got her picture, Matthew and I left and went back home.

I decided to cut all ties with my family. I blocked them all on my social media; my brother, sister, nieces, aunts, cousins—everyone. I was going through a deep spell of depression, and my family really caused me a lot of stress. For a while, I was the only one calling my mother. She never called me. When I did call her, the conversation was always less than ten minutes. I got to the point where I was just tired of being the only one putting forth the effort in this relationship. I stopped calling her and didn't hear from her for over three months. I was testing her to see how long it would take for her to call me if I stopped calling her. I told Matthew that we were no longer going down to visit her or any of them.

My brother, Theo, just bought a house and wanted us to come down and see it but I refused. At this point, we had already been in our house for three years, and not once had he ever came to see our house. Theo's in-laws owned a cabin fifteen minutes away from me, and he was up for an entire week, saying he was going to stop by and never did. He was too busy. I was very upset and angry. I was tired of being the only one to put forth the effort in a relationship with any of them, so I cut them all off.

My mom started calling me, but the more I ignored her, the more she kept trying to call me. Then she got my niece and my brother, Theo, to try and contact me through Matthew's social media because I had them all blocked. I had to write my mom a letter and send it to her in the mail, explaining to her how much she had hurt me and that I no longer wanted any contact with any of them to get her to stop calling me.

It was extremely difficult for me to do this. I cried over this and went into deep depression for having to do this because I wanted more than anything to have a relationship with them, but I realized that no relationship with them was better than a stressful toxic relationship with them that brought me nothing but grief and disappointment, and that was never going to change. I had to do what was best for me and my mental health, even though it was very painful.

Each time that my mother called me and I had to ignore her, it was painful. I knew that I was hurting her, but it was time to put myself first and do what I felt was best for me. This had been one of the hardest things that I ever had to do because I already felt like I was alone with hardly any family to speak of, and now I was isolating myself even more. Now I was truly alone aside from Matthew's family and a few select friends that were more my family than my own family.

During the first year of being in our own house, we decided to get another puppy. Esmae was becoming quite the daddy's girl, and I was jealous and wanted a momma's boy. Matthew's friend who lived just a few miles from us had a litter of Yorkie poodle puppies for sale. They had one male puppy in the whole litter, and he was mine. Matthew and I went over to see him when he was six weeks old and put a deposit on him. We paid $450 for him, and he was worth every penny. He was all black with a little nub for a tail. He was the cutest little guy we ever did see and so tiny. He fit right in our hands. Waiting two more weeks to get him was the longest two weeks of our lives.

We named him Remington Ruger after a brand of gun. We called him Remy, for short, or Remy Roo Roo or Mister Roos. He has a lot of names. Matthew was a big hunter, so we wanted to give him a hunting name. Esmae took to him right away and was a good big sister.

Nine months later, Remy decided that he wanted to be a little stud and have a little fun with Esmae. Esmae was not fixed, and we had planned on getting Remy fixed, but we thought we had time, and we were trying to save up the money to do so. We had made the appointment, and just before his appointment, he decided to use them before he lost them and got her pregnant. We never planned on having a litter of puppies, but we had to make preparations for their arrival, and as her belly grew and I could feel the puppies move around, my excitement grew with each passing day, and I couldn't wait to see what their puppies would look like. Esmae was half Maltese and half poodle, and Remy was half poodle and half Yorkie, which made their puppies Morkiepoos.

Esmae was going into labor, and Donna came over to watch the puppies be born, but Esmae was just having a terrible time, and the puppies just weren't coming. Donna was there all day, waiting on the puppies. She ended up going home after dinner. I stayed by her side, waiting for the puppies to come out. It was late at night when Esmae started to have black discharge coming out of her, and I got very worried. I looked it up online and found that was a sign of a dead puppy, and I became very distraught. Matthew wasn't home. He was at his parent's house, and I called him up, crying, saying that we needed to take her to the emergency vet right away because she was losing the puppies.

We called the family vet that Matthew's family had used for years, and he wanted the money up front before he would even see her. We had a few hundred dollars, so I wrapped her up in a blanket and we rushed her up there, but we didn't have enough money. The vet was going to refuse to see her at first and let her and the puppies die unless we came up with the rest of the money. We begged him to save her and gave him all of the money we had, which left us with nothing until payday. He told us that if she did not have an emergency c-section that she would die along with all of the puppies. There was a dead puppy blocking the birth canal and was causing her serious distress. The vet finally agreed to take her back to do the c-section with a promise to pay.

Esmae had six beautiful puppies. All of them survived. Two of the puppies were much smaller than the rest, and the vet told us that Remy most likely got her pregnant twice. The first time, she got pregnant with four, and the second time with two, and the two small ones were really early and might not make it. They didn't even have all of the hair developed on their faces, and they were half the size of the other four. There were three white ones and two brown ones and a black one with the traditional Yorkie markings. She had three boys and three girls.

The vet told us that Esmae was not producing enough milk and that we may end up having to bottle feed them and sent us home with some puppy formula. He wanted us to especially focus on the two little ones to make sure they got enough nourishment since they were so weak.

We took the little family home and placed Esmae and her puppies in the box we prepared for them inside a little pen area in the living room. Matthew went to bed with Remy, and I slept on the cold hard floor next to the box of puppies in the living room. I didn't sleep at all that night. I couldn't sleep. I was so worried about the puppies.

Since Esmae didn't give birth to them naturally, she didn't get that chance to bond with them as they came out. She went under anesthesia and woke up to having six puppies, so she rejected them. She didn't want to nurse them, and we had to force her to lay down to nurse them. She wasn't a very good mom, and the vet said that was because she was too spoiled, and that happens a lot with little dogs like that. They don't make good parents.

Eventually, she got used to being a mom and wanted to mother them but still didn't always want to lay down to feed them. She flipped out every time Remy even came near the living room and went after him, growling at him and beating him up. She was very protective of her babies. I called my brother, Joshua, up and asked him to take Remy for a week or so until Esmae could calm down and get used to being a mother. Joshua only had him for one week, and we missed him so much we had to go get him. We just had to keep yelling at Esmae and telling her to be nice, and eventually, she calmed down and didn't flip out. We introduced Remy to all of the puppies with Esmae right there to get her to realize that Remy wasn't going to hurt her babies. He was just curious, and they were his babies too.

Before they were even born, we had decided that we were going to keep a female out of the litter. Esmae was very "licky" and loved to give kisses, and so was Remy. So we knew that there was a chance that their puppies would be "licky" as well. We decided to name the female puppy that we were going to keep Ellicka Lou Mae. Licka, for short, and Mae after Esmae. We kept the black one with the traditional yorkie markings, and she did turn out to be the queen of licks, so the name fit her perfectly. We joke that naming her Licka was a self-fulfilling prophecy. Little Licka Lou grew to be bigger than her parents, and she is quite solid and all muscle.

The two runts thrived and grew to be strong and healthy puppies. They were little fighters. The male runt went to a good friend of ours, Dave Ryan, and his sister, Mary, got the female runt, and their names are Cooper and Lacey Rose. I loved that her name had Rose in it since Esmae's middle name was Rosalie. Cooper actually grew to be the biggest out of all of them with really long legs. Lacey Rose is a pampered spoiled princess, just like her mom.

Dave Ryan's stepson got one of the male brown puppies and named him Hunter. So three out of the six puppies all went to the same family, and they all had play dates and saw each other, which I was very pleased with.

I worked in home health care, taking care of a client that lived in my subdivision, and they really wanted a puppy as well. They chose the biggest one, which was a female, and named her Bella.

My brother, Joshua, begged me for a puppy for his girlfriend, but I really didn't want to give him one. Joshua didn't stay with the same girl for very long, and what would happen to the puppy when they split up? I made him sign a contract with me before giving him the puppy. If he and his girlfriend ever split up, he would be the one to keep the puppy because I wanted to keep track of him to make sure that he was taken care of and wanted him to stay in the family. If he ever got to the point where they didn't want him or couldn't take care of him, then he would relinquish him back into my care, and I would take him back. He was not to put him into another home or sell him.

They only had him for maybe eight months, and during that time, he got Parvo and almost died. Joshua worked in a mobile home park, cleaning out trailers so that they could rent them back out, and he always took the puppy with him to his jobsites, and that is where he picked up Parvo. After nursing him back to health, Joshua and his girlfriend split up, just as expected, and Joshua's new girlfriend didn't want the puppy, so he gave him back to me. They named him Rebel, but I didn't like that name, so we renamed him Charles Emerson Winchester after a character on the old TV show, *M*A*S*H*. It was also a gun name. We call him Charlie for short.

Poor Charlie was so malnourished, dirty, matted, and covered in fleas when we got him back. He was in rough shape. We gave him a bath when we first brought him home, and that's when we saw just how skinny he really was. We were very upset that this was how they treated this poor puppy. The matting were so bad on his ears that even after taking care of them, the tips of his ears were curled in and stayed that way for quite some time.

Charlie is now happy, fat, and thriving. Aside from being a little food aggressive from being starved, he is doing very well and is the sweetest little guy. He loves to cuddle and give hugs and will play fetch 24/7 if you let him.

So now we have four dogs—Esmae, Remy, Licka and Charlie. We never planned on having this many dogs, but we wouldn't change it for the world because we love all four of them, and they are the most spoiled dogs in the world.

After the litter of puppies were weaned, we took Esmae in to have her spayed. Remy was neutered shortly after getting her pregnant. When the two puppies were old enough, we got them spayed and neutered right away. We were not going through this again. Having a litter of puppies was fun, but we were so happy to see them all go. It was a lot of work bottle-feeding them every couple of hours and cleaning up after them. Having these puppies almost killed Esmae and racked up a huge vet bill. We had our fill of puppies. We enjoyed it while it lasted but were relieved when the last puppy went to their forever home.

Matthew and I have been trying to conceive for the last six years, and I want a baby in the worst way. I was diagnosed with PCOS and I have really irregular and erratic cycles, so it has been really hard and frustrating. I think this has been one of the hardest things about being married and also being a Christian.

My whole life, the one thing I knew I wanted more than anything was to be a mother. I've wanted to be many things in my life, but this was the one thing that has always remained the same. Why am I thirty-two years old and married for six years and still have no baby? I really struggled with my faith over this and shook my fist at God. I was mad at God. Why did He give Jordan two children and not me? Why am I seeing stories on social media about kids getting abused or abandoned or murdered by their own parents, and Matthew and I would be great parents and can't get pregnant? I just didn't understand. Why are kids being born to mothers who don't want them or deserve them, but I want them in the worst way and can't have them? What was the reasoning behind this? What was God's plan in this?

My thirtieth birthday was the hardest. Each year that came closer to thirty was extremely hard and depressing. I knew that trying to conceive after the age of thirty would be harder and harder and decreased my odds of getting pregnant, so approaching that number became very difficult for me to deal with, and I became very angry and very bitter. Seeing everyone around me having children, especially their third or fourth baby, was very upsetting. It was hard for me to be happy for my sisters-in-law who kept getting blessed with children, and I couldn't even get pregnant with one.

Once I hit thirty, I became very depressed. I hated my birthdays. Why wasn't God giving me the one thing that I wanted more than anything? What was His purpose behind this? After everything that I had been through, I felt that I deserved the one thing that I had been asking for. Why was God denying me the desire of my heart when the Bible says that He gives us the desires of our hearts?

To rub salt on a wound, my mother always talked about Jordan's baby and kept sending me pictures of him. I felt like she was rubbing it in my face that he had a baby. She may have been just a proud grandma showing him off, and like I said before, she is a very selfish person, and I believe that she is just incapable of thinking about the feelings of others, so when she offends someone, she is not meaning to. It's just her selfish nature to only think about herself.

Nobody understands just how painful infertility is unless you have been through it. What hurts the most is growing up, my mom had made comments on multiple occasions, telling me that she hoped I would never have children of my own. I believe that there is power in your words, and I told her that I believed that she put a curse on me when she told me that. Of course, she denies ever saying that, but the pictures of Jordan's baby kept coming. She just didn't get it that I didn't want to see any pictures of him or hear about him. What made it worse was that it was Jordan's baby. She didn't send me pictures of any of the other grandkids. She seemed to be very good at hurting me and offending me in every way possible without even trying, especially when it came to her precious son, Jordan.

I did the right thing by cutting her out of my life, at least for now. Maybe someday, things will be different, and I will be able to have a good relationship with my mother.

When I wrote her that letter, I did tell her that I was writing this book and that I was going to get it published, and she would probably hate me anyway when it all came out. I told her that it was my story to tell and that I needed to tell it.

I have probably taken about a few dozen pregnancy tests over the course of our marriage, hoping and praying to see two little lines only to be left disappointed time and time again. I have pleaded with God and begged God to give us a child. I think what made it even worse for me was the fact that I didn't have much of a family to speak of, so making one of my own was extremely important to me. I didn't want to be eighty years old in a nursing home with no children to come and visit me. Being old and alone was a scary thought for me.

Matthew and I have already picked out names at the beginning of our marriage. For a girl, we are going to name her Alyceondriah Rosalie Marie Sherman, and we will call her Alyce for short. Matthew's grandmother's name was Alice, and his other grandmother's name was Rosalie, and I loved that name. Marie was after my grandmother and mother. It was their middle name as well as Jennifer's. The initials, ARMS, were my grandmother's married name. So there was a lot of meaning behind this name, and it really meant a lot.

For a boy, we picked out Matthias Kenneth Nathan Sherman, and we would call him Thias for short, not Matt. Matthias is a biblical name and also close to Matthew. Kenneth is after Pastor Ken Sandefur who meant so much to me and played a huge role in my life. Nathan is Matthew's middle name. I also had the name Moses Samuel Alan Sherman picked out for a boy. Moses is a biblical name, and Samuel is after my grandfather, Francis Samuel Bush, who I am also named after. Alan is a Sherman name. It is Matthew's dad's middle name and is used as a middle name for other male boys in the family as well. I also love the name Allanah Heavenliegh Rose Sherman. Allanah is pronounced Uh-lawn-uh. It has the name Alan in it, which is a Sherman name. A lot of the Sherman girls have Leigh somewhere in their names, and I want to keep some kind of Rose form in every girl's middle name.

I wanted at least four kids, and the older I got, the more doubts I had of ever having one, let alone four. I even prayed for them by name. "Please, God, bless me with Alyce and Thias. When am I going to hold them in my arms?"

A couple of years into my marriage with Matthew, God did give me a vision of a little redhaired girl about two or three years old. She had curly red pigtails, wearing a white dress, running through a grassy field of flowers, laughing. I believe that was a promise from God telling me that he will bless me with a child one day. I just have to be patient and not get caught up in my age. It will happen in his perfect timing. I just have to trust God and in his timing.

Despite this vision, I had little faith. With every year that passed, every birthday, my faith diminished even more. I have always been a very impatient person, and I was so bitter and upset that God wasn't hearing me about this one request. I was starting to give up hope. What hurt the most was mourning a child that had a name but only existed in my mind. I can imagine how painful it is to mourn a dead child, but to mourn a child that never existed is just as painful.

I know that God has a plan, and that vision of little Alyceondriah will come to fruition one day. I believe now that God has been waiting for his very moment to take me on this journey of healing and writing this book to bring me to a place of growth and wisdom so that I can be the best parent I can be. It was His plan all along, and I just couldn't see it until now.

Despite the lack of family, God has blessed me immensely with great close friends. God has separated me from my natural family, but he has replaced them with great Christian role models who have guided me and prayed for me and encouraged me along the way.

Donna Sherman, my dear mother-in-law, sadly passed away March 8, 2019, in her sleep in her own home. I got the news while I was at work and was devastated. I thought highly of Donna and loved her dearly, and she and I became very close. I was blessed with five great years of her in my life, and I know that I will see her in heaven one day and that she is no longer in pain. God taking her when he did was actually a blessing because she suffered from pulmonary lung disease, and that was a slow painful death that he spared her from as she was approaching that tragic point. I found a mother in Donna and loved her dearly.

Cris Archer lost her husband, Jim, and a few years later. She decided to put her house up for sale and buy a much smaller house almost two hours away in my neck of the woods, just a few minutes away from me in my subdivision. I couldn't have been more happy to have her live nearby. I just wish that I didn't have to work so much so that I could spend more time with her. God has blessed me with her in my life, and I am forever grateful for all of her prayers and the pep talks and words of wisdom she has provided me. She shares a love for animals and God's creation and has such a positive, uplifting attitude that is contagious, and I can only hope to have as much faith as she has one day.

God has also blessed me with a wonderful job that pays very well for my area working in an AFC home for Community Mental Health, and an added bonus is the opportunity to work the night shift with Kathy Davidson who has become a very close and dear friend of mine. She has been like a mother to me and a spiritual mother as well. She has prayed for me and encouraged me through this whole journey.

When I felt like giving up on life and giving up on myself, she was there to pray me through. She refused to give up on me, even when I wanted to give up on myself.

Writing my story has been very difficult. It has brought things back to my memory that I have forgotten, and I have had to relive through everything all over again, and it is extremely painful. Kathy was there to give me a hug when I needed it the most. She was a listening ear and a prayer warrior that prayed me through the most difficult times. She was my biggest fan and encouraged me to get my story heard. She has cried with me through this whole journey, and I couldn't have finished this book without her, and I am forever grateful for God sending her my way.

Matthew received a job promotion with a large increase in income, and our house will be paid off in less than a year. God is pouring out his many blessings on us, and I can't wait to see what the future holds for us. I believe with all my heart that I will hold a child in my arms from my own womb one day. Patience has been one of the hardest things that I have had to learn, aside from forgiveness, but I believe that it will be worth the wait because God needed me to be brought to this point of healing so that I could finally put the past behind me and move on with my future and fulfill *His will* over my life, whatever that may be.

The past has always held me back and affected my present, and this story will now put an end to that and close that door once and for all, propelling me into the future. I know that God has a great calling on my life and that he had me write this book, not only for my healing but for my readers as well. I have learned that *I am worthy* of a life of happiness and that the past does not define who I am today. What I went through is not who I am. I am who I am because God has strengthened me and brought me through the vilest of storms to show me just how strong and victorious I am and how great a God He is. God has been there for me every step of the way, and He has never forsaken me. Even when I felt all alone, He was there right by my side. I may have been through *hell* and back, but I am here today because God has a purpose for me.

I should have died many times throughout my life, but God brought me through all of the fiery trials of this life because He wanted me to give you a message. God loves you. No matter what you have been through, you can cry out to God, and He will see you through any storm. You are worth more than the sparrows, and He has a purpose and a plan for you. Things may seem grey right now, but I promise you that there is a rainbow at the end of each storm. If you surrender your life to the one who created it, He will use you in a mighty way and bless you more than you can ever imagine. All you have to do is hold out your hand and let Him take it and show you just how mighty and great He really is.

If God can bring me through all that I've been through, He can bring you through your storm too. No problem is too great for a God that spoke everything into existence. This is not the end of my story. This is only the beginning.

26

7 x 70 = The Power of Forgiveness

Then said he unto the disciples, It is impossible but that offences
will come: but woe unto him, through whom they come! It
were better for him that a millstone were hanged about his
neck, and he cast into the sea, than that he should offend one of
these little ones. Take heed to yourselves: If thy brother trespass
against thee, rebuke him; and if he repent, forgive him.
And if he trespass against thee seven times in a day, and seven times
in a day turn again to thee, saying, I repent; thou shalt forgive him.

—Luke 17:1–4 (KJV)

Then came Peter to him, and said, Lord, how oft shall my brother
sin against me, and I forgive him? till seven times?
Jesus saith unto him, I say not unto thee,
Until seven times: but, Until seventy times seven.

—Matthew 18:21–22 (KJV)

I had such hatred in my heart for Jordan, Clayton, Devlin, Craig,
and especially my mother. I loathed Jordan, Clayton, and Devlin
the most. I let that anger fester and boil beneath the surface, and it
worked its poison into every fiber of my being.

304

Many people would say that I have every right to hold hatred and unforgiveness in my heart for those who have hurt me. I have been through a lot in my young life, and I have a reason to be bitter and angry.

Clayton is a pedophile and ruined my whole family, and because of his example, Jordan molested me and sent me into a whirlwind of pain and suffering and depression, attempted suicide which lead into being admitted in a psychiatric hospital multiple times, self-harming behavior, anorexia, bulimia, and a whole childhood that was robbed from me. My mother neglected me and wasn't there for me emotionally or mentally. She dismissed my obvious suffering and basically told me to get over it because "back in the old days, incest was normal." She refused to hear about the details of what her son did. She minimized my emotional distress and took away counseling. She forced me to deal with this all on my own.

My mother shoved Jordan in my face and tried to force him into my life whenever she could. She placed a lot of blame on me as to why the family was split up and made me feel guilty for my feelings. My mother probably caused the most damage because not only did I not have a father in my life, but I also did not really have a mother in my life either. I was very isolated in my pain, which is why I was forced to cope the best way I knew how with self-harmful behaviors. I really think that regardless of what Jordan and Clayton did, if she would have been there for me, to console me, comfort me, was there for me to talk to; if she was supportive and got me help, if she would have told me that she loved me, listened to me, hugged me, cried with me, and fought for me and told me that it wasn't my fault, I think I would have been much better off and further ahead.

If there was one thing that my mother has taught me in all of this, it is this: though my mother and father may forsake me, my Father in heaven will never forsake me. There is only one that each of us can count on, and that is our Father in heaven.

> Fear thou not; for I am with thee: be not
> dismayed; for I am thy God: I will strengthen
> thee; yea, I will help thee; yea, I will uphold thee

with the right hand of my righteousness. Behold,
all they that were incensed against thee shall be
ashamed and confounded: they shall be as nothing; and they that strive with thee shall perish.
Thou shalt seek them, and shalt not find them,
even them that contend with thee: they that war
against thee shall be as nothing, and as a thing
of nought. For I the Lord thy God will hold thy
right hand, saying unto thee, Fear not; I will help
thee. (Isaiah 41:10–13 KJV)

Man will let us down and disappoint us every time, no matter
who it is, but remember the one who created us. He will never leave
us nor forsake us. He loves us more than we could ever imagine.

I spent my entire life wasting a lot of energy on hating those
who hurt me. I spent a lot of energy on being angry and bitter toward
my mother. Forgiving them seemed like a foreign concept to me. I
believed in my heart that they deserved to burn in hell for what they
had done to me. How could God let them in heaven? They were the
villains in my life. They ruined my life. They are evil right down to
the core.

I tried to forgive them over and over and over again, but it
was only a matter of time before the anger and resentment bubbled
up beneath the surface again and spread its poison of hatred and
unforgiveness in my heart and in my mind once more. Bitterness
is the most natural response in the world. We as humans are easily
offended, and offense leads to anger, hatred, and retaliation which
tends to end up in a vicious cycle.

I agree with Dan Hamilton who wrote in *Forgiveness*:

Suppressed resentment will never die; it will
be held in reserve and nurtured like malignant
toadstools in a cellar. Resentment suppressed will
never lose its power; like a spark in a gasoline
tank, a bit of momentary friction will set off a
devastating explosion.

It's so true. Every time I remember what they did to me and how much pain they had caused me and the childhood that was robbed from me, it was like ripping tape off an open wound. My memory kept replaying like old reruns, replaying the same old scene, and with each new play came a whole new wave of bitterness and anger which was the spark in a gasoline tank that set off a resonating explosion of more hurt and more pain which morphed into more hatred and more bitterness. It was just an endless vicious cycle that wouldn't go away. This was the result of unforgiveness.

Something that I had to learn the hard way and a whole lifetime to figure out was that the people who hurt me and caused me great pain carried on with their lives as if my unforgiveness and hatred toward them had no effect on them. They could care less if I forgave them or not. My unforgiveness had no bearing on their lives, so what good was it? The only person that my unforgiveness, hatred, and bitterness hurt was me. What did I have to gain by holding unforgiveness in my heart? Nothing but more pain and heartache and the inability to move past it. The resentment, the anger, the bitterness, and hatred I held in my heart was like a raging fire that kept consuming everything in its path. Unforgiveness leads to more sin. My hatred and unforgiveness led to attempted suicide, eating disorders, cutting, and other self-harmful behaviors which are all sin.

My unforgiveness kept me in a state of emotional bondage to the wrong that was done which perpetuated more sin and gave place to hate. Charles Stanley said it best:

> Unforgiveness is emotional bondage and your mind gets thinking about the wrong and the pain that the person has caused you and then it festers deep inside your soul and turns into utter hatred and revenge which is a sin.

Unforgiveness can wreak havoc on your life, and it is such a dangerous thing to hold on to. It can leave you in bondage and tie you down with your thoughts, and it can turn into bitterness in your heart.

I was a very bitter and hardened person, and I know God is still working on me and softening my heart. I got frustrated and angry so easily. I didn't have patience for people. I didn't know how to handle people because of all of the years of isolation in my bedroom. I spent so much time alone, thinking and dwelling on the past. I really internalized everything, and it festered into hatred and anger. God really could not move in my life because of all of the hatred and bitterness I held in my heart. I believe that is why I kept jumping from one traumatic experience to another.

I had a death grip on my bitterness and anger, which was caused by the unforgiveness I held toward all those that hurt me. I believed that I had every right to be angry, which kept me in emotional bondage to the past. I refused to let go of it and give it all to God. I had little faith and tried to do things on my own. That is why I jumped from Craig to the Shuecrafts, to Devlin, and to Frank. I jumped into another bad situation to escape the one before. And that was all because I refused to let go and trust God to see me through. That all stemmed from the unforgiveness that I held in my heart.

This has not been an easy journey by any means, and I'm telling you that forgiveness has been one of the *hardest* lessons to learn. It doesn't come easy, especially if you have been severely traumatized as I have. It wasn't until I was in my late twenties and into my thirties that I finally realized just how much the hatred and bitterness really affected me. It affected my relationships with people. I had people telling me that I was hard to approach and hard to read because they thought that I was mean. I didn't realize that I was coming off that way, but they saw that in my body language and the way I carried myself. I was a very angry person and was blind to it. I didn't realize that I was that way. My anger came out in the way that I talked to people, which gave people the impression that I was mean and unapproachable. It was a real slap in the face because I had no idea that I was that way. I didn't mean to be. That unforgiveness and anger and bitterness I held in my heart really blinded me to the effects it had on my life and my interactions with people.

When someone pointed it out to me and made me face that fact, I was forced to ask God to take it from me, and I had to repent and ask for forgiveness. I couldn't change until I came to that realization. God is still working on me, but I was able to really pay attention to how I talked with people and pay attention to my body language. I never wanted to come across mean and angry and bitter, and I feel like I have come a long way from where I was. God has really been healing me and restoring me, and that is only because I chose to finally surrender completely to Him, which meant that I had to give Him my anger and bitterness so that I was finally able to forgive.

You see, unforgiveness harbors passengers. It harbors anger, bitterness, resentment, and hatred. The anger and hatred and bitterness gives power to unforgiveness, but it can also cause depression, and depression can lead to many things, such as self-harm and thoughts of suicide. It all becomes a tangled web of poison, but the only cure and hope you have is Jesus Christ. He is the only one that can take it all away so long as you let Him.

Jesus Christ led by example, what it means to truly forgive. Every single one of us is born into sin, and it was our sin that put Him up on that cross. It was our sin that arrested Him. It was our sin that spit in His face. It was our sin that shouted, "Crucify Him! Crucify Him!" It was our sin that beat Him until he was unrecognizable as a man. It was our sin that mocked Him and shoved a crown of thorns upon His head. It was our sin that made Him carry a wooden cross up a hill after being beaten, kicked, spat at, and mocked. It was our sin that drove the nails into His hands and feet and hung Him up on that cross where He slowly died of asphyxiation.

One thing you have to remember is that Jesus was completely innocent, blameless, and without sin. They hated Him. His own followers denied Him and turned against Him. He had every right to be angry and bitter, but He wasn't. In spite of all of that, with His last dying breath, He called out to his Father, "Father, forgive them, for they know not what they do!" He loved us in spite of the beating we gave Him. He loved us in spite of the nails we drove into His hands and feet. He loved us in spite of the mocking and spitting in His face. He loved us so much that He willingly laid His life down for us so that we can have forgiveness of our sins. He is the perfect example of what it means to truly forgive.

> Ye have heard that it hath been said, Thou shalt love thy neighbour, and hate thine enemy. But I say unto you, Love your enemies, bless them that curse you, do good to them that hate you, and pray for them which despitefully use you, and persecute you; That ye may be the children of your Father which is in heaven: for he maketh his sun to rise on the evil and on the good, and sendeth rain on the just and on the unjust. For if ye love them which love you, what reward have ye? do not even the publicans the same? And if ye salute your brethren only, what do ye more than others? do not even the publicans so? Be ye therefore perfect, even as your Father which is in heaven is perfect. (Matthew 5:43–48 KJV)

Jesus not only died for me, but He also died for Jordan, Clayton, Craig, Devlin, and my mother. He died for us all, no matter what we have done. Every sin that man could ever commit has the same price, and that is the blood of Jesus.

I don't have that right to harbor unforgiveness in my heart because I, too, am a sinner and guilty and worthy of hell. My sins have the same price as the sins of my enemies.

> For if ye forgive men their trespasses, your heavenly Father will also forgive you: But if ye forgive not men their trespasses, neither will your Father forgive your trespasses. (Matthew 6:14–15 KJV)

Every sin we commit is a direct trespass against God because of the price that was paid for us on the cross for our sins. That is why it is important to ask God for forgiveness when we sin. We would want

God to forgive us, and because we ask that of God, we must extend the same grace and mercy to those who trespass against us, even when we think they don't deserve it because we also don't deserve the same grace and mercy that we ask of God.

It is better to secure our own character by being ready to forgive seven times seventy times, even if that person is not sincere in asking for forgiveness or if they don't ask for forgiveness at all than to hold a grudge to a truly repentant soul and be in danger of putting a stumbling block in their way. Repentance demands forgiveness, and forgiveness demands grace.

As a Christian and Christ follower, we are charged with the responsibility of emulating Christ and being Christlike, which includes extending forgiveness to those who have wronged us and showing them love and compassion just as Christ has done for us. How can we show the love of Christ if we let our unforgiveness stand in the way?

Forgiveness means canceling a debt. It does not mean overlooking a mistake or the wrong that was done nor does it mean excusing it by any means. Forgiveness means seeing the wrong or the debt for what it is and canceling the debt owed. It means showing the very same grace and mercy that God shows us when He forgives us of our sins.

C. S. Lewis explained it very well when he said:

> Real forgiveness, the kind that comes from God, means looking steadily at the sin, the sin that is left over without any excuse, after all allowances have been made, and seeing it in all its horror, dirt, meanness, and malice, and nevertheless being wholly reconciled to the man who has done it.

Being a Christian means forgiving the inexcusable because God has forgiven the inexcusable in you. We refuse God's mercy and grace for ourselves when we refuse to forgive without exception.

When you choose to forgive someone, you are choosing love just like God extended to us.

The subject of forgiveness is not something I am ignorant to because I have been there. I have been used and abused and neglected by the very people who were the closest to me. You have taken this journey with me and read my story. I have been through unimaginable hell throughout my whole life. I harbored resentment, hatred, bitterness, and anger toward the very people who have hurt me. I know what it is like to hold onto all of that poison.

Unforgiveness is like drinking poison and waiting for the other person to die. I have wasted so many years being angry and bitter. It wasn't until people started pointing out to me just how bitter and unapproachable I was that I started to realize that I had to let go of that once and for all. I didn't want to be known as mean or harsh, and I was deeply grieved when I found out that I was perceived that way.

I cried out to God and begged Him to take it from me. I begged Him to soften my heart and take away all of the years of anger and bitterness. I asked Him to forgive me of my unforgiveness and asked Him to help me to forgive those who have hurt me. I thought that I forgave Jordan and Clayton years prior, but a part of me took a hold of that anger and bitterness and held onto it. I didn't give it up completely. I had to search deeply within myself and examine where all of the anger and hatred stemmed from so that I could take it as a whole and give it up to God once and for all.

It is not something that God can just take from us. It is something that we have to see for ourselves and *want* to surrender to him. Only then can He mold us and start to heal us from the pain and wounds that were inflicted upon us because of the unforgiveness and bitterness and anger that was stored in us. It is not something that can be done overnight, and it does take time. We just have to continue to trust God and have faith that He will continue to work on us and restore us and make us new and whole again.

Holding a grudge doesn't make you strong. It makes you bitter. Forgiving doesn't make you weak. It sets you free. Forgiveness is the only thing that heals wounds. Once I finally forgave those who had wronged me, I felt a huge burden being lifted off my shoulders. I was finally set free. Do the pain and the memories from those people ever go away? No! But I can finally see it for what it was, and I'm able to move on and grow from it and take those experiences and use them to help others who are going through the same things and offer them hope and guidance through it with the help of my heavenly Father.

This world is so evil and wicked that sometimes we are innocent bystanders and fall victim to someone else's crimes and sins. That's just the fallen and broken world that we live in. I spent my entire life asking God why things happened to me. We may not understand why certain things happen, but I do know that God sees it all, and He knows the end from the beginning and can take the pain, the heartache, and any bad situation and turn it into something good and use it for His glory. My story, however painful it may be, could bring hope to the hopeless and be the very thing that God uses to help others through their situations, whatever they may be.

I have forgiven Clayton. He is an old man now and haven't seen him since I was a young teen. My forgiveness does not require a relationship with him by any means. It only means that I have released myself from the resentment harbored against him and have given it to God. My only hope for him is that he will find himself on his knees, begging God to save his soul before he takes his last breath. Despite what he has done to the family and the impact his sin had on my life, I know that one day, he will stand in front of God to answer for what he has done.

I have forgiven Jordan. He was a kid himself when he did what he did. We can all remember doing stupid things as kids. His sin impacted my life in a mighty way that he will never realize. The scars run deep and spider out to other scars which stemmed from what he did to me. I don't know where his heart lies and if he has remorse for what he did, but that is not my business to know. That is between him and God, and only God can judge him. It took me a whole lifetime to forgive him and find peace in my heart and finally move on with my life. I can say that I'm a stronger person because of it. My forgiveness does not require me to embrace him with open arms or have any kind of a relationship with him. Too much damage has been done. I know that forgiving him has brought me peace and healing and the ability to finally move on with my life and use the pain of the past for God's glory to give witness to others about the mightiness of God.

You see, my God is a mountain mover. He has the power to turn your valleys into mountains, but the only one standing in the way of Him doing that is you. You have to be willing to let go and trust God in every situation and have faith that He will see you through. All you need is faith the size of a mustard seed.

I have forgiven Craig for taking advantage of my vulnerability. I'm sure a life of abandonment by his parents and growing up in a foster home hasn't been easy. It doesn't excuse what he has done by any means, and I know that he knows the truth because he attended the same church that I did. I pray that God gets a hold of him and that he repents and turns his life around and dedicates his life to serve the kingdom of heaven, giving God all of the glory.

I forgive Devlin as God would forgive me. He was a tough one to forgive because of how evil that man is. I only revealed a portion of what that man has done to me. Some of the things that he has done are way too horrifying to repeat and put into words. Even mustering up the words to describe just a hint of what he put me through was extremely difficult. I had to relive a lot of the things that I spent years trying to forget. Writing about it brought it all back to the surface, and I had to remember things that I had suppressed and had forgotten, which was very painful. It sent me into a dangerous depressive state.

I am very thankful God has blessed me with my good friend, Kathy Davidson, who prayed incessantly for me, encouraged me, lent me a shoulder to cry on, and reminded me of the whole purpose of writing this in the first place because I was ready to throw in the towel and give up. It was too hard for me to relive and remember things I had forgotten.

I have never known such wickedness as I have in that man. Writing about him has been the most difficult part of my story to write about. I have forgiven him, but I still have to keep asking God to take it from me. I still have to ask God to heal those wounds that Devlin had incurred and ease the pain that he had caused. I never realized just how much pain I still had from him until I wrote about it. I have always just suppressed it and hidden it away beneath the surface and chose not to deal with it. I pray that somehow, he gets a hold of this book and reads the effect that he had on my life and that God will grab a hold of him and convict him to the point where he falls to his knees, crying out for forgiveness, begging God to save him and have mercy on his soul. God wishes for none to perish, and that includes him.

It doesn't do any good to harbor unforgiveness in your heart because we all have to stand before God and answer for the things we have done anyway. Everybody will get their due justice at that time. That is when God will deal with the wicked once and for all.

I forgive my mother. I know nothing about her childhood because she never talked about that with me. I'm not sure if that has something to do with how she was as a parent or how she is now. I know things must have been hard for her as well. She married a much older man who turned out to be a pervert, and she tried to deal with that the best way she knew how, which was to deny reality. She became a single mom with no job or driver's license and had five kids to worry about. I get that it must have been hard on her. She had to hurry up and find a man to support her and her kids, and Dwayne came along, and she moved us in right away.

Dwayne was very short-tempered and things had to be his way. She had to make the best of the situation. I know it must have been hard to have to choose between two of her kids. The best way she knew how to deal with that was to shove it under a rug and pretend as if nothing ever happened, and she tried to force me to do the same. Her coping method was denial, just like mine was cutting and starving to death. My mom has always been a very selfish person and has only thought about her own feelings, and I have accepted that. None of us want to see ourselves in a negative light. We don't want to admit when we are wrong, so we remain ignorant to our own attitudes. When it gets pointed out to us, we become defensive and denial ensues. That is human nature. I forgive my mom because I believe that she does not realize the effect she has had on my life, partly because there has been little communication between us. I have faith that if she ever does read my story that God will work His miracles in a mighty way and restore our relationship where it needs to be.

I have chosen to sever all contact with my family. That includes my mom, brothers, sisters, aunts, uncles, cousins, nieces, nephews, and anyone associated with them. There was too much negativity and drama, and my mother kept throwing Jordan and his kids in my face, and I just needed time to breathe and analyze my life. I tested my mother to see how long it would take before she took the initiative to call me because I was always the one calling her. It took her about three months to call me. Shortly after that, I decided that I could no longer handle the disappointment. I never felt like a priority to any of my family. I was cast aside as an afterthought.

If they were in town, they didn't bother to visit me. I was the one always going to them, and I was sick of making the effort when I got nothing in return. I felt like every one of them chose Jordan over me. My mom sent me pictures of Jordan's baby on social media all the time, not caring that it bothered me, especially since I was struggling with infertility. I just felt like it was time to finally put me first and sever all contact with all of them for the time being. I needed time to heal and reflect on what was truly important in my life without any distractions from people bringing me down.

It was extremely difficult to ignore my mom every time she called. I had to write her a letter and tell her that I was severing contact with all of them and that I didn't want her or any of them to call me or contact me in any way. Every time she called, it was like a dagger to the heart because I felt guilty for ignoring her calls. I felt like I was hurting her. But I had to stick to my guns and tell myself that this was what was best for me. I needed time to heal, which meant that I had to sever all contact with them because all they did was stir up strife and anger and bitterness inside of me, which was detrimental to my healing process. I was never allowed the opportunity to heal and finally put the past to bed, so I felt like this was very important to me.

I fear that if they ever read my book, they may not want anything to do with me, anyway, and I have prepared myself for that. I do, however, have faith in my heavenly Father that He will work in a mighty way and mend the things that are broken and make all things new. This book is bigger than myself, and whatever comes of it is God's will, whatever the outcome may be. God laid this book on my heart not to hurt them but to help others who have gone through similar trials as I have. Writing this book has also been a journey of healing for me as well as a learning experience. God has revealed so many things to me through this that I have not realized before.

One more person that I need to forgive is myself. I have put myself through a tremendous amount of hell and made some pretty awful decisions, which resulted in more unnecessary trauma that I put myself through. I was extremely hard on myself throughout my entire life and tried to do things on my own instead of releasing it to the One who spoke everything into existence. I was as stubborn as they come, and though I titled myself as a Christian, I had very little faith and resisted complete surrender to a God who can make everything new. I did many things that I'm not proud of as every human that has ever lived has. Through this journey, I have gained wisdom, and through wisdom, peace in knowing that my story does not define who I am today. What defines me is where I go from here and how I apply it to help others.

We are not our past. We should not let our past define us. God has so many things in store for us, but as long as we define ourselves by our past, we will never be able to move on and fulfill the destiny that God has laid out for us.

I lost myself and spent my whole life searching for me when I was right here all along. I just needed to be set free. Sometimes in our journey, we get lost in our mistakes. It is time to let go and let God take control. I want to be nothing less than who I'm meant to be. The rearview mirror is small for a reason, and gone are the days where I am constantly looking back, wishing that my life turned out differently.

The past has prepared me for my future and made me who I am today—strong, fearless, and victorious. If God can bring me through all that I have been through, then look out because my God can bring me through anything.

Now is the time to release the past, the hurt, the pain, the trauma, and all of the negativity to God because he is the only one who can make you whole and new again as long as you surrender it all completely to Him. God is going to show up in the darkness. Where you think you are going to be destroyed, God will be there to carry you through and lift you up.

Dark times is a conclusion—it means that yesterday is over. The night is the end of a day, but tomorrow is a fresh new day and a new beginning. It's the first part of a new day, a period on the past. It means yesterday is over, and there is a new sunrise over the horizon. Everything in the past has lost its influence over the present. Everything yesterday has no influence over tomorrow. God brings us through storms so we can appreciate the rainbow. He brings us through darkness to purge us of the things that do not belong in our futures.

Look at the mountain that is in front of you, the circumstance you are in, and say, "Nothing is impossible for my God. He can do anything. He creates out of nothing. He speaks it and it is so. My God is a waymaker and a miracle worker. My God is a mountain mover."

When you look at your situation through the lens of your own eyes, yes, it may seem *big*, but through the lens of a mighty God, it is actually small because *nothing* is too big for a mighty God we serve. Your purpose is already complete. He has already spoken it. God has already done it.

> For I know the thoughts that I think toward you, saith the Lord, thoughts of peace, and not of evil, to give you an expected end. Then shall ye call upon me, and ye shall go and pray unto me, and I will hearken unto you. And ye shall seek me, and find me, when ye shall search for me with all your heart. (Jeremiah 29:11–13 KJV)

God is present, now and forever. God transcends time, and in our patience, he tells us to be still and know that He is God. God is a restorer and makes all things new. He turns a mess into a miracle and our darkness into light. God's plan is greater than your pain. He is greater than your situation and whatever you may be going through. Cry out to Him, and He will hear you.

Don't pray for God to take this mountain away. Pray that through Him, you will be able to climb it and remain victorious over it and be stronger because of it. The race is not given to the quick or to the strong but to the one who endures to the end. What builds up endurance? The more mountains you face, the stronger you get. The stronger you get, the easier it is to climb, building up endurance. Don't ask God to relieve you from this burden or to take it away, but ask God to give you the strength to weather this storm so that you can find yourself standing on top of that mountain, singing praise and glory to God for seeing you through it.

Life is about mountains and valleys, so trust God to get you through. God is able to do immeasurably more than we can ever ask or imagine. He can calm a storm by simply saying, "Peace, be still." He can part a sea so that you can walk across dry land. He can raise the dead and heal the sick. God is *able*. He is able to bring deliverance to the most impossible circumstances. He delivered Daniel from the lion's den and three men from the fiery furnace. He delivered Joseph from Pharaoh's prison. God brought water out of a rock and provided manna for forty years. He is able to change the hearts of men and women.

Jesus Christ is the same today, tomorrow, and forever. He has the power to replace fear with faith and to mend broken relationships. I believe that one day, my mom and I will be able to sit down and talk things out and begin to heal our broken relationship. My God can heal brokenness and make things whole and new again. My God is able. He is big enough to run the universe but small enough to dwell in my heart and able to do more than I can ever ask for or dream of. Whatever you are carrying, God is able. Whatever you are longing for in your heart, God is able. The same God who brought you through yesterday's crisis will bring you through today's crisis. Sometimes God will allow you to go through things to develop you spiritually. With God, you are able to go through anything and come out an overcomer. With everything you go through, God is preparing you for the next battle, making you stronger and wiser with each one. You can't enjoy today if you are still crying about yesterday.

Yield to His purpose and His plan. Being a follower of Christ does not exempt you from fiery trials. Trials will visit everyone. Expect trials not from a standpoint of fear but of victory because with God on our side, we can remain victorious over anything—spoken from one who has been through the deepest valleys and climbed the tallest mountains.

God has brought me through so much. I should have died on a number of different occasions throughout my life, but God made sure that I made it through because He had a purpose and a plan for my life, and He has a purpose and a plan for your life too. Whatever you are going through, hang in there and call on the name of Jesus. He is the only one who can see you through the storms of life. No other can mend a soul and make the broken beautiful like Jesus can. God is a restorer and makes all things new. He can turn your mess into a miracle. Just trust in *Him* because He is the only one that will never leave you nor forsake you. He is the only one that will never let you down.

About the Author

A ndrea Sherman is a thirty-something overcomer who grew up navigating some of life's hardest adversities, including childhood sexual abuse and anorexia, which resulted in numerous suicide attempts, cutting, and running away from home. She has made it her life mission to tell the story that has long been stifled under family embarrassment.

Andrea was born in Erie, Pennsylvania, in 1988 but moved to a small town in the thumb of Michigan with her family when she was eight. Growing up, she struggled throughout her teen years, and yet her twenties were even more difficult. She found a counselor and a friend in her pastor and his wife who prayed for her.

In a life of uncertainty, one thing was certain: there was only One who could see her through the darkest pits of life, her heavenly Father. Andrea's newfound faith gave her strength and hope for a future filled with purpose. God has given her a mission: Tell the world her story, and use her adversities to help those who have similar experiences. Share the hope and goodness of the One who can make all things new—Jesus Christ.

Currently, Andrea resides in a small town in northern Michigan with her husband, four dogs, and three cats. She enjoys painting, gardening, nature, and remodeling her home with her spouse. She finds joy in taking care of others with special needs. She experiences peace and solace in her Creator and gives Him full glory for where He has brought her to this day.

CPSIA information can be obtained
at www.ICGtesting.com
Printed in the USA
LVHW030949170721
692931LV00002B/120

9 781098 091590